Gender and Spanish Cinema

Gender and Spanish Cinema

Edited by
Steven Marsh and Parvati Nair

Oxford • New York

First published in 2004 by
Berg
Editorial offices:
1st Floor, Angel Court, 81 St Clements Street, Oxford OX4 1AW, UK
175 Fifth Avenue, New York, NY 10010, USA

Berg is the imprint of Oxford International Publishers Ltd.

Library of Congress Cataloging-in-Publication Data
A catalog record for this book is available from the Library of Congress.

British Library Cataloguing-in-Publication Data
A catalogue record for this book is available from the British Library.

ISBN 1 85973 786 2 (Cloth)
1 85973 791 9 (Paper)

Typeset by JS Typesetting Ltd, Wellingborough, Northants.
Printed in the United Kingdom by Biddles Ltd, King's Lynn.

www.bergpublishers.com

Contents

Contents

Acknowledgements

The editors would like to thank Kathleen May, Anne Hobbs and Caroline McCarthy at Berg for the help and support that they have provided. Thanks are also due to the students of HSP 662 in 2002–2003 at the School of Modern Languages, Queen Mary, University of London for useful discussion of issues of gender in Spanish cinema.

Notes on Contributors

Julián Daniel Gutiérrez-Albilla is currently completing his doctoral dissertation in the Department of Spanish and Portuguese, University of Cambridge. His research re-reads the Spanish-language films of Luis Buñuel from a sexually dissident subject position by drawing on psychoanalysis, feminist and queer film theories of spectatorship and surrealist-informed visual arts. His publications include an article for a forthcoming book on the cinema of Pedro Almodóvar and his major teaching and research interests lie in Spanish and Latin American cinema and Spanish culture and gender theory.

Jo Labanyi is Professor of Spanish and Cultural Studies in the School of Humanities, and Associate Dean (Research) in the Faculty of Law, Arts, and Social Sciences, at the University of Southampton, UK. Her most recent publications include *Gender and Modernization in the Spanish Realist Novel* (Oxford University Press, 2000) and the collective volume *Constructing Identity in Contemporary Spain: Theoretical Debates and Cultural Practice* (Oxford University Press, 2002). She is currently completing a book on 1940s Spanish cinema, and is coordinator of a five-year collaborative research project *An Oral History of Cinema-Going in 1940s and 1950s Spain*, funded by the Arts and Humanities Research Board of the United Kingdom. She is also a research partner in the project *Europe: Emotions, Identities, Politics* coordinated by Luisa Passerini, European University Institute, and funded by the Kulturwissenschaftliches Institut, Essen. She is a founding editor of the *Journal of Spanish Cultural Studies*.

Steven Marsh teaches film and Spanish cultural studies at the University of South Carolina. He is the author of the forthcoming volume *Spanish Popular Cinema Under Franco: Comedy and the Weakening of the State* (Palgrave, 2005). He is currently working on a history of popular film in Spain from 1930 to the present day (I.B. Tauris, 2006) and writing a book on the cultural politics of everyday life in the city of Madrid since 1975. He is a co-author on the collaborative book project and CD-Rom *Cinema* *and the Mediation of Everyday Life: An Oral History of Cinema-Going In 1940s and 1950s Spain* and one of the joint editors of the journal *Studies in Hispanic Cinemas*.

Celia Martín Pérez is a lecturer in Spanish at Thames Valley University. She is currently finishing a PhD thesis on the cultural recycling of historical Spanish women. Her research interests are in gender and cultural studies.

Alejandro Melero Salvador is currently working towards a doctorate at Queen Mary University of London, where he obtained his MA in films Studies and Communication. His thesis explores new sexual discourse in the films of the Spanish transition to democracy. He has already published on George Orwell and the adaptation of Tennessee Williams´ texts onto screen.

Parvati Nair is a lecturer in Spanish at Queen Mary, University of London, Assistant Fellow of the Institute of Romance Studies and Fellow of the Royal Society of Arts. She is the author of *Configuring Community: Theories, Narratives and Practices of Community Identities in Contemporary Spain* (2004). Her research and publications focus on representations of ethnicity and migration in music, film and photography. She is currently working on representations of Islamic identities in contemporary Spain and also preparing a monograph on the photography of Sebastião Salgado.

Eva Parrondo Coppel is an independent scholar based in Madrid. She has published in various journals and edited books on Hollywood and Spanish film, psychoanalysis and the construction of sexual difference in culture. She recently participated in a European Union project on gender stereotyping in media and film and is currently writing a book on *Gilda* (Paidós).

Tatjana Pavlovic is Assistant Professor of Spanish at Tulane University, New Orleans. She is the author of *Despotic Bodies and Transgressive Bodies: Spanish Culture from Francisco Franco to Jesús Franco* (SUNY Press, 2003). Her next major book project, tentatively entitled *España cambia de piel* (Spain Sheds Her Skin). The Mobile Nation (1954–1964), focuses on a little-studied period of transition (1954–1964) in the history of Spanish mass culture.

Notes on Contributors

Chris Perriam is Professor of Hispanic Studies at the University of Newcastle. His research interests are in contemporary Spanish Cinema, poetry in Spanish, and queer writing in Spain. His publications include *Desire and Dissent: An Introduction to Luis Antonio de Villena* (Berg, 1995), A *New History of Spanish Writing from 1939 to the 1990s* (Oxford University Press, 2000) (ed. and co-author) and *From Banderas to Bardem: Stars and Masculinities in Recent Spanish Cinema* (Oxford University Press 2003).

Rob Stone directs film studies in the Department of Media and Communication in the University of Wales at Swansea. He is the author of *Spanish Cinema* (Longman, 2002), *Flamenco in the Works of Federico Garcia Lorca and Carlos Saura* (Edwin Mellen, 2004) and co-editor of *The Unsilvered Screen: Surrealism on Film* (Wallflower, 2005). His book on film-maker Julio Medem entitled *The Symmetry of Chance* will be published by Manchester University Press and Ocho y Medio in 2005. In addition to a number of academic articles on Spanish, Basque and Cuban cinema, he has also written for the popular and specialist film press including *Time Out* and *Vertigo*.

Kathleen M. Vernon is Associate Professor of Hispanic Studies at the State University of New York at Stony Brook. She is the editor of *The Spanish Civil War and the Visual Arts* (1990) and *Post-Franco, Postmodern: The Films of Pedro Almodóvar* (1995) and the author of numerous essays on Spanish cinema. She is currently completing a book on cinema, music, and popular memory in post-war Spain.

Eva Woods is Visiting Assistant Professor in Hispanic Studies and Media Studies at Vassar College. She is currently finishing a book called *White "Gypsies": Racing for Modernity in Spanish Stardom and Folkloric Musical Films, 1923–1954* (Minnesota University Press, 2005) and is co-editor with Susan Larson of a collection of essays entitled, *Seeing Spain: Vision and Modernity, 1850–1939* (Berg, 2004). She is also involved in the collaborative book project, *Cinema and the Mediation of Everyday Life: An Oral History of Cinema-Going In 1940s and 1950s Spain*.

Introduction

Steven Marsh and *Parvati Nair*

The aim of this volume, *Gender and Spanish Cinema*, is to offer diverse perspectives on the treatment and conceptualizations of gender in Spanish cinema of the twentieth and early twenty-first centuries. Bearing in mind the important political and socio-cultural changes that occurred in Spain over the course of the twentieth century, in particular the experience of nearly four decades of dictatorship, followed by the transition to democracy and the cultural effects of the country's consolidation as a modern European nation, the studies in this volume refer directly to those aspects of Spanish cinema that can be highlighted as providing landmarks to the ways in which gender intersects with the course of culture and politics. This introduction will begin with an examination of the conceptual conjuncture of cinema, gender and the nation. It will then move on to a discussion of reading gender in Spanish cinema and will conclude with a summary of the chapters that follow.

Cinema, Gender and the Nation

From its inception at the end of the nineteenth century and throughout its subsequent development as a key mass medium of the twentieth century, cinema has effectively carried out the twin roles of providing social diversion and conveying social messages. Herein lie both the attraction and the force of cinema: on the one hand it invites, entertains and enthrals while on the other it has the capacity to reinforce, challenge and subvert configurations of identity among its viewers. The curiosity and vivid interest that cinema inspires, therefore, arises not so much from its potential to represent reality as from the possibilities that it puts forward to transform, refract and breach the imagined horizons of social identity. There is, nowadays, a widespread recognition that film, as a central medium of modernity, is charged with a political weight that cannot be ignored; furthermore, the aesthetic of film is directly linked to the means by which it reproduces, legitimizes or challenges social values and cultural imaginations.

Indeed, what makes cinema the subject of scholarly study is the fact that, far from being a mere copy of the real world, it is an art form that has an active and dynamic relationship with existing models of identity. Its engagement can be viewed as a double-edged dynamic that both bridges social norms relating to established patterns of identity with cultural processes of change and contestation and, simultaneously, acts as pure entertainment, habitually termed escapist, a safety valve designed to neutralize contestatory energies. Such ambivalence has proved the hallmark of critical writing on cinema. In the course of the development of the film industry in most, if not all, parts of the world, its consistent popularity has been exploited for the purposes of both the reinforcement and the subversion of given ideologies. By the same token, the politics of film must, therefore, be viewed by scholars and students of cinema within a larger context of the politics of social and cultural identity.

Parallel to the development of film studies as a discipline over the past twenty or so years has been the equally exciting growth of gender studies, itself a product of the interest in feminism that began and so revolutionized conceptions of identity from the 1950s onward. Much quoted in these contexts are, of course, the seminal works of Simone de Beauvoir, who with her *The Second Sex* (1949) launched the debate on sex and gender, and the more recent work of Judith Butler on performative theory (*Gender Trouble* [1990]) that has provided a rich vein of inspiration for queer theorists. For scholars of gender and film today, the work of these two theorists must stand as key reference points in the complex and evolving map of understandings and imaginations of gender in advanced modernity. In terms of epistemologies of identity – seen here as ideological construction – gender and nation have been established as central focuses of what Althusser defined as interpellation: subjectivity forged and defined as a glancing shield of historical and social inflections charged with political intent. In turn, as the already vast and growing corpus of scholarship attests, gender has become one of the key means of analysing social and cultural representations.

An especially marked link can be discerned between the fields of gender studies and film studies. One of the connections between these two areas of enquiry can be traced to a common indebtedness to psychoanalytic theory. In turn, this latter discipline found new dimensions in terms of its application of theories of desire that lead to gendering in the two emerging fields of psychoanalytic feminism and film studies. Indeed, it is possible to state that some of the foremost works on psychoanalysis as well as on feminism have themselves taken place in the context of film analysis. Thus, discussions of sexual politics in cinema have opened up debates that can be applied directly to social patterns and norms. Laura Mulvey, Teresa de Lauretis, Annette Kuhn, Christian Metz and Kaja Silverman are but a few of the key contributors to such debates. While the work of such theorists provides students of film with important referential milestones, it is important to bear in mind that, almost thirty years on, both film and gender studies have expanded to occupy areas that intersect with other conceptualizations of social and cultural identity.

Gender and film interact in another very important way: perhaps the most frequent 'dichotomy' cited in the name of gender studies is that between the private sphere and the public. Cinema in many ways bridges that opposition. Cinema and, more specifically, the experience of sitting in the movie theatre watching films provides a window onto the outside world from the most intimate of spectatorial perspectives. Films open up a panorama of experience that temporarily transports the cinema-goer away from private domestic routine to public, global horizons, and in that movement lies the disturbing power of film.

A particularly potent zone of contact that film thus effectively projects is that between gender and national identity. One of the central paradoxes of the idea of cinema as agent of exclusive national identity lies in the fact that since its very origins it has been a multinational product. Long before the invention of the term 'globalization', cinema's industrial and artistic infrastructure (its studios, financing, distribution and protagonists: screenwriters, cinematographers, directors and actors) had breached national frontiers. This inherent contradiction (one that is frequently either overlooked or is willfully misread in much critical writing) is further destabilized by the intervention of gender. Recent scholarship has tended to foreground the juncture between gender and national identity with the increasingly strong drive to emphasize the specificities of historical, cultural and social contexts in film. Film studies, therefore, take into account the narrative and visual potential of cinema to release historical constellations and thus construct imaginations of national identity. However, in keeping with film's potential for contesting the status quo, cinema has also provided a key means by which to refigure national identity or, indeed, to challenge its very foundations. In light of gender's central position in the construction of the individual's private and public identity, such rethinking often relies upon a revision of gender perspectives and imaginations. In order to frame national cinemas – often considered in opposition to the global hegemony of Hollywood and frequently categorized by director or *auteur* – it is useful to seek analytic inroads via gender theory.

In the context of Spanish cinema, this is particularly apt. Not surprisingly, given the social and cultural relevance of gender, both during the dictatorship and in the more recent period of democracy, the construction of gender in Spanish cinema has been charged with ideological intent aimed at specific imaginations of national identity. Cinema has also been one of the most salient forms of Spanish cultural manifestation with consistently vibrant production and high box-office takings (in spite of claims to the contrary by its leading spokespersons). While Spanish cinema is incontrovertibly distinctive, the transnational borrowings of cinema as a fluid art form have produced important interventions in terms of how gender, and in turn nation, is imagined. For all these reasons, gender considerations, as we will see, provide a useful theoretical perspective from which to study the specificities of Spanish cinema.

The Historical Specificities of Spanish cinema

It is almost a commonplace for books on Spanish culture to refer to the fact that Spain is a country that has still to come to terms fully with its divided past, and this book is no exception. The Spanish Civil War (1936–1939) is an ineludible caesura in the nation's memory, whose consequences have come to mark not only cultural production but also its critical priorities. As is made explicit by certain texts in this volume, the prevailing hostility to film production of the early period of Francisco Franco's dictatorship has led until recently to its being woefully overlooked and dismissed as mere propaganda by some quarters within Spain. As Jo Labanyi points out in her chapter, such an attitude is not only founded on misinterpretation (it is largely untrue that propaganda cinema predominated), but also ignores the potential for pluralistic readings of the films of the 1940s.

Such readings inform the thrust of this volume. While Spanish cinema has been dominated by the presence of men and remains so today, it has also produced film-makers – marked by the times in which they were obliged to live – who are strikingly concerned to the point of obsession with gender and sexuality. From Luis Buñuel to Pedro Almodóvar, Spanish film is distinguished by a parodic interrogation of the Catholic Church's teaching. Catholicism provided a central ideological plank for Francoism, but it is also a national-popular field where high and low cultures meet. For both the aforementioned film-makers, the symbolism and rituals of the Catholic Church have provided rich pickings for ironic inversion.

Introduction

For most of Spain's bourgeois critics, Spanish cinema of 'quality' commenced after 1950 with the emergence of the first promotion of the Madrid Film School, among whose most celebrated members were Juan Antonio Bardem and Luis García Berlanga. There is indeed no doubt that the moment signalled a turning point in the fortunes of the nation's cinematic history. This was the first generation of film-makers who had come to adulthood after the war and the first to actively engage the regime. In 1955, this group (and particularly Bardem) were prominent participants at the 'Conversations' in Salamanca; an attempt at dialogue between liberal elements close to the regime and its opponents from the world of cinema aimed at reorientating Spanish film. It is rather telling that many of those present such as Berlanga, Fernando Fernán Gómez and, significantly for this volume, Jesús Franco, have since both disavowed the elitist reframing of cultural politics that Salamanca proposed and proved to be interesting contributors to debates surrounding gender discourse – a fact that goes either largely unnoticed by the critics or is otherwise crudely misrepresented. It would seem, thus, that discourses of gender have a relation to the very production of non-canonical culture, albeit a tangential one.

There is no record of female intervention at the Salamanca Conversations, but women film-makers – as Susan Martin-Márquez has demonstrated – have, in fact, been present in Spanish cinema almost since the beginning. The lack of visibility of women's presence reflects a general patriarchal attitude in cultural production and certainly not one limited to Spain. What is perhaps more distinctive to Spanish critical production is the enduring nature of such an attitude and the apparent impermeability to outside influence. While there are currently a significant number of established women directors, many of whom emerged in the 1990s, and the last three presidents of Spanish Cinema Academy have been women, women are underrepresented in terms of critical writing. (The overwhelming majority of men in proportion to women present at the biannual conferences of the Spanish Association of Cinema Historians in 1999 and 2001 was illustrative.) It is noteworthy that Valeria Camporesi and Eva Parrondo Coppel, whose special edition of the film magazine, *Secuencias*, on women and cinema in the year 2001 was an unheard-of event in Spain's critical film history, both did their graduate work outside Spain. Moreover, the influence of queer studies or any form of analysis of homosexual presence in Spanish cinema remain very much in their infancy, marginalized and confined to the minority ghetto. Spanish cultural hegemony remains firmly in the hands of the critical conservatives. (The irony of this is that, almost to a *man*, these arbiters of taste would consider themselves politically of the Left.)

Among the very few exceptions to the general disinterest in interrogating cultural power structures are to be found appropriately enough in the field of the 'popular'. The recently deceased novelist Terenci Moix and journalist Maruja Torres, who first became known because of her work on the popular film magazine *Fotogramas,* drew attention to and delighted in stars, film icons and the fascination with 'transportation', engagement with the exotic Other, that cinema has always produced in its spectators. Neither of these writers has received any noticeable academic recognition within Spain; indeed their principal engagement has been with the general public, yet in many ways their concerns with gender fluidity, sexuality and the body draw them closer to the intellectual work that for the last two decades has been carried out abroad. In this they coincide, albeit in a very different register, with the recent extraordinary work of Giuliana Bruno who describes the cinema-going experience as akin to travel. Aptly for our purposes, she also links this to the effects of 'moving pictures' on schematic constructions of gender:

> Facilitating the female subject's journey through the geography of modernity, [cinema] expanded the horizons of female pleasures, opening doors of power and knowledge. The movie "house" moved gender divisions by removing their fixed borders. (Bruno, 2002: 82)

Outside of Spain almost all critical writing on Spanish cinema prior to 1999 – with a few significant exceptions[1] – concerned itself with the post-dictatorship period, particularly in the light of the highly marketable and marketed figure of Almodóvar from the mid-1980s onward. However, more recently there have been several attempts to revisit – with the aim of revising assumptions, of which those concerning Francoist cinema are symptomatic – cinematic production prior to democracy.

Susan Martin-Márquez was the first writer to engage with the issue of gender and Spanish film in a single volume. Her 1999 book *Feminist Discourse in Spanish Cinema: Sight Unseen* has established itself as the benchmark for subsequent studies in the field and, among its many virtues, it performed a greatly needed service by disinterring a tradition of woman film-makers – from the early sound era to the late 1990s – buried beneath the weight of patriarchal cultural history. Moreover, Martin-Márquez's theoretical focus brought a contextual feminist framework into the fold of Spanish cinema studies for the very first time. While this volume owes and acknowledges its enormous debt to work such as Martin-Marquéz's,[2] it does not focus primarily upon female *auteurs*. It is perhaps indicative of new, more fluid approaches to gender that no single chapter in this volume is devoted exclusively to a woman director. Instead, the editors

Introduction

have adopted a perspective that views gender through a varied prism, one that recognizes the complexities inherent in sexual difference. Drawing on recent innovative work in gender and queer theory, we have sought to subject the notion of fixed identities to interrogation.

It was, of course, the eruption in the mid-1980s onto the scene of world cinema of Pedro Almodóvar, as the single most hyped representative of a new liberated and democratic Spain, that heralded new ways to approach Spanish cinema. Prior to Martin-Márquez's volume, Paul Julian Smith had produced the first full-length book in English on Almodóvar and made a point of defending him against criticism that he was guilty of being 'ahistorical', a defence that is pertinent to this volume's chapter on the same film-maker. Identifying new forms of resistance, Smith wrote that 'Almodóvar anticipates that critique of identity and essence that was later to become so familiar in academic feminist, minority, and queer theory' (1994: 3).

However, Almodóvar also represents an important strain in Spanish film that stretches back to its origins. Much as he has been constructed by European and North American critics as an *auteur*, Almodóvar breaks with the tradition of Spanish *auteurism* that had been inherited from the French and which came to art-house dominance in the 1960s and early 1970s. He stands as the latest in a long line of popular cineastes – that is of 'the popular', including many that are discussed in this volume – who have consistently proved to be the stalwarts of Spanish cinematic history since the onset of the Second Republic in 1931. Like his ancestors of the early 1930s, Almodóvar combines Hollywood borrowings with local autochthonous customs and – pertinently to this volume – once more like his forerunners, he insists on of the fluid malleability of the human body as a means to express complication.

Gender is, of course, a broad and heterogeneous field. That field is one that is reflected in this volume. Its contributors have employed a wide variety of theoretical tools ranging from psychoanalysis to urban geography; from innovative approaches to costume design to consumerism and commodification; from melodrama to cultural history; from the function of stars in destabilizing gender categories to complex explorations of masculinities; the effects of globalization and migration on refiguring perceptions of genders.

The Contents of the Volume

In his chapter on Buñuel's film, *Viridiana,* Julián Daniel Gutiérrez-Albilla approaches the notion of gender through the relation between categories that are conventionally considered opposites, such as the sublimated and the desublimated, the visible and the invisible. By focusing on the body of the vampire from a psychoanalytic perspective, Gutiérrez-Albilla highlights the positive dynamic offered by the film of dissident pleasure, obtained through the transgression of taboos. In terms of the vampire, this transgression is one that challenges not only the limits of embodiment, but also those of life itself. This in turn leads to a collapse of gender and other boundaries and the blurring of distinctions.

Jo Labanyi's chapter, 'Costume, Identity, and Spectator Pleasure in Historical Films of the Early Franco Period', analyses three films set between the early eighteenth and nineteenth centuries and made in the first decade of Francoism. Here, Labanyi discusses the role of costume in representing gender, and the impact of the latter on the representation of history. Stating that costume, by its very definition, allows for the blurring of conventionally defined aspects of identity, such as gender and social class, she stresses the relation between the spectacle of such early modern fashion and its portrayal of history as a parodic spectacle.

In the fourth chapter, Steven Marsh explores the connections between gender and urban geography in his analysis of Almodóvar's *Carne Trémula*. Arguing that the critical tendency to label Almodóvar's cinematic output as ahistorical is more complex than has been depicted, Marsh suggests that this film marks a pivotal moment in the director's career, given its close engagement with recent Spanish political history. It also constitutes Almodóvar's most serious exploration of heterosexual masculinity. The urban space of Madrid serves as a means of interpreting such historically constructed and conflicting masculine identities. To this end, the film hinges on the corporeal interface of public and private spheres, connecting the teleological narrative of the city's space with the individual human body.

Celia Martín Pérez, in Chapter 5, focuses upon the contrasting portrayals of the historical figure of sixteenth-century Spanish Queen Juana I of Castilla in the 1948 *Locura de amor* directed by Juan de Orduña and in Vicente Aranda's recent *Juana la loca* (2001). In her ideological critique, Martín argues that, in spite of Orduña's proximity to the Franco-ist regime and the efforts made to tailor his depiction of Juana to the regime's historiographical project, the earlier film permits a reading that proves more progressive than that of the contemporary director in spite of the latter's self-avowed feminism.

Alejandro Melero Salvador's Chapter 6 examines the new sexual politics of recent post-Francoist Spain. He argues that the phenomenon of sexual liberation and experimentation that accompanied this period

Introduction

was indicative of a time when new constructions of gender relations were posited via film. His essay centres on Eloy de la Iglesias's film, *El diputado* (1978) as a landmark in the struggle for homosexual social acceptability. Melero outlines depictions of homosexuality in numerous films made between 1975 and 1985, where homosexuality is represented as a 'problem'. *El diputado*, according to him, was a deliberate didactic attempt by de la Iglesias, aimed at offering Spanish spectators, long conditioned by the patriarchal and heterosexist discourses of Francoism and the Catholic Church, representations of 'other' gender relations.

Among the most significant social transformations of the last two decades in Spain has been the arrival of large numbers of immigrants from North and Sub-Saharan Africa. The interface between gender, displacement and migration provides the central argument of Parvati Nair's analysis of two of these films in Chapter 7. Migration – with concomitant consequences of racism, social invisibility, and marginalization – argues Nair, produces cultural reconfigurations in both the arriving immigrants and the host population. Looking to the theories of Third Cinema, the author argues that these films problematize gender and other central aspects of identity, by presenting them in overall contexts of displacement and migrancy; in so doing, they force a rethinking of such categories in terms of mobility and disempowerment.

Eva Parrondo Coppel in Chapter 8 brings to this volume a sophisticated psychoanalytical reading of Miguel Bardem's 1999 futuristic film *La mujer más fea del mundo* (1999). Through her close reading of the movie she details the political implications of transnational cinema on and off screen. In doing so she comes to comment on the place of Spanish film in a global context from a historical perspective by exploiting her detailed knowledge of both psychoanalysis and Hollywood. Moreover, Parrondo reveals the film's narrative concern with contemporary social commentary and its mapping of the evolution of modern feminism.

In Chapter 9 Tatjana Pavlovic reviews the work of the prolific but critically ignored Spanish film-maker Jesús Franco as a radical representative of low popular culture specializing in horror, muscle-man epic, sexploitation movies and pornography. This director – better known outside of Spain as Jess Franco – began making films in the late 1950s and has worked, in varying capacities, with many of the country's most renowned cineastes. Indeed he was present at the Salamanca Conversations. Pavlovic interrogates the reasons for his marginalization within the country of his birth (he is far better known in Germany). She also focuses upon his portrayal of powerful and witty women characters and discusses his appeal to lesbian audiences. Drawing extensively upon

Steven Marsh and *Parvati Nair*

Zizek, she notes the parallels between this film-maker and his namesake, Francisco Franco, and in doing so maps a bodyscape of Spanish history.

Chris Perriam, in Chapter 10, analyses two of a spate of films to emerge at the turn of the new millennium which manifest signs of what Maddison has termed 'heterosocial dissent'. That is, alliances between heterosexual women and gay men that both challenge patriarchal power relations and offer a critique of 'the discourse of homosociality'. Primarily, this is an essay that recognizes the complexity of social and political alignments in liberal affirmative (and sometimes complacent) discourse and one that subjects such discourse to interrogation.

In Chapter 11 Rob Stone provides an analysis of gender constructions as represented by the female star. By concentrating on the actress Victoria Abril and her portrayal of the character Gloria in *Nadie hablará de nosotros cuando hayamos muerto* (1995), this chapter explores problematics of feminist spectatorship. Stone's analysis of the complexities of spectator identification with this star raises important questions concerning gender and feminist politics.

In Chapter 12 Kathleen M. Vernon discusses what was in its day a major box office hit, *El último cuplé* (1959), a movie that remains in the Spanish popular imaginary as a highpoint in the nation's film-making history in spite of the critical reception concerning its 'quality'. In the context of enduring contested nationalistic readings, Vernon approaches the film with a discussion of its star vehicle, the indefatigable Sara Montiel. Furthermore, in detailing the evolution and significance of the song form, the *cuplé*, the author proposes an analysis of the movie's 'highly effective' deployment of melodrama.

In the final chapter of the volume Eva Woods relates gender to cultural production in her discussion of the film *Torbellino*, made during the early years of Francoism. She argues that Andalusian musical comedies subvert dominant cultural forms, and in doing so foreground popular cultural products, such as the radio, traditionally considered effeminized. By analysing the role of popular mass media in the construction of gender and other hierarchies she further locates them within an ongoing contemporaneous debate aimed at inventing national identity. A triangular relation emerges in this chapter between the concepts of gender, culture and nation.

Notes

1. The most significant exceptions of course are works on Luis Buñuel, whose ambiguous relationship to the country of his birth is perhaps exemplified by the fact that he is often not thought of as a Spanish film-maker but as either Mexican or French, and Carlos Saura who, prior to Almodóvar, was the best known Spanish director outside of Spain.

2. Jordan and Morgan-Tamosunas devote a chapter of their book *Contemporary Spanish Cinema* (1998) to interrogating the limits of gender representations in recent Spanish cinema. Likewise, Stone addresses numerous gender-related issues in his *Spanish Cinema* (2002).

References

Althusser, Louis (1971), *'Lenin and Philosophy' and Other Essays*. London: New Left Books.

Beauvoir, Simone de (1972), *The Second Sex*, trans. H. Parshley. Paris: Gallimard.

Bruno, Giuliana (2002), *Atlas of Emotion: Journeys in Art, Architecture, and Film*, New York: Verso.

Butler, Judith (1990), *Gender Trouble: Feminism and the Subversion of Identity*, New York and London: Routledge.

Camporesi, Valeria and Parrondo Coppel, Eva (eds) (2001), *Cine y mujer: Secuencias 15*, Madrid: Universidad Autónoma.

Ferrán, Ofelia and Glenn, Kathleen M. (eds) (2002), *Women's Narrative and Film in Twentieth Century Spain*, New York and London: Routledge.

Jordan, Barry and Morgan-Tamosunas, Rikki (1998), *Contemporary Spanish Cinema*, Manchester: Manchester University Press.

Martin-Márquez, Susan (1999), *Feminist Discourse in Spanish Cinema: Sight Unseen*, Oxford: Oxford University Press.

Smith, Paul Julian (1994), *Desire Unlimited: The Cinema of Pedro Almodóvar*, London and New York: Verso.

Stone, Rob (2002), *Spanish Cinema*, Harlow: Longman.

–2–

Between the Phobic Object and the Dissident Subject: Abjection and Vampirism in Luis Buñuel's *Viridiana*
Julián Daniel Gutiérrez-Albilla

> Climbing, some years later, the hill which leads to her grave, the memory of that first ascent returns. And there returns, as well, the special darkness of that night, for he steps across the threshold of his house in the direction of the burial site into a night whose darkness is, as it were, inexplicable. His pilgrimage is marked by a sudden intensity of terror and by an experience of splitting, of possession by the body and spirit of the dead woman, and it culminates in an ecstatic recapturing of love lost.
>
> Michelson (1986: 111–27)

The epigraph to this essay encapsulates both symbolically and literally some of the issues that I attempt to argue in my analysis of Luis Buñuel's *Viridiana* (1961).[1] As suggested by the quotation, which points to the threshold of the visible, this chapter considers the ideological and psychic implications of the dialectical relationship between the desublimated and the sublimated, the seductive and the repulsive, the visible and the invisible, the identifiable and the unidentifiable, as well as between the phobic object and the dissident subject. I will pay, thus, attention to Buñuel's emphasis on 'these gaps, breaches, openings, and wounds by which communication, sexual and social, is attained' (Michelson 1986: 112). This chapter focuses on Buñuel's treatment of examples of subversive bodies in *Viridiana*. These can be understood in relation to Julia Kristeva's notion of abjection, which itself relates to Bataille's notion of *hétérologie*. This notion allows Bataille to celebrate those objects that are prohibited or censored. These are objects of revulsion, excluded from daily contact or touch, abstracted from use because of their heterogeneous and excessive nature.

This chapter explores how *Viridiana*, by alluding to the heterogeneous image experienced in the semiotic *chora*, is concerned with and obtains pleasure (*jouissance*) from the transgression of sexual, social, religious and psychic taboos. I argue that *Viridiana* engages implicitly with the vampire, who desires to return to the maternal body, where there is arguably no understanding of the Freudian castration crisis. Can we, then, reinterpret the film from a sexually dissident subject position? As we shall see, the spectator defines himself/herself as an unstable, propulsive, and multiple erotic subject.

Viridiana,[2] a beautiful novice (Silvia Pinal), visits her uncle don Jaime (Fernando Rey) before pronouncing her religious vows. Since the death of don Jaime's wife the night of their wedding, he has lived alone with his servants. When Viridiana arrives at the house, don Jaime is astonished by her remarkable resemblance to his late wife, who was Viridiana's aunt. Don Jaime attempts to coerce Viridiana into rejecting her religious vocation and into becoming his sexual partner. One night, don Jaime persuades Viridiana to wear his late wife's wedding dress, drugs her, and finally attempts to make love to her in a necrophilic manner. However, we are left in doubt as to whether he violated Viridiana.

The following day, a disgusted Viridiana decides to leave the house. However, don Jaime's suicide obliges her to stay and to renounce her monastic life. Subsequently Viridiana dedicates herself to charitable concerns by inviting a group of beggars into the house. Jorge (Paco Rabal), an illegitimate son and heir to don Jaime, begins to share the house with Viridiana. Jorge wishes to transform the estate into productive land. His pragmatic spirit contrasts with Viridiana's sterilized sense of the world. One night, when the house is vacant, the beggars take advantage of the situation and decide to organize a kind of bacchanal banquet and orgy. One of the beggars pretends to take a picture of the others as they pose around the dining table in a clear parody of Leonardo Da Vinci's *Last Supper*. The debacle ends with an assault on Viridiana, whose rape is only prevented by Jorge's intervention. Once the beggars are expelled from the house, the bourgeois order is reestablished. This coincides with Viridiana's abandoning her religious inclinations. She decides to seek the sexual company of her cousin Jorge. The latter accepts Viridiana's company as well as that of the maid. The final sequence of the film shows the three characters playing cards in Jorge's bedroom, clearly suggesting that the three have agreed to opt for a *ménage à trois*.

Let us begin with a brief description of Kristeva's problematic theoretical concept of abjection and its operational function within psychoanalytic thought. Kristeva's term contributes to a theory of subjectivity based on the infant's relation to the pre-Oedipal mother. This theory was first formulated by Melanie Klein, who revised Freud's work on the pre-Oedipal stage of the infant subject by referring to a psychic stage prior to the acquisition of language. Kristeva's definition of the abject is bound up with a theoretical perspective that may be defined as a feminist position.[3] Her psycho-linguistic re-reading of Freudian and Lacanian formulations of the construction of human subjectivity allows her to decentre the position of Freud and Lacan in relation to the paternal function by reintroducing or re-emphasizing the maternal body at the central axis in the process of the formation of the child's subjectivity. Kristeva 're-inscribes the maternal metaphor in the Oedipal triangle, just as Klein had insisted earlier on the centrality of infantile ambivalence to the maternal body' (Fer 1997: 185). Kristeva argues:

> Through frustrations and prohibitions, this authority shapes the body into a *territory* having areas, orifices, points and lines, surfaces and hollows, where the archaic power of mastery and neglect, of the differentiation of proper-clean and improper-dirty, possible and impossible, is impressed and exerted. It is a 'binary logic,' a primal mapping of the body that I call semiotic to say that, while being the precondition of language, it is dependent upon meaning, but in a way that is not that of *linguistic* signs nor of the *symbolic* order they found. Maternal authority is the trustee of that mapping of the self's clean and proper body; it is distinguished from paternal laws within which, with the phallic phase and acquisition of language, the destiny of man will take place (Kristeva 1982: 72).

There are significant problems with Kristeva's theory, especially in relation to her ambiguous position toward biology. According to Stephen Frosh, this feminist object-relations theory runs the risk of falling into biologistic categories. The account given of the particular nature of mothering, Frosh argues, might reinforce gender division (Frosh 1987: 180). Frosh suggests that Kristeva's conceptualization of motherhood might rely on essentialist views that have foregrounded the social differences between the feminine and the masculine gender within a biological framework.

However, Kristeva's definition of the abject reinscribes the body into signification. This strategy subverts what Lacan sees as the loss of the Real self through his/her symbolic construction in language. For Lacan, the definition and construction of subjectivity is, moreover, bound up with lack and imperfection (*manque-à-être*). As such, the subject fears losing control of language and discourse, which is equivalent to the loss of one's self. Kristeva also redefines the Freudian theory of the Oedipus complex and castration crisis. As Kelly Oliver explains, 'in traditional

Freudian and Lacanian psychoanalysis it is the paternal function that finally propels the infant into both language and subjectivity' (Oliver 1993: 3). If the paternal imago functions as the centre of prohibition and sublimation, by reinscribing the maternal body into subjectivity, Kristeva succeeds in challenging the two most canonical psychoanalytic models that have been associated with privileging patriarchal and therefore 'compulsory' heterosexual identity and subjectivity. Hal Foster persuasively argues that 'in a world in which the Other has collapsed, Kristeva implies a crisis in the paternal law that underwrites the social order' (Foster 1996: 156).

In *Powers of Horror*, Kristeva introduces the category of the abject in order to describe the constitution of acceptable forms of subjectivity and sociality of the self. According to Kristeva, the subject achieves autonomy through the process of rejecting improper and unclean elements that are reminiscent of his/her initial fusion with the maternal body. Hence, the separation of the child from the mother takes place through the semiotic aspect of language. Kristeva argues that 'the abject confronts us within our personal archaeology, with our earliest attempts to release the hold of *maternal* entity even before existing outside of her, thanks to the autonomy of language' (Kristeva 1982: 13). For Kristeva:

> The abject has only one quality of the object – that of being opposed to *I*. If the object, however, through its opposition, settles me within the fragile texture of a desire for meaning, which is a matter of fact, makes me ceaselessly and infinitely homologous to it, what is *abject*, on the contrary, the jettisoned object, is radically excluded and draws me toward the place where meaning collapses (Kristeva 1982: 2)

This quotation suggests the extent to which desire and identity occupy a paradoxical position. On one hand, the subject is caught in the desire for the original object (the mother), which, structurally speaking, occupies the position of death. On the other hand, the subject anxiously desires satisfaction, which is associated with life. The subject is also constituted through its struggle against separation, developing an endless process of translating the unnameable other. Hence, separation is a vital necessity in the formation of the subject. As I shall suggest, the subversion implied in Kristeva's definition of the abject allows us to understand the extent to which some punctual details in *Viridiana* refer to fantasies and anxieties, which, in the same way as Kristeva's concept, reject the theories of psychic and social organization that privilege genital sexuality, which can be attributed to the theories of Freud and Lacan.

Abjection and Vampirism in Buñuel's *Viridiana*

In *The Monstrous Feminine*, Creed successfully applies Kristeva's theory of abjection in the context of film theory. Creed attempts to unpack how gender, more specifically the feminine, has been represented in the Hollywood horror film genre. Creed questions why in most of these horror films the feminine character reveals destructive powers which are 'castrating' for the male characters and for the male spectator. In the horror film, these horrific figures of formlessness emerge from that terrifying borderline between the 'clarity' of the masculine and the 'obscurity' of the feminine. This tension between control and loss of control is central to patriarchal discourses of the masculine. For this reason, the monstrous-feminine is one of the ways in which male anxiety might figure in cinematic representation. The theory formulated by Kristeva provides Creed with an important theoretical framework to draw the following conclusion; the monstrous-feminine in the horror film is usually constructed as a figure of abjection. This particular representation of femininity is ultimately punished psychically, and even physically, by the different elements that constitute the cinematic apparatus, restoring the power of patriarchy within conventional signifying practices. As Creed argues, 'the horror film stages and re-stages a constant repudiation of the "maternal figure" (the abject)' (Creed 1986: 70).

Creed suggests that the abject has been excluded and repressed in our patriarchal society in order to keep the symbolic and therefore the social order securely protected. According to Creed, these feminine representations produce a disturbance in the male spectator because they reveal that ambiguity (the maternal body) repressed (abjected) in the collective unconscious of patriarchal culture. As Creed says: 'Abjection is above all ambiguity, because, while releasing a hold, it does not radically cut off the subject from what threatens it' (Creed 1993: 9). The maternal body, which is related to the notion of fluidity, challenges the boundaries rigidly established by the dominant society. The notion of fluidity, which is itself linked to that of contradiction, drive or frustration, is either repressed or marginalized in the fictional construction of a rational model of thought. The modern subject (presumed to be a heterosexual man) fights against these 'othernesses'. However, his fear and anxiety at that fragmented and liquid body return traumatically. Sexuality and the unconscious, desire and drives are thus associated with *jouissance*. It is this psychic pain or pleasure, thus, that shatters the subject and surrenders it precisely to the fragmentary and the fluid. Creed's examination of the representation of femininity as abject in the horror genre also suggests that these figures of the abject, represented in a sublimated or desublimated manner, open up the possibility of their being a site of inscription of bodily alterations, wastes and decay or death. The ultimate (non-) subject of abjection is death. Foster states that such 'images evoke the body turned inside out, the subject literally abjected, thrown out. But they also evoke the outside turned in, the subject-as-picture invaded by the object-gaze' (Foster 1996: 149).

In her genealogical study of abjection, Rosalind Krauss attributes the first articulation of the term to the sociological studies of Bataille, which were concerned with the exclusionary forces that operate within modern state systems in order to strip the labouring masses of their human dignity and reduce them to dehumanized social waste. Particularly celebrated in the French critical journal *Tel Quel*, Bataille became a central stimulus in French post-structuralist thought, such as in the theories of Barthes, Foucault, and Derrida. The theoretical work of these authors had previously been published in the journal *Critique* (1946–64) of which Bataille was an editor. Kristeva, who was a prominent figure of the *Tel Quel* intellectual group, rethought Bataille's term of abjection from an anthropological and psychoanalytical perspective in order to address the constitution of the subject in its negative aspect, emphasizing a subject position located at the 'border' between its own subjecthood and objecthood. Subsequently, Bataille's theories were taken up in the critical discourse of art in the United States through the reception of post-structuralism and through new readings of Surrealism, such as in the writings of Krauss. The latter championed Bataille's dissident journal, *Documents*, rather than André Breton's association of Surrealism with idealized love and liberation.

Some American visual artists in the 1990s, such as John Miller, Kiki Smith, Paul McCarthy, Robert Gober, Andres Serrano or Cindy Sherman, have attempted to link Bataille with Kristeva in order to deal with the abject through the representation of the body as vulnerable, wounded, gendered, sexual, fragmented, horrific, uncanny, scatological or excessive. As there has been an increasing emphasis on the body in the visual arts, so there has been a parallel-intensified interest in body theory in the academic field. Since the late 1980s, Western society has also developed a growing fixation on the body due, for example, to the crisis of the AIDS epidemic, which involves invasive disease and death. Therefore, relatively recent fundamental, social and political questions have been deeply implicated in the problematic of the body. However, Krauss objects to the way in which these visual artists have unproblematically attributed to the abject the function of describing the properties of objects, as is the case with John Miller's pile of excrement. According to Krauss, these artists have literalized and reified the abject. For Krauss, the appeal to essence and substance in such artworks might paradoxically be seen as culturally stereotypical, thereby reconfirming the symbolic order and retracing the fragile limits of the speaking being.

To what extent does the abject blur the boundaries between self and other or relate to Bataille's notion of 'base materialism' in which he challenged established notions of mind/body dualism? It is at this point that we should explore how the commonality between Kristeva and Bataille confronts social and psychic taboo issues related to gender and sexuality in *Viridiana*. This theoretical approach may uncover retrospectively some reasons why the film was so controversial at the time it was produced. This controversy resulted in the prohibition of its distribution within Francoist Spain. The Spanish authorities even denied that the film existed (Edwards 1982: 144).

In one of the sequences of the first part of the film, the beautiful Viridiana is persuaded by don Jaime to play out one of the sexual fantasies of this old patriarchal figure. Don Jaime obsessively wants Viridiana to dress up in his late wife's wedding dress, which is a fetishistic object throughout the film, so that he can traumatically relive, in a ritual manner, the tragic night of his wife's death. Hence, don Jaime attempts to retrieve a disappeared female by remodelling another. Robert Stam explains:

> Don Jaime is haunted by the memory of his first wife, who expired in his arms on their wedding night. Just as the heartbroken Tristan weds a second Isolde in order to sustain the memory of the first, so don Jaime attempts to transform Viridiana, the physical double of his espouse, into a reincarnation of his former love. He dresses her in his wife's wedding clothes, drugs her, and beds her, caressing her ankles and running his hands along her satin gown to the accompaniment of Mozart's Requiem (Stam 1991: 128).

This obsessive sense of repetition through substitution reminds us of Hitchcock's film *Vertigo* (1958), in which the male protagonist also generates a hypothetically endless play of the illusion of substitution through similarity. Moreover, this spiral-like image that we conjure from this repetitive action emphasizes the sense of openness of the film's dramatic construction. Don Jaime's wife's death threw him into a melancholic depression. The patriarchal subject therefore dedicates the rest of his life to the poetic celebration of the lost object. Don Jaime's search for eternity through his attempts to transform Viridiana into his dead wife implies, according to Peter Evans's association of the film with the death instinct, a 'process that bears all the hallmarks of the artist's transformation of the chaotic material of reality into the highly wrought patterns of art' (Evans 1988: 66).

The old aristocratic-looking gentleman is reminiscent of the characters portrayed in the eighteenth-century scatological writings of the Marquis de Sade, who was praised by surrealist artists of the 1920s. The representation of this character in the film suggests the close intertextual relationship between Buñuel's work and that of Sade. Buñuel himself recognized that 'In Sade I discovered a world of extraordinary subversion, in which everything entered: from insects to the customs of human society, sex, theology... In a word, he dazzled me' (Sánchez Vidal 1993: 221). The controversial nature of Sade's literature lies in the way in which Sade managed to resist situations of prohibition by the social mores of the time. In the same way as Sade, Buñuel also enjoyed allowing the viewer's imagination to have complete control of its own domain. Buñuel returns to Sade in order to 'scrutinize the very idea of evil, or of crime, or of blasphemy: the borders of nature. Sade for Buñuel represented not vice but a form of principled pathology, a refusal of all illusions about the ruthless propensities of humankind' (Wood 1993: 94).

The patriarchal figure sadistically persuades Viridiana to dress up in his late wife's wedding dress and to promenade in his haunting *château*. Here don Jaime will attempt to perform one of the most 'bestial' of the sexual perversions. The camera pays attention to the wedding dress, which is made of white silk and tightly fits Viridiana. The dress accentuates her feminine figure, yet constrains her body to the point of immobilization. Hence, the wedding dress fulfils the material function of a rope, which is a constant motif throughout the film, and also serves as a metaphor that suggests the extent to which desire and subjection, dominance and submission, love and death, pleasure and punishment, phobia and dissidence are mutually interconnected in the film. Viridiana's blonde hair is drawn back with a beautiful crown of flowers. Although the white material covers the whole of Viridiana's female body, close-ups and medium shots of Viridiana allow the spectator to imagine Viridiana's voluptuous naked female body. In this case, one could argue that Viridiana is defined only in terms of heterosexual male desire. Buñuel's representation of Viridiana's femininity implies what later Allen Jones explicitly revealed in his sculptures known as 'women as furniture'.[4] According to Laura Mulvey's psychoanalytic interpretation of these 'punished women', the female figure has been visually represented in history in order to fulfil the function of a socio-psychic commodity fetish at both levels: the economic and the sexual. Viridiana or Allen Jones' women exist 'in a state of suspended animation, without depth or context, withdrawn from any meaning other than the message imprinted by their clothes, stance and gesture' (Mulvey 1989: 7). Viridiana's image might therefore function as a spectacle: an object or piece of furniture to be displayed, to be looked at, gazed at, stared at and even to be consumed and exchanged by predominantly men of different social and economic backgrounds.

In this sadomasochistic performance, after having being drugged by her uncle, Viridiana recreates the dead feminine body of don Jaime's wife both as a sublimated phantom and as a fulfilment of the material function of a corpse.[5] In his analysis of Hitchcock's *Vertigo*, whose thematic concerns with sublimation and the male protagonist's over-identification with the lost female object remind us of *Viridiana*, Slavoj Zizek rightly points out that sublimation has to do with death. The power of fascination exerted by a sublime image always announces a lethal dimension. Zizek argues:

> The sublime object is precisely an ordinary, everyday object that undergoes a kind of transubstantiation and starts to function, in the symbolic economy of the subject, as an embodiment of the impossible Thing. This is why the sublime object presents the paradox of an object that is able to subsist only in shadow, in an intermediary, half-born state, as something latent, implicit, evoked. As soon as we try to cast away the shadow to reveal the substance, the object itself dissolves; all that remains is the dross of the common object. (Zizek 1991: 84)

If we follow Zizek's notion of sublimation, Viridiana may be read as the necrophiliac patriarchal figure's beloved apparition. The sublimated image of Viridiana implies an illusion that transcends itself, destroys itself, by demonstrating that it is only there as a signifier. Viridiana's sublime image is equivalent to a lid that covers up something else and therefore, conceals its contents. As an attractive and seductive surface, Viridiana's sublime image is so resplendent that it is dazzling and irresistible. Her image invites speculation, yet resists explanation or fixed meaning. Viridiana lies horizontally in the nuptial bed as if she lies in the coffin, so radiantly beautiful that she seems the *Sleeping Beauty*. The camera lingers on her body to emphasize Viridiana's horizontal pose, conjuring in the spectator a corpse lying in a wake. If Viridiana fulfils the function of a corpse, her dead body does not awaken to become once more the bride of her perverse uncle (or father figure).

Kristeva distinguishes between three main forms of abjection. These are constituted in relation to food, bodily waste and sexual difference. For Kristeva, the ultimate in abjection is the corpse. Although the body expels its waste in order to continue to live, the corpse is a body that can no longer expel its waste. Kristeva argues:

> The corpse, the most sickening of wastes, is a border that has encroached upon everything. It is no longer 'I' who expel, 'I' is expelled. The border has become an object. The corpse, seen without God, and outside of science, is the utmost of abjection. It is death infecting life. Abject. It is something rejected from which one does not part, from which one does not protect oneself as from an object. (Kristeva 1982: 3–4)

If Viridiana is seen as a corpse, the camera's constant attention to her hair may no longer be read as displaying hair as a sign of cosmetic beauty, since women's hair is conventionally equated with femininity. Viridiana's blonde hair becomes a bodily part highly related to the abject. Hair is defined as a bodily waste element, which even transcends the death of the subject, as it continues to grow after we are dead. I now bring into the discussion a contemporary art installation produced by the contemporary British-Palestinian female artist, Mona Hatoum's *Recollection* (1994) in order to explore this 'other' function that hair fulfils.

The installation is composed of the artist's own hair hanging from the ceiling. The lines of hair are so thin that they seem almost invisible. In a corner of the gallery's space, there is a kind of hand-operated machine that weaves hair as opposed to wool. This machine parodies the kinds of domestic labours that have been historically located within the realm of femininity. Hatoum also displays balls made of the same hair that spread across the exhibition's floor. This peculiar art installation disrupts the boundaries between the art object and the privileged spectator's space, generating an anxiety and disturbance in the spectator's field of vision. The claustrophobic effect is reinforced by the hair's physical contact with the face and body of the spectator. Hatoum's art installation attempts to reaffirm the notion of tactility. The latter is often repressed in the construction of a rational model of thought that privileges sight. Hatoum thus challenges the conventional obsessional neuroticism in relation to the taboo of touch. Hatoum's redefinition of the function of hair enables to reread the hair in the corpse as a haunting 'abject body'.

Hatoum's redefinition of hair as a haunting abject body tends to render the body a territory of cultural self-redefinition. This mobilization of the *strangeness* within oneself may be seen as emancipatory, as well as defining a more complex account of the self. With particular references to another installation work by Hatoum entitled *Corps étranger* (1994), Ewa Lajer-Burcharth has argued that 'Hatoum's visual self-interrogation inspires one to account for the work of hyphenations within oneself.

Abjection and Vampirism in Buñuel's Viridiana

This idea must have posed itself with particular urgency to the artist as a culturally "hyphenated", British-Palestinian subject. Hatoum exposes the work of hyphenations as the routes of an internal migration, rather than division and stagnation, of psychic and cultural meaning' (Lajer-Burcharth 1997: 202). Lajer-Burcharth's complex analysis of Hatoum's installation work enables us to suggest that the redefinition of Viridiana's hair as an abject body during the necrophiliac ritual of don Jaime can also be seen as a kind of internal mobility. This mobility allows for a more complex sense of subjectivity and a greater awareness of its psychic and social implications.

The necrophiliac don Jaime subsequently commits suicide by hanging himself with the rope that has also functioned as an erotic object. Through subjective shots from the point of view of don Jaime, the legs of Rita (the maid's daughter) are observed voyeuristically while she plays skipping. As Raymond Durgnat observes, 'don Jaime, instead of taking advantage of Viridiana, hangs himself with the skipping-rope which he had given to his servant's illegitimate daughter' (Durgnat 1968: 123). By hanging himself, we assume, don Jaime will achieve a full erection and his male body will become a site of unbridled eroticism. If we read the rope symbolically as a penis that 'penetrates' the neck, in don Jaime's body there coexists a 'penetrated' neck and an erect penis. Therefore don Jaime's body now unsettles the polarities between penetrator and penetrated. The association of torture rendered in an erotic manner allows us to link Buñuel's film to the erotic and terrible universe of the dissident Bataille, who had a fascination with the combination of desire with violence.

Don Jaime's 'sublime object' has involved the mortal danger that the sublime object always entails. The sublime object allows the subject to recognize that the condition of life for human beings is the recognition of death. Bataille asserts that eroticism affirms life to the point of death, as well as life even in death. Hence, death and sex are bound up with a remainder that is experienced at a primitive level. This remainder is linked to anguish, which appears when the desiring subject, caught in a double bind, wishes to return to an undifferentiated stage before or beyond life. In this universe, all differences are abolished. The notion of good is synonymous with that of evil. Even death dies, or ceases to exist, since it is no longer distinguishable from life. Death, thus, haunts Bataille's fiction and Buñuel's films. More importantly, death is a reality embodied in representational practices. However, during this performance, don Jaime, like the vampire, is still condemned to live. This perverse aristocratic man is unable to forget the defilement, this incestuous relationship between uncle and niece, or father and daughter. This explicit Sadean incestuous scenario is indeed a challenge to bourgeois morality, as the dominant society punishes any consensual act of incestuous union. Moreover, incest is a clear violation of the symbolic order, as it is a challenge to reproduction.

In her essay 'Fetishism and the Problem of Sexual Difference in Buñuel's *Tristana*', Jo Labanyi rightly suggests that Cathérine Deneuve becomes 'increasingly vampire-like towards the film's end, her pallor emphasised by her garish make-up and her black shawl echoing Dracula's cape' (Labanyi 1999: 82). In *Viridiana*, it is the morally depraved old patriarchal figure who leans over his dead niece 'like a vampire over its victim' (Labanyi 1999: 82) in order to grieve for the loss of his desired object. We could make an analogy between don Jaime and the Count Dracula. Both characters are depicted as sinister heterosexual males who dwell in a kind of Gothic castle. The latter is characterized by long winding stairs, dark corridors, or cobwebs. The issue of incestuous love intertwines, then, with the anxieties or pleasures associated with the vampire trope. The vampire not only sucks the victim's blood. Often his first victims are those whom he has most loved. In the case of Buñuel's film, the 'vampire' don Jaime takes his own niece as the first prey. Viridiana, like most victims of the vampire, is a young virgin. The issues of incest and vampirism are not mutually exclusive. Rather, they are complementary primordial transgressions that the pervert is subject to repeat endlessly by subjecting himself/herself to a fragmentary perception of the Real.

The camera cuts to shots of Rita (the maid's daughter) looking at this performance from one of the room's windows. Marsha Kinder's analysis of the film concentrates on the extent to which the gaze is captured by female characters from lower classes (Kinder 1993: 314) at various points in the film. The camera cuts from an objective shot of Rita looking at the scene inside from the room's window to a subjective shot from Rita's point of view of the old patriarchal figure lying over his niece's 'dead' body in order to satisfy a coital urge. In symbolic terms, although it does not appear graphically on the screen, we might, perhaps, read his ejaculated semen and Viridiana's post-coital blood as substitutes for the victim's blood. In the vampire film, semen, blood and milk are signifiers that allow mixture and confusion. This demonstrates once more the close relationship between Buñuel's work and Bataille's. In *L'Histoire de l'oeil*, the dissident surrealist author argues that the display of the blood and body of Christ in Catholic liturgy is a metaphorical masquerade of Christ's sperm and urine. Penetration is therefore an equivalent to the act of sucking the blood of his victim. The 'absent' signifiers of semen and blood in *Viridiana* contribute paradoxically to the breakdown of a taboo in the dominant ideology with regard to the display of semen. In order to emphasize this heretical act, Buñuel juxtaposes the incestuous relationship between the necrophiliac don Jaime and the 'dead' Viridiana with religious music coming from another place off-screen. Like the vampire, Viridiana's body does not elicit compassion, but the morbid attraction of a sublimated body fully covered in white silk that reveals simultaneously and paradoxically its possibility of decaying. Through this particular imagery and these conventions, the *mise en scène* recalls explicitly the vampire film. As Evans has rightly suggested, Buñuel, moreover, uses the contrast between light and dark, associated with the style of *chiaroscuro*, to enhance the film's analogy with the Gothic style and genre. Moreover, the contrast between light and shadow is further emphasized by the uniform temporal pattern established between day and night in which the action of the film takes place.

At this point, we can relate the vampire body of don Jaime to the uncanny return of the Real. In addition, Viridiana's body may also be read as a vampire body when it lies in the nuptial bed. On the one hand, the representation of vampirism in *Viridiana* can be interpreted as a retrogressive phobic critique of perversion. On the other hand, the vampire trope can be seen as a progressive challenge to patriarchal ontology. In the latter case, the vampire figure is an 'abject' space reclaimed by a contemporary sexually dissident viewer. Although Viridiana seems to be the victim of the necrophiliac vampire, her sublimated body lies in the bed as if in the coffin. Like the vampire, Viridiana rests 'in her coffin like an unborn baby nestled in the dark comfort of the mother's womb' (Creed 1993: 69). Moreover, the vampire body alludes to an oral relation of *jouissance*, since vampirism can only be achieved through sucking the victim's neck, which is a displacement of the breast. According to Joan Copjec, vampirism provokes an anxiety in the complete ego. The breast is a partial object that the subject needs to abject in order to constitute itself as a unified subject. Copjec argues that it is not the image of the mother's child at the mother's breast that provokes anxiety in the subject's psyche. The vampire body is rather located beyond the relationship between the child and the object of desire, the breast. Vampirism refers to the point at which desire disappears, as the breast has been dried up. The drying up of desire thus asphyxiates the subject.

Hence vampirism is a threat to the notion of the body as being securely protected in the symbolic. The vampire body is a bodily double that the subject cannot recognize intelligibly. In a previous sequence, Viridiana plays a sleepwalker, who reminds us of the figure of the phantom. The latter, like the vampire, positions itself between the material and the immaterial, the visible and the invisible, the recognizable and unrecognizable, presence and absence. The phantom, born out of the shadow, transgresses the threshold of the visible world by going beyond culture, beyond the signifier and therefore inhabiting a domain of non-meaning. Copjec's emphasis on the Real allows us to suggest that vampirism is a fragmented body that is located in the semiotic *chora*. In opposition to the semiotic, in the thetic phase, the subject, qua subject, is always already in language, and thus in the symbolic. The semiotic focuses rather on the imperfections of the body. The fragmented body breaks the skin that functions as the boundary between the inside and the outside of our bodies by suggesting that the self is in an unfinished state. It envisions the instability of the internal psychic boundaries as a concrete embodied experience. The vampire disrupts the dominant society's teleological conception of resurrection by pointing to a cyclical notion of return. The body is no longer subject to cultural signification but is now part of an arbitrary process of fluid 'schizo'-symbolization.[6] If Lacan has defined identification as an incorporation that transforms the subject, identification here is less assimilation than a kind of spectral decomposition of the self.

The morning after this sinister performance, Viridiana believes that her uncle possessed her during this ritualistic and masochistic act. The audience never finds out whether he indeed had sex with her or whether it was just an excuse to force Viridiana to not return to the convent and to stay near him as his lover. What interests me in this sequence is how this female character's sense of disgust with her uncle's actions and with the fantasy space of sublimation in which the action took place provokes her to leave abruptly the bourgeois house. Viridiana is no longer securely protected either in a bourgeois social and symbolic order or in a world governed by perverse relations. It seems as if any trace of the Real should vanish from her repressed consciousness. In psychoanalytic terms, this reaction of repulsion on the part of Viridiana could be the response of Buñuel's heterosexual and patriarchal anxiety at the danger associated with the Real that remains inaccessible to the subject and yet structures its functioning. Copjec suggests that the subject 'flees into a symbolic domain which implies a hedge against the Real. For this reason, the evasion of the Real can only be secured through the negation of the Real' (Copjec 1991: 31).

At the end of this sequence Buñuel punishes Viridiana by perpetuating her sense of disgust. He also punishes don Jaime by having him commit suicide. Don Jaime becomes the corpse that was sublimated in the previous ritual that alluded to the vampire. This effect reinforces a rereading of the vampire film in which the Real is retrogressively associated with monstrosity. Although the reading that follows might be considered anachronistic, a contemporary, embodied reading of vampire films can function as a theoretical object that allows us to perform a close reading of this sequence from *Viridiana*, adding and inferring a queer perspective hitherto largely ignored by critics of the film.[7] From our contemporary dissident subject position, we may in retrospect suggest that Buñuel perhaps anticipates a kind of psychic anxiety that was later explicitly manifested and associated with sexual disease in the filmic representations of the vampire produced during the Reagan years in the United States. This historical context coincides with the development of a growing fixation on the body in relation to progressive and retrogressive social and political questions, mainly associated with the AIDS crisis.

In this context, the representation of bodily fluids in mainstream vampire film became metaphorically associated with the AIDS epidemic of the 1980s. As Simon Watney suggests, the media coverage of AIDS was aimed at the heterosexual groups, especially an imaginary national family unit (Bersani 1987: 203). The homosexual was portrayed as a monster, infecting the harmonious heterosexual society with his poisonous blood. It is interesting to note in this specific socio-political context that Cathérine Deneuve, who collaborated with Buñuel in *Belle de Jour* (1966) and *Tristana* (1970) in two of his films, later played a bisexual vampire in Tony Scott's 1982 movie, *The Hunger*. Harry M. Benshoff observes that the sequence in which Deneuve is making love with Susan Sarandon, the harmonious melody of Delibe's *Lakme* is suddenly disrupted by discordant sounds. Benshoff argues that 'the Scene slowly turns from tender and erotic to menacing and evil. What had begun as a beautiful scene of making love ends as yet another monstrous horror' (Benshoff 1997: 243). In response to this homophobic coverage, many gay and lesbian cultural productions have tried to dismantle the relationship between the vampire, the monster and the queer. From this perspective, Buñuel's representation of vampirism might function as a negative stereotypical representation of the sexual outlaw as a monster that needs to be expelled from hegemonic society.[8]

On the other hand, the vampire body allows for the possibility of a sexually dissident pleasure dynamic. The vampire, as a figure of abjection, contributes to the collapse of the boundaries between the human and the non-human subject. In this utopian space, there is no longer any distinction between masculine and feminine. From this perspective, the vampire does not work in the dimension of gender and sexual difference, but rather at the site of ontology. The boundaries that separate life from death are disrupted in the vampire's 'unnatural' being. Sue-Ellen Case argues that the vampire challenges

> the Platonic parameters of Being, the borders of life and death. Queer desire is constituted as a transgression of these boundaries and of the organicism which defines the living as the good. The Platonic construction of a life/death binary opposition at the base, with its attendant gender opposition above, is subverted by a queer desire which seeks the living dead. (Case 1991: 3)

Buñuel's representation of vampirism becomes, then, a cultural space in which sexual dissidence can be positively addressed. *Viridiana*'s allusion to the performative vampire body is a gratifying revenge by a minority on dominant heterocentrist hegemony. The vampire has been extracted from the monolithic patriarchal and heterosexist discourse it once inhabited. Moreover, the vampire's separation of gender-based categories contributes to the collapse of the hierarchical distinction between the dominator and the dominated. Contemporary sexually dissident spectators who observe the vampire body in the nuptial bed, which stands metaphorically for the coffin, are able to celebrate that socially and psychically 'abjected' space that, paradoxically, dominant society has obliged the sexual outlaw to inhabit. Hence, the Real is critically reclaimed in order to install a kind of doubt as an imaginary basis for a more complex and flexible sense of the self.

Acknowledgements

I would like to thank Paul Julian Smith and Jo Labanyi for their help and valuable advice with this chapter, and the AHRB for generously supporting my doctoral research on which this chapter is based.

Notes

1. In this chapter, I shall not be concerned with providing a historical account of the film. For a historical analysis of Spanish cinema under Francoism and democracy, see P. Besas (1985).

2. The title of the film derives from a religious painting by Chávez, which depicted a female saint with Christ's attributes praying. This portrait inspired Buñuel to make the film, but never appears in it.
3. Kristeva has been strongly criticised by many feminists. For instance, in 'The Horrors of Power: A Critique of Kristeva', Jennifer Stone analyses how Kristeva supports Freudian notions of 'nothing to be seen'.
4. Allen Jones emerged in the early 1960s as part of the pop movement that dominated the art of a decade. He held his first solo exhibition in 1963 at Tooth & Sons, London where he continued to exhibit until 1970.
5. For a discussion on death, femininity and aesthetics, see E. Bronfen (1992).
6. According to Elisabeth Bronfen, vampirism preserves a fluid boundary with the unconscious.
7. I am thinking of the most recent work on Buñuel by Peter Evans, Marsha Kinder, Victor Fuentes, Agustín Sánchez Vidal, Virginia Higginbotham, or Gastón Lillo. Rather than undermining their valuable and inspiring arguments, this article attempts to give a more radical reading of Buñuel's film.
8. In *Viridiana*, there are explicit references to sexually contagious diseases.

References

Bataille, G. (1985), *Histoire de l'oeil*, Paris: Pauvert.

—— (2001), in M. Dalwood (trans.), *Eroticism: Death and Sensuality*, London: Penguin.

Benshoff, H. (1997), *Monsters in the Closet,* Manchester: Manchester University Press.

Bersani, L. (1987), 'Is the Rectum a Grave?', *October,* 43: 197–222.

Besas, P. (1985), *Behind the Spanish Lens*, Denver CO: Arden.

Bronfen, E. (1992), *Over Her Dead Body*, Manchester: Manchester University Press.

Case, S.E. (1991), 'Tracking the Vampire', *Differences*, 3(2): 1–20.

Copjec, J. (1991), 'Vampires, Breast-feeding and Anxiety', *October*, 58: 25–43.

Creed, B. (1986), 'Horror and the Monstrous-Feminine: An Imaginary Abjection', *Screen*, 27: 44–70.

—— (1993), *The Monstrous Feminine,* London: Routledge.

de Zeguer, C. (1996), *Inside The Visible*, London: Whitechapel.
Durgnat, R. (1968), *Luis Buñuel*, Berkeley: University of California Press.
Edwards, G. (1982), *The Discreet Art of Luis Buñuel: A Reading of His Films*, London: Marion Boyars.
Evans, P. (1988), 'Viridiana and the Death Instinct', in P. Evans and R. Fiddian (eds), *Challenges to Authority: Fiction and Film in Contemporary Spain*, London: Tamesis.
Fer, B. (1997), *On Abstract Art*, New Haven: Yale University Press.
Foster, H. (1996), *The Return of the Real*, Cambridge, MA: M.I.T. Press.
Frosh, S. (1987), *The Politics of Psychoanalysis*, Basingstoke: Macmillan.
Herpe, N. (1992), '*Viridiana*: Autour du retour', *Nouvelle Revue Française*, 47: 77–86.
Kinder, M. (1993), *Blood Cinema: The Reconstruction of National Identity in Spanish Film*, Berkeley: University of California Press.
Krauss, R. (1996), 'Informe without Conclusion', *October*, 78: 89–105.
Kristeva, J. (1982), in L. Roudiez (trans.), *Powers of Horror: An Essay on Abjection*, New York: Columbia University Press.
Krzywinska, T. (1995), 'La Belle Sans Merci', in P. Burston and C. Richardson (eds), *Queer Romance: Lesbians, Gay Men and Popular Culture*, London: Routledge.
Labanyi, J. (1999), 'Fetishism and the Problem of Sexual Difference in Buñuel's *Tristana* (1970)', in P. Evans (ed.), *Spanish Cinema: The Auteurist Tradition*, Oxford: Oxford University Press.
Lajer-Burcharth, E. (1997), 'Real Bodies: Video in the 1990s', *Art History*, 20(2): 185–213.
Michelson, A. (1986), 'Heterology and the Critique of Instrumental Reason', *October*, 36: 111–27.
Miller, D.A. (1990), 'Anal Rope', *Representations*, 32: 114–33.
Miller, J.A. (1992), *The Seminar of Jacques Lacan: Book VII The Ethics of Psychoanalysis, 1959–1960*, New York: Routledge.
Mulvey, L. (1989), 'Fears, Fantasies, and the Male Unconscious', in *Visual and Other Pleasures*, Basingstoke: Macmillan.
Oliver, K. (1993), *Reading Kristeva: Unraveling the Double-bind*, Bloomington: Indiana University Press.
Sánchez Vidal, A. (1993), *El mundo de Buñuel*, Zaragoza: Caja de Ahorros de la Inmaculada Concepción.
Smith, P.J. (1996), *Vision Machines: Cinema, Literature and Sexuality in Spain and Cuba, 1983–1993*, London: Verso.

Stam, R. (1991), 'Hitchcock and Buñuel: Authority, Desire, and the Absurd', in W. Raubicheck and W. Srebnick (eds), *Hitchcock's Rereleased Films from Rope to Vertigo*, Detroit: Wayne State University Press.

Steihaug, J. (1999), *Abject, Informe, Trauma: Discourses on the Body in American Art of the 1990s*, Oslo: Institute for Research within International Contemporary Art.

Stone, J. (1983), 'The Horrors of Power: A Critique of Kristeva', in F. Barker (ed.), *The Politics of Theory*, Colchester: Essex University Press.

Taylor, S. (1993), 'The Phobic Object', in *Abject Art: Repulsion and Desire in American Art*, New York: Whitney Museum of American Art.

Twitchell, J. (1981), *The Living Dead*, Durham, NC: Duke University Press.

Wood, M. (1993), 'God Never Dies: Buñuel and Catholicism', *Renaissance and Modern Studies*, 36: 93–121.

Zizek, S. (1991), *Looking Awry: An Introduction to Jacques Lacan through Popular Culture*, Cambridge, MA: M.I.T. Press.

3

Costume, Identity and Spectator Pleasure in Historical Films of the Early Franco Period

Jo Labanyi

As Pam Cook notes (1996: 67), one of the problems when talking about historical films is that the term covers a wide range of disparate genres: biopics, epics, adventure stories including westerns, period romances, musicals – any kind of film that is set in the past. They can be divided into those whose plots are or are not based on historical events, but here too the distinction blurs, since the former always include invented elements while the latter often include historical events as a backdrop. What they all have in common is that they 'dress [history] up in period clothes and décor' (Cook 1996: 67). In this chapter, I shall not distinguish between films based on historical events and those with fictional plots (usually termed costume films), since both rely on period costumes to create their effects. In the case of Spanish cinema of the early Franco period, there are tactical advantages in refusing this distinction, since it allows the meanings created by visual spectacle to emerge in apparently more serious films, which have tended to be interpreted in terms of their plot and dialogue.

I shall rely heavily on Cook's perception that costume is a key element in the blurring of boundaries, not only between genres, but also between gender, class and national identities, since the reliance on spectacle, created by the décor and costumes, necessarily represents history as a masquerade. Modernity's insistence on the construction of clearly defined identities (Foucault 1987) is complicated by the fact that an equally important aspect of modernity has been its insistence on the new. Baudelaire, Simmel and Benjamin are just some of the cultural critics who have analysed the key role played in modernity by fashion (Squicciarino 1998: 149–90). Costume, which bolsters individual identity, is not only put on and taken off, but under modernity must constantly be changed

Jo Labanyi

and updated. Identities are defined – and deconstructed – in historical films not only by what the characters wear but also by the number of times they change their clothes. Cinema has from the start been embedded in the fashion system, promoting stars and the 'look' of the studio that employed them through publicity that encouraged the public to imitate their clothes, hairstyles and make-up (Stacey 1994; Kuhn 2002). In 1940s Spain as elsewhere, film magazines ran fashion pages and fashion magazines had film features. Audiences did not, of course, imitate the costumes in historical films, for the point of the imitation was to be up to date with the latest fashion – especially in a post-war Spain cut off (save for its consumption of movies) from the outside modern world. Audiences nevertheless projected their modern assumptions about fashion onto the historical films they watched, in that they expected to be dazzled by the stars' successive changes of costume – even in films set in a period prior to the modern equation of fashion with the new.

In their desire to dissociate themselves from cultural production under the early Franco regime, critics have, until recently, tended to give the impression that Spanish cinema of this period was dominated by the big-budget patriotic epics on national historical subjects produced by CIFESA (Compañía Industrial Film Español S.A.). While it is true that the period saw a large number of historical films, CIFESA made only four patriotic epics, all directed by Juan de Orduña: the spectacularly successful *Locura de amor* (1948) whose focus on private emotion makes it more of a melodrama, *Agustina de Aragón* (1950), *La leona de Castilla* (1951) and *Alba de América* (1951) – the last two of which flopped, throwing CIFESA into crisis. The number of films on national historical subjects rises if one considers the output of other production companies. And if one includes films set in the past but not based substantially (or at all) on historical events, the number of historical films increases dramatically, extending from 1938 – continuing the production of historical films in the silent and Republican eras (Hernández Ruíz 1999) – through to the mid 1950s, peaking 1944–50.

While a large number of these films encourage an exceptionalist reading of Spanish history, defined by its 'difference' from that of northern Europe (especially France representing Enlightenment values), we should not conclude that the vogue for historical films in early Francoist Spain is itself a sign of the exceptionalism of Spanish cinema. For, as Harper (1994: 186–7) notes, historical films were hugely popular in British cinema between 1933 and 1949, after which the genre declined. As she observes, in the period 1942–49 these movies celebrated the same kind of aristocratic-plebeian alliance found in early Francoist historical films (which cannot therefore be attributed solely to Francoist ideology) – as well as allowing female pleasure (something that I hope to show characterizes the Spanish equivalents).[1] The 'look' – that is, costumes and décor – of Spanish historical films of this period is clearly influenced by Hollywood's historical productions of the 1930s and 1940s. Gubern (1994: 361) observes that Perojo's *Goyescas* drew on the German and Italian costume-film traditions – which Hay notes (1987: 152) were themselves massively modelled on those of Hollywood – Perojo having worked at UFA (Universum Film A.G.) and Cinecittà in 1938–39 and 1939–40 respectively.[2] Gubern notes that the film's German set designer, Sigfrido Burmann, had worked with Perojo and Florián Rey at UFA, as costume and set designer; while its chief cameraman was the Russian-French Michel Kelber, a Jewish refugee from Nazi-occupied France, who had worked with Duvivier, Sirk, Pabst, Clair, Siodmak, Feyder and Ophuls among others. Burmann – who had modernized Spanish stage design from 1917 through the 1930s (Gil Fombellida 2003) – would become the art director responsible for the 'look' of CIFESA's historical productions, including (but not only) its historical epics, while working also for other companies (Gorostiza 1997: 219–22). And the German Ted Pahle – who had worked for Paramount in the late 1920s, and in Britain, France and Germany in the 1930s, fleeing Nazism for Spain in 1940 – was chief cameraman for *Agustina de Aragón*, among other CIFESA historical films (Llinás 1989: 544).[3] That CIFESA, in particular, should have relied for the 'look' of its historical productions on foreign professionals suggests that we should not assume too quickly that these films – notwithstanding their patriotic marketing – should be read as imposing a monolithically National-Catholic view of Spanish history.

The three films discussed below – made between 1942 and 1950 – comprise one epic based on historical events (*Agustina de Aragón*, Orduña, 1950); a comedy (despite its tragic end) with musical elements whose fictitious plot centres on a historical figure (*La princesa de los Ursinos*, Luis Lucía, 1947); and a musical comedy whose entirely fictional plot alludes obliquely to a historical backdrop (*Goyescas*, Perojo, 1942). The fact that two of these three films were made by CIFESA does not reflect the proportion of historical films for which CIFESA was responsible, but the fact that it was the production company that most successfully created a sustained period 'look', which required a large budget to hire stars on exclusive contracts and to commission lavish costumes and sets. Aurora Bautista made *Agustina de Aragón* under the three-year exclusive contract she signed with CIFESA at the age of 23, following her success in *Locura de amor*, for a record 500,000 pesetas per film:

Jo Labanyi

this contract involved her full-time in fashion sittings and marketing activities such as being photographed, attending social and charitable events, and appearing on radio programmes. The budget for *Agustina de Aragón*, whose crowd scenes involved more than 600 extras, was nine million pesetas, almost double that of *Locura de amor* (Castillejo 1998: 24–5, 97). The budget for *La princesa de los Ursinos* was just under three million pesetas; its star Ana Mariscal, despite the prestige of her lead role in the 1941 epic *Raza* scripted under a pseudonym by General Franco, occupied a lower echelon in CIFESA's constellation at a salary of 70,000 pesetas per film (Fanés 1989: 247, 259). *Goyescas* – made by UNIBA (Universal Iberoamericana de Cinematographía S.L.), formed solely for that purpose – cost three million pesetas, most of which went on the sets and costumes whose extravagance set a precedent in Spanish cinema which CIFESA would later emulate (Gubern 1994: 359).

The historical time-span covered by these three films goes from the early eighteenth to the early nineteenth century. I have chosen this time-span – and will discuss the films in order of the period depicted – so as to focus on the early stages of the emergence of the modern concept of fashion, in which costume becomes an indicator specifically of the new. *La princesa de los Ursinos* is set during the War of the Spanish Succession (1701–13). This is the time when the concept of fashion, which emerged in the previous decades, first established itself, as the court of Louis XIV broke with the tone of (relative) sobriety set by the Spanish court (Squicciarino 1998: 151). The battle over dress codes was part of Louis XIV's bid to establish France as the major European power, definitively breaking Spain's former political hegemony: the War of the Spanish Succession, which forms the film's backdrop, was fought out across Europe by Austria, England, Holland, Portugal and Savoy against France and Spain, to stop the threat to the balance of power caused by the 1701 accession of Louis XIV's grandson Felipe V to the Spanish throne. Lucía's decision to represent this conflict via a costume drama shows an acute cultural insight into the political importance of fashion. Here we should remember that other famous event of the eighteenth century: the 1766 Motín de Esquilache (filmed by Josefina de Molina in 1988), triggered by the attempt to force citizens to replace the Habsburg cape and *chambergo* with Bourbon coats and cocked hats.

Goyescas and *Agustina de Aragón* are both set in 1808, though one would not guess this from their very different visual styles. For *Goyescas* depicts a period – that of the preceding decades, in fact – when it was still normal for men to be as ornately dressed as women. Whereas *Agustina* documents a new unease about ornate male dress, anticipating modernity's imposition of sexual difference, from around the 1820s, via gender-specific dress codes that relegated men to sober attire (suits, dark colours), reserving elaborate dress for women. The choice of different period costumes to represent the same year of 1808 in these two films is striking since both had the same art director (Burmann) and costume designer (Manuel Comba). To be precise: in *Goyescas*, Comba shared responsibility with the fashion designer Julio Lafitte who designed Imperio Argentina's costumes; in *Agustina de Aragón*, Comba shared responsibility with E. Torre de la Fuente. Comba and Torre de la Fuente also designed the costumes for *La princesa de los Ursinos*, with Comba having the role of 'historical consultant'. In all, Comba was responsible for costume research and design for nearly 80 historical films, many for CIFESA including *Locura de amor* (Gorostiza 1997: 51).

It was normal in other countries, too, for the costume designer to be responsible for historical research, with the chief sources being paintings. But in early Francoist Spain the self-conscious use of pictorial sources is especially notable (Gubern 1994: 363; Hernández Ruíz 1999: 156, 160; Pérez Rojas and Alcaide 1992). CIFESA had close links with the Italian film industry (*Hacer memoria* 1990: 42–4), which in the late 1930s and early 1940s had specialized in historical films that drew on paintings (Affron and Affron 1995: 85–7). Comba's father had been Court painter to Alfonso XII and Alfonso XIII, and his wife was granddaughter of the famous nineteenth-century historical painter Rosales, whose painting *El testamento de Isabel la Católica* (1864) is recreated in tableau form in *Locura de amor*. The difference in visual style between *Goyescas* and *Agustina de Aragón* is explained by their recourse to pictorial source-material from different periods. The 'look' of *Goyescas* (as suggested by its title, taken from Granados's opera of the same name, whose music it uses but not its plot) is based on a range of paintings by Goya which in fact are from earlier years: his festive paintings of *majos* from the 1780s and early 1790s; his 1797 painting of the Duquesa de Alba in black; and his 1803–5 *Maja vestida* (also depicting the Duquesa de Alba). *Agustina de Aragón* recreates Goya's famous 1814 painting, *Fusilamientos en la Moncloa* (*Tres de Mayo de 1808*), plus assorted mid-to-late nineteenth-century historical paintings of popular resistance in the War of Independence. These pictorial citations are highlighted by frequently being presented in tableau form, interrupting the narrative flow and enhancing the sense of history as a masquerade.

In all these films, the stress on spectacle produces a self-consciousness bordering on parody, if not the camp: this is particularly the case with the comic romps *La princesa de los Ursinos* and *Goyescas*. The fact that these are musicals (with the singing limited to the male lead in the former) by definition turns the real into performance, since the characters burst into song in 'life' as if they were on stage. Indeed, one of Goyescas's two protagonists (Petrilla) is a music-hall singer, whose performances on stage and in 'life' are indistinguishable; the other protagonist, the Duquesa de Gualda, acts out the part of Petrilla on several occasions, again blurring performance and 'life'. However, this self-consciousness also typifies those serious films, such as *Agustina de Aragón*, that dramatize actual historical events: the pleasure of such films lies in the spectator's wondering how the film will deal with events that are known in advance. Thus the concern is not with what happens but with how it is restaged. The defining characteristic of the epic genre is its re-enactment of historical events through a 'cast of thousands' – something that Orduña excelled in, *Agustina de Aragón* being the best example. The audience pleasure consists in being dazzled by the magnitude of the spectacle. Those that have criticized CIFESA's historical films for their histrionic quality have missed the point.

At the time of Felipe V's 1706 evacuation of the court from Madrid under pressure from the advancing Austrian-Portuguese army – the key historical event in Lucía's otherwise fictitious plot – the real-life Marie Anne de la Trémouille (aka Ana María, Princesa de los Ursinos) was aged 64 and not the beautiful young woman played by Ana Mariscal at

Figure 1 From pressbook for *La princesa de los Ursinos*. Courtesy of Video Mercury Films, S.A. and Filmoteca Española.

her aloof best. The film's opening title warns us that it will dramatize 'a famous diplomatic duel whose vicissitudes are silenced by history'. Lucía is interested in the legend, not the facts, of the Princesa's political power at the Spanish court, true to his love – in his films generally – of playing with clichés for camp effect. (I define 'camp' broadly as style playfully imitating itself.) In fact, the Princesa de los Ursinos came to Spain with Felipe V's thirteen-year-old bride, María Luisa of Savoy, in 1701 immediately after the seventeen-year-old Felipe's arrival in Spain that year to take up the Spanish crown. She had secured appointment by Louis XIV as Head of the Queen's Household through the mediation of the Spanish Prime Minister, Cardinal Portocarrero, who had persuaded the dying Carlos II to name Felipe (grandson of Louis XIV) as heir. In the film, the Princess is depicted as arriving in Spain for the first time, alone, when Felipe is already married and established on the throne; and she is pitted against Cardinal Portocarrero, cast in the film as head of the anti-French faction at court. Different historical accounts of the political intrigues of this period (Bleiberg 1968; Kamen 1969) give conflicting versions, but it seems that they clashed chiefly as rivals for influence over Felipe V (with the Princess mostly winning) rather than because of different attitudes to France. The film collapses the evacuation of the court from Madrid (1706) with the arrival of French military aid which in reality the Princess secured from Louis XIV in 1710, tipping the war in Felipe's favour. In the film, Portocarrero is present throughout though in reality he had left the Spanish court in 1705, after a clash with the Princess, subsequently switching allegiance to the Habsburg pretender. The film's stress on his sober costumes and solid build construct him as the epitome of fidelity and reliability, back-projecting onto the War of Succession the early Franco regime's construction of the Church as the bedrock of Spanish nationalism.

The Franco regime's anti-Enlightenment rhetoric is picked up and played with in Lucía's film, with the War of Succession – in which France and Spain were allies – recast as a fashion war between the two nations. The film's opening title announces that Louis XIV is threatening the 'irrepressible, independent Spanish character ... for whom the Pyrenees have never disappeared and never will'. This cliché is turned on its head in the course of the film. Roberto Rey, playing the Cardinal's aristocratic nephew Luis Carvajal, who is masquerading as the adventurer Javier Manrique in order to spy on the Princess on his uncle's behalf, declares to Ana María (who has fallen for his horse-riding and singing skills) that their love is doomed since 'the Pyrenees stand between us'. This prompts her to ask the French Prime Minister to send French troops, not to invade Spain but to help it against attack from the Austrians and Portuguese, since the way to abolish 'the Pyrenees that exist in Spaniards' hearts' is for the two countries to pledge friendship. The fictional love plot transmutes the initial anti-French rhetoric into the 'marriage' of the two cultures – but with the film's end arbitrarily killing Luis off on the battlefront, leaving the 'marriage of cultures' as a desirable goal rather than a reality.

The sparring between Luis and Ana María is enacted via the 'duel' between their contrasting costumes – or rather, sets of costumes because both are constantly changing. She, representing the height of modern French fashion, appears in a succession of dazzling period costumes: elaborate white wigs decked with ostrich feathers and bows, beauty spots, low-necked, if not off-the-shoulder dresses, covered in frills and with multi-layered, hooped skirts. It is not true that cleavages were not allowed in early Francoist cinema, but they were confined to women who represented a negative model of the *femme fatale* – except that we as spectators, like Luis/Javier, are totally seduced by Ana María's visual splendour. This is enhanced by Ana Mariscal's manipulation of her lavish costumes as a form of power dressing, gliding majestically in her hooped skirts, her tall wigs giving her a phallic power. (See Triana-Toribio 2000 on Mariscal's star persona.) Her costumes do, however, get slightly more sober toward the end of the film as she admits her attraction to Luis. The latter, masquerading as the adventurer Javier, is equally seductive in Douglas-Fairbanks-Junior-style open white shirt and jerkin, with loose, shoulder-length hair. As the aristocratic Luis, he wears a sober, dark jacket with braid trim, his hair simply tied back: he and his Cardinal uncle are the only characters who do not wear wigs. It is important that he seduces us (and the Princess) as the adventurer Javier: the film proposes a populist aristocratic-plebeian alliance. His dress constructs him as traditional in both of his roles, but he is nonetheless a master of disguises. When the camera closes on his head and shoulders, dressed as Javier in open white shirt, his 'traditional' popular image comes over as more modern than the period costume ('modern' for its day) of the Princess – and, indeed, more modern than his own period costume when dressed as Luis Carvajal. This makes Javier Manrique appear to be his 'real' self, while Luis Carvajal, in aristocratic period costume, comes over as 'dressed up'. This encourages a very Hollywood identification with the 'commoner' who wins the love of a Princess.

Ana María's seductive deployment of French fashion is contrasted with the ridiculous French-influenced costume of the men at court: the Bourbon Felipe V, played by Fernando Rey at his foppish best, in white satin jacket and poodle-like wig; and the comic *afrancesado*, with similar poodle-wig, who constantly twirls his lace handkerchief in an overtly camp gesture. Luis/Javier will mimic this camp gesture when he disguises himself as the *afrancesado*, absurdly kitted in highwayman gear, to gain access to Ana María's apartments. In this third-degree disguise (Luis masquerading as Javier masquerading as the *afrancesado* masquerading as highwayman), he is sending up French male fashion to enamour Ana María of his traditional Spanish brand of masculinity. It seems that modern French fashions masculinize women (seductively) and feminize men (ridiculously). A series of visual gags are built around Ana María's pet poodle, whose visual likeness to the absurd male wigs is stressed by the way in which the lapdog is petted by the male characters – including Luis/Javier. At one point, Luis/Javier gets confused with the poodle when he hides behind Ana María's sofa: when she investigates, he has disappeared and the poodle emerges in his place. What we are to make of this moment is not clear, but we should note that Roberto Rey's acting and singing style is that of the Hollywood beau, who combines swashbuckling male prowess with a feminine display of emotion.

The debt of *La princesa de los Ursinos* to the visual sumptuousness of Perojo's 1942 *Goyescas* is evident. *Goyescas* is another comic romp, this

Figure 2 From pressbook for *Goyescas*. Courtesy of Video Mercury Films, S.A. and Filmoteca Española.

time with a more or less happy ending as the two female protagonists get their respective men (though we only see Petrilla setting out, reins of the carriage in hand, to be reunited with her wayward lover). Like Lucía's film, *Goyescas* is oriented toward the pleasures afforded by stylized visual spectacle and in particular by the successive changes of female costume – except that these are more complicated since Imperio Argentina, as the film's opening credits tell the spectator, plays both female protagonists: the Duquesa de Gualda and the *tonadillera* Petrilla. The audience's knowledge that both roles are played by the same star – who had been the biggest Spanish box-office draw to date in the 1936 *Morena Clara* – produces huge enjoyment in tracking her role-switching, as well as admiration for the technical skill with which Perojo handles the scenes where both Imperio Argentinas appear on screen. By having the same actress play both parts, the film suggests that costume is what determines identity. The class fluidity is compounded by the fact that the Duquesa (like her real-life prototype, the Duquesa de Alba) has a penchant for dressing in popular *maja* dress, in another aristocratic-plebeian alliance. Unlike Luis Carvajal, who dons popular clothes for strategic reasons, the Duquesa does so for the pure pleasure of 'passing' as what she is not.

The Duquesa's class cross-dressing leads to the two women repeat-edly being mistaken for each other. The second time they meet on screen – having got caught up in the Aranjuez Mutiny – they are both in *maja* dress, Petrilla's bejewelled costume being the more ornate. When the Duquesa asks Petrilla if she is surprised to see her in popular dress, Petrilla replies 'The habit doesn't make the monk', suggesting that ident-ity is inherent and not constructed through costume. She reinforces this by adding 'I know we are not the same'. We have here the beginnings of a modern anxiety about the difficulty of telling the different classes apart as fashion starts to encourage the imitation of dress styles across classes. The plot restores each woman to her original lover but this is not a return to class hierarchy: the fickle Duquesa ends up with a common – if dashing – guardsman, Captain Pizarro; whereas Petrilla sets off to rejoin the Marquis Luis Alfonso de Nuévalos, fickle lover of both herself and the Duquesa. So the happy end, giving each woman the man she loves, creates two contrary cross-class alliances.

The film marks the onset of modernity by rewarding the Duquesa with a self-made man. However, his elegant dress – frilly cravat, white breeches, silky white wig tied back with a bow – suggests the assimilation of the bourgeoisie into the aristocracy, rather than a bour-geois challenge to aristocratic hegemony. We have a converse class cross-dressing with the Marquis Luis Alfonso de Nuévalos who, having killed the Corregidor in a duel, flees to become a bandit leader. There is no question of him returning to his aristocratic status since he is wanted for a crime which carries the death penalty (Gubern 1994: 367). The ease with which he moves from Hollywood-beau version of (anachronistically) late eighteenth-century costume – as in the opening theatre scene where he wears a dazzlingly white powdered wig and white satin jacket – to stereotypical bandit dress – kerchief knotted round head, bolero – produces a more radical questioning of the stability of identity than the Duquesa's 'passing' as a *maja* since, while she remains an aristocrat beneath the popular dress (as Petrilla observes), his change of class is irreversible and for real. Unlike the Duquesa, Luis Alfonso or Captain Pizarro, Petrilla is not allowed to cross-dress in class terms; she can only dress up as what she is – a popular performer who performs herself both on and off stage. The suggestion seems to be that only the popular classes have any authenticity – but this consists in the ability to perform the stereotype of one's own class identity to perfection. The film anticipates Judith Butler's postmodern perception (1990) that identity is the effect resulting from a repeated performance.

The ease with which the Duquesa moves across class lines by changing her clothes allows her to cross-dress as a postilion with equal facility. She is, in fact, at her most seductive as she strides down her palace steps, whip in hand, in riding jacket, cravat, breeches and riding boots, with her hair (no wig) tied behind her neck. The moment when, captured by Luis Alfonso's bandits, her long hair comes tumbling down over her riding jacket is the sexiest moment in the film, for this is the only time we see her immaculately contrived image come 'undone'. With this moment, Perojo is suggesting something perhaps more interesting than the notion that all identity is performed: if Butler enjoins us to escape rigid gender identities through conscious impersonation, Perojo's film suggests that the escape from socially sanctioned roles which define one as *either* this *or* that occurs when something goes wrong with the performance and the fluidity beneath the impersonation comes tumbling out.

In this sense, part of the pleasure produced by the film derives from the slight misfit – playfully highlighted – between original and copy at the moments when it restages particular Goya paintings. In the boudoir scene that starts with the Duquesa in *maja vestida* pose, she is wearing an anachronistic Hollywood-style slinky satin nightdress and chequered bed-jacket, her loose dark hair looking more like that of a 1940s Hollywood vamp than the Duquesa de Alba. In the scene that starts with a recreation of Goya's portrait of the Duquesa de Alba in black, the camera zooms out to reveal that it is the Duquesa de Gualda composing her image in a full-length mirror – but the landscape behind her remains in the mirror as she walks away: a logical impossibility since this is an interior shot. I take these to be visual jokes, rather than carelessness, given the studied, painterly quality of the film throughout.

Indeed, the film produces audience pleasure precisely because it plays with the historical reality – centred on the Aranjuez Mutiny of 17 March 1808 – to which it alludes. The figure of Godoy, Charles IV's hated favourite, is evoked by the Minister who asks Petrilla to perform for him in private, in return granting her request to send Captain Pizarro to the Indies – but also in Captain Pizarro himself, whose enjoyment of the Duquesa de Gualda's favours mirrors Godoy's spectacular ascension from common guardsman to grandee of Spain as a result of Queen María Luisa's favours (reputedly sexual). Captain Pizarro's role in suppressing the Aranjuez Mutiny which sacked Godoy's palace and secured his dismissal by Carlos IV, who abdicated in favour of his son Fernando VII two days later, mirrors the fact that Godoy was saved from the mob by the Guardia de Corps. The Aranjuez Mutiny was triggered by rumours that Godoy – having moved the court to Aranjuez on Napoleon's military occupation of Spain (sanctioned by Carlos IV) – was planning to evacuate the court to Andalusia or America: Captain Pizarro's despatch to America on Godoy's orders seems to be a travesty of this. What is extraordinary is that the film ends with Godoy apparently restored to power and – even more so – that there is a complete lack of mention of Spain's occupation, in December 1807, by Napoleon, who would in April 1808 force Fernando VII to abdicate in favour of his brother Joseph Bonaparte, triggering the 2 May 1808 popular uprising in Madrid that evolved into the War of Indpendence (Carr 1966: 79–90; García de Cortázar and González Vesga 1994: 413). The contrast with the anti-French rhetoric of *Agustina de Aragón*, dramatizing the siege of Zaragoza by the French in June–August 1808 and December 1808– February 1809, could not be greater. Gubern (1994: 367) cites a 1950 publicity blurb which bills *Goyescas* as a 'Struggle between homegrown Madrilenian customs and imported foreign-ness', but this critique of *afrancesado* customs, while it may be implied by the Duquesa's flightiness, is not present in the representation of costume. The elaborate white wigs and opulent, low-necked, frequently off-the-shoulder satin gowns of the Duquesa de Gualda are as much, if not more, a source of pleasure than the cheeky *maja* costumes of Petrilla (and of the Duquesa in lower-class 'drag') with their above-ankle skirts, tight bodices, and natural hair adorned with flowers and lace coifs or nets with pompoms. Petrilla is not represented as more authentic than the Duquesa, for the film's emphasis on period costume produces a scenario where everyone is dressing up.

In *Agustina de Aragón*, the focus is on the enactment of historical events, with costume being used not to perform the fun of dressing up, but to give credibility to the historical account. This does not mean that costume is less important in shaping the audience's response, or that it is not a source of pleasure. Although the film is set just three months later than *Goyescas*, wigs have now disappeared, men have cut their hair short and are more soberly clad (dark frock coats) – with two exceptions: the military, and the *afrancesado* Luis, the fiancé with whom Agustina breaks. The film more or less respects military uniform of the day – with both Spanish and French officers in tight white breeches and tails – but the Napoleonic officers' jackets have an ornate braid design, with the generals in plumed hats sporting a silly feather cockade. The Napoleonic officers fold their arms in a foppish gesture, while the Spanish military stand erect, their arms stiffly at their side. The *afrancesado* Luis also folds his arms and gesticulates in camp fashion as he talks, drawing attention to his lace cuffs. Luis's fashion-consciousness makes him odious, with his light-coloured jackets and tight white hose over his podgy thighs, and immaculately groomed blond curls. What definitively condemns him is his penchant for flashy patterns: in the scene when Agustina ditches him, he is wearing a Regency-stripe tailcoat over a brocade waistcoat, with tartan cravat. Here, attention to fashion signifies modernity in the sense of being a 'turncoat', adopting foreign fashions. In fact, Luis's foppish attire is out of date, for the other French civilians in the film have adopted the new sobriety. As Luis repents of his pro-French stance, his clothes will become progressively simpler and darker.

The other men in Zaragoza wear traditional rural costume (short hair, short jacket or waistcoat over a white shirt, knee-length breeches, sometimes with cummerbund and bandana). This inevitably undermines the film's exaltation of the 'authenticity' of the *pueblo*, since the actors give the impression of being in fancy dress. In a comic scene, Agustina helps 'lace' her uncle into his new military uniform, in a parody of the lacing of women into their corsets; this suggests that joining the army is another form of dressing up. The women in Zaragoza (and in the village sacked by the French early in the film) also wear peasant costume, with flowery shawls tucked into their gathered skirts. Just as Luis is the only male bourgeois, so there is one female exception: the Condesa de Bureta who – in another aristocratic-plebeian alliance – lends her person and palace to the anti-French cause. We first see her in a white satin, embroidered, empire-line dress with plunging neckline, short puff

Figure 3 Double-page spread from pressbook for *Agustina de Aragón*. Courtesy of Video Mercury Films, S.A.

tan dispares como la Reina Juana la Loca en LOCURA DE
·e a la pantalla, para recreo de su legión de admiradores, en un
los anteriores. Ni austeridad ni grandeza regia, ni lujosos salo-

mujer patriota, todo fuego y corazón, que ante la injusticia de
a en española, ofreciendo a lá Patria el sacrificio de cuanto es y
mpulso insigne que la hace convertirse en combatiente de pri-
·r que destaca en una lucha en que los héroes son todos los que
·e el personaje de Agustina, y nos responde:
no de esos personajes providenciales que nunca dejan de surgir

iotismo y feminidad despiertan en mí. No le exagero si digo que
·ustina· son tan acusados; limitan tan maravillosamente su per-
·n tantos sus matices y contrastes..., feminidad, heroísmo, temple
·» a· su interpretación verdaderamente entusiasmada como mujer

zaragozana que asombró al mundo, ha quedado en la Historia
·na, que fué una entre otras muchas, ha sido quien más ha que-
·lla producto nato del alma popular española, invencible e indo

·ar ese personaje que, de la vulgaridad de una vida oscura, alcan-
·idad de los elegidos. La fuerte línea dramática de AGUSTINA
·s de lucimiento para Aurora Bautista, que alcanza con esta pelí-
·uerda en la historia del Séptimo Arte.

Figure 3 (continued) Double-page spread from pressbook for *Agustina de Aragón*.
Courtesy of Video Mercury Films, S.A.

sleeves, cameo brooch on a black velvet ribbon, and elaborate curls piled on top of her head: she is allowed to be elegant to demonstrate her patriotic sacrifice. Toward the end of the film she is nursing the wounded, still in empire-line dress but covered with an apron. Luis imitates French fashions badly; she imitates them well – her empire-line dresses (a simplification of earlier female fashion) are the latest Napoleonic trend – without thereby ceasing to be a patriot. The figures of Luis and the Condesa show how similar kinds of costume – French-influenced in both cases – can be used to create contrasting meanings.

The film's protagonists – Agustina (Aurora Bautista) and the guerrilla leader Juan Bravo (Virgilio Teixeira) – stand out for the modernity of their image. In their costumes, the historical marking is kept to a minimum, as is the number of their costume changes. This makes us almost forget that they are 'dressed up', encouraging audience identification. Throughout, Luis wears an open white shirt (sometimes open down to his waist) with its sleeves rolled up above the elbows, and rolled-up trousers: this, and his short hair, makes him an entirely modern figure. The only variations are the occasional addition of an open black waistcoat or short jacket and/or bandana; his cummerbund also varies in thickness, making his costume correspondingly more or less historically marked. As the siege progresses, his white shirt is torn, revealing his body, particularly in the scene when he bends over Agustina to seal their love. Agustina does have several costume changes but mostly wears the same clothes for several consecutive episodes. Her clothes are dark (plain, short fitted jackets and full skirts), apart from a light blouse or neck-trim, and once she gets to Zaragoza she takes to wearing a shawl, identifying her as a woman of the people. The only time we see her looking at herself in the mirror is as, dressed in a plain white nightdress, she braids her hair. As the siege progresses, she rolls up her sleeves, and her blouse becomes decorously torn at the neck (as it does when she is nearly – actually? – raped by a French soldier). In the scene where she rallies the men to the barricades, with her loose hair and white blouse (the white shawl over it is barely visible), she – like Juan – looks entirely modern. At the end, as she finds the dying Juan and rushes to fire the cannon, she is dressed just in a torn white blouse, open almost down to her cummerbund, and full, dark skirt – the historical markings are minimal. When the film cuts back to its narrative frame – the later moment when Fernando VII, restored to the throne, pins a medal on Agustina's dress to honour her role in the Independence Struggle – it is impossible to reconcile this free-moving, modern figure with the demure Victorian matron at the Royal Palace, in black lace veil, cameo pendant, and elegant, pin-striped dress. This narrative frame strips Agustina of her agency, confining her to bourgeois femininity, but it also – as she closes her eyes and returns in a flashback to the events of 1808–9 – constructs the past as a moment of nostalgia. The contrast between the modernity of her dress in the battle scenes and the meticulously recreated period costume of the narrative frame also constructs the former as the 'real' Agustina and the latter as a masquerade.

I claimed earlier that these films, despite the regime's prevailing misogyny, are sources of female pleasure. Gubern (1994: 369) notes that *Goyescas* is a 'rare' example of a 1940s Spanish woman's film, but the majority of early Francoist films – even most of the historical epics – are woman-centred. No doubt the camera's focus on the spectacle of female stars in often lavish period costume provided pleasure to male as well as female spectators, not least because the period costume allowed a seductive mix of plunging necklines and various forms of veiling. The open shirts of Roberto Rey and Virgilio Teixeira, and even the tightly-hosed crotches of the foppish males, are likely also to have been a source of pleasure, to both sexes in various ways, but at the expense of feminizing the male by making him, through soft-focus close-ups, an erotic object. However, when the female protagonists are made into objects of the gaze, their eroticization coincides with their narrative agency. The emphasis on spectacle blurs gender categories by feminizing the heroes (even in the case of men of action like Luis/Javier in *La princesa de los Ursinos* and Juan in *Agustina de Aragón*) and masculinizing the heroines (such as the Condesa de Gualda and Petrilla in *Goyescas* who live only for love, but take the reins of the plot entirely in their hands). Only *Goyescas* allows a woman to cross-dress as a man; but both Perojo's and Lucía's films, with their stress on masquerade and especially on class cross-dressing, construct identity as unstable. Both films also allow the pleasure of losing oneself in a past prior to the mid-nineteenth-century consolidation of gender difference which confined women to the home. This pleasure is especially strong in Orduña's epic, which does not encourage pleasurable fantasies of dressing up, but suggests that bourgeois femininity itself was the imposition of a masquerade onto an earlier freer form of femininity (embodied by the Condesa de Bureta as well as by Agustina). It is no coincidence that the majority of costume films of the early Francoist period are set in the mid- to late nineteenth century, the period when this dramatic separation of male and female roles was enforced. That, however, is the subject of another discussion.

Notes

1. It was not only in Franco's Spain that historical films served as government propaganda. Harper (1994: 3) reminds us how the British Foreign Office and Ministry of Information, as well as civil institutions, sought to influence the production of British historical films in the 1930s and 1940s.
2. Landy (2002: 250) notes that Italian cinema of the fascist period is marked by 'a reflexive use of gesture, costume, and mise-en-scène, stressing artifice of cinema and high-lighting impersonation, disguises, doubling, carnival, and spectacle'.
3. The press book for *Agustina de Aragón* (1950) notes the contribution of 'valores técnicos extranjeros', stressing Pahle's work in Hollywood and the length of time Burmann had worked in Spain. Another foreign refugee from Nazism who worked on CIFESA costume films was the Russian art director Pierre Schild, who had worked with Perojo in France 1924-6 and on Gance's *Napoléon* and Buñuel's *Un Chien andalou* and *L'Âge d'or*.

References

Affron, C. and Affron, M.J. (1995), *Sets in Motion: Arts Direction and Film Narrative*, New Brunswick, NJ: Rutgers University Press.

Agustina de Aragón (1950), press book, n.p., CIFESA.

Bleiberg, G. (ed.) (1968), *Diccionario de Historia de España*, 2nd rev. edn.

Butler, J. (1990), *Gender Trouble: Feminism and the Subversion of Identity*, New York and London: Routledge.

Carr, R. (1966), *Spain 1808–1939*, Oxford: Clarendon.

Castillejo, J. (1998), *Las películas de Aurora Bautista*, Valencia: Fundació Municipal de Cine, Mostra de Valencia.

Cook, P. (1996), *Fashioning the Nation: Costume and Identity in British Cinema*, London: British Film Institute.

Fanés, F. (1989), *El cas CIFESA: Vint anys de cine espanyol (1932-1952)*, Valencia: Filmoteca de la Generalitat Valenciana.

Foucault, M. (1987), *The History of Sexuality: An Introduction*, Harmondsworth: Penguin.

García de Cortázar, F. and J.M. González Vesga (1994), *Breve historia de España*, Madrid: Alianza.

Gil Fombellida, M.C. (2003), *Rivas Cherif, Margarita Xirgu y el teatro de la II República*, Madrid: Fundamentos.

Gorostiza, J. (1997), *Directores artísticos del cine español*, Madrid: Cátedra/Filmoteca Española.

Gubern, R. (1994), *Benito Perojo: Pionerismo y supervivencia*, Madrid: Filmoteca Española.

Hacer memoria, hacer historia: CIFESA, de la antorcha de los éxitos a las cenizas del fracaso (1990), monographic issue of *Archivos de la Filmoteca* 1(4).

Harper, S. (1994), *Picturing the Past: The Rise and Fall of the British Costume Film*, London: British Film Institute.

Hay, J. (1987), *Popular Film Culture in Fascist Italy: The Passing of the Rex*, Bloomington: Indiana University Press.

Hernández Ruiz, J. (1999), 'Historia y escenografía en el cine español: Una aproximación', in J.E. Monterde, *Ficciones históricas: El cine histórico español*, monographic issue of *Cuadernos de la Academia*, 6 (September): 167–77.

Kamen, H. (1969), *The War of Succession in Spain 1700–15*, London, Weidenfeld & Nicolson.

Kuhn, A. (2002), *Dreaming of Fred and Ginger: Cinema and Cultural Memory*, New York: New York University Press.

Landy, M. (2002), 'Theatricality and Impersonation: The Politics of Style in the Cinema of the Italian Fascist Era', in J. Reich and P. Garofalo (eds), *Re-viewing Fascism: Italian Cinema, 1922–1943*, Bloomington: Indiana University Press, 250–75.

Llinás, F. (1989), *Directores de fotografía del cine español*, Madrid: Filmoteca Española.

Pérez Rojas, J. and Alcaide, J.L. (1992), 'Apropiaciones y recreaciones de la pintura de historia', in J. Díez (ed.), *La pintura de historia en España en el siglo XIX*, Madrid: Museo del Prado, 103–18.

Squicciarino, N. (1998), *El vestido habla: Consideraciones psico-sociológicas sobre la indumentaria*, Madrid: Cátedra.

Stacey, J. (1994), *Star Gazing: Hollywood Cinema and Female Spectatorship*, London and New York: Routledge.

Triana-Toribio, N. (2000), 'Ana Mariscal: Franco's Disavowed Star', in U. Sieglohr (ed.), *Heroines without Heroes: Reconstructing Female and National Identities in European Cinema, 1945–51*, London and New York: Cassell, 185–95.

4

Masculinity, Monuments and Movement: Gender and the City of Madrid in Pedro Almodóvar's *Carne trémula* (1997)

Steven Marsh

One of the oft-observed paradoxes of the cinema of Pedro Almodóvar is that his apparently progressive stance on issues of gender or sexual orientation enmasks a failure to invest in more committed ideological affiliation. Indeed, one particularly vehement Spanish commentator recently suggested that Almodóvar's latest films do little other than provide a luscious cultural alibi for the Right. For Antonio Elorza, writing in the Madrid daily *El País*, movies such as *Todo sobre mi madre* (1999) and *Hable con ella* (2002) constitute

> A local Madrilenian variant of the Spielberg style, in all its astuteness as well as its tricks, applied to the sentiments of a human life taken out of context and which in its excesses confirms order. Transgression has become conservative. (Elorza, 2003: 14)[1]

Such sentiments are not new. While Almodóvar's films have long been proclaimed as marking the most significant cultural symptoms of Spain's break with its dictatorial past and associated repression, conformity and drabness, the film-maker himself has been viewed – together with his generation – as apolitical and ahistorical: a paradigm of a new postmodern Spain. Critics have been quick to draw attention to his mixture of styles, his kitsch recycling of religious imagery, his musical appropriations from the past and his profligate borrowing from international sources. Although for his hostile observers, his spectacular espousal of gender fluidity obscures a dilettante attitude to politics, for his invariably unconditional admirers, Almodóvar's cinema – with its emphasis upon 'desire' and 'identity' – has been delightedly seized upon precisely because, while self-consciously proclaiming its own radicality, it eschews more meaningful engagement.

Carne trémula [*Live Flesh*, 1998], Almodóvar's twelfth feature, however, signalled a new direction in his career. Uniquely in his corpus, this taut sex thriller is a film that considers recent Spanish history. Furthermore, it is also the first of his films to explore heterosexual masculinity with any degree of seriousness. For a film-maker often labelled a director of women, *Carne trémula* marks another departure.[2] In this film the men are, for once, more than ciphers. Yet the two novelties are connected; each of the film's male characters is more than simply imbued with history, each is constructed by it.

Almost all of Almodóvar's films have been shot in the city of Madrid. *Carne trémula* is in some ways a pivotal film in that to date it is the last of his movies to be shot principally on the city's streets. Subsequently, Almodóvar has tended either to move away from his adopted home city or to distance himself from the urban landscape – that of central Madrid – with which he is most closely associated. Most critics, while acknowledging the importance of the Spanish capital to the director's work, have often regarded it as mere film set, camped-up, transformed and reinvented for the purposes of pleasure. For Marvin D'Lugo, Almodóvar's Madrid is a 'city of desire' in which 'the ideas and icons of francoist cinema are set up as foils to stimulate the audience to embrace a new post-francoist aesthetic' (D'Lugo 1995: 125). Meanwhile Barbara Morris and Kathleen Vernon describe Almodóvar's 'almost utopian rendering of Madrid as *locus amoenus*, a space of infinite possibilities' (1995: 8). While there are few directors who are more defined by a sense of place than Almodóvar, it is rare that the historical dimension of this relationship is engaged with. In this chapter I will argue that the politics of Almodóvar reveal themselves precisely in his engagement with Madrid, in continuities and discontinuities with the past as manifested in its buildings, streets and monuments.

The period following the death of Francisco Franco in 1975 is distinguished by two times running simultaneously. The very negotiated nature of the Spanish transition to democracy has resulted in politicians and policemen from the dictatorship overlapping with those who came to prominence or began work during the later period. Spain is also a country in which gender roles have been radically and very swiftly transformed, although more so in legislative terms than in the reality of wider society. Meanwhile, the influence of the Catholic Church on the State may have diminished but its presence as a powerhouse of ideological production among the population remains significant at least in the popular imaginary. Thus, together with historical economic subdevelopment, Spain is enmeshed in a cultural and social set of contradictions from which, as

D'Lugo himself suggests, Almodóvar can not be excluded. While the country's uneven economic evolution and its class society is graphically represented in its cities, so too is the shift in gender relations. Any discussion of gender and urban geography inevitably draws upon issues of private and public space. The ultra-modern, state-of-the-art office blocks of business Madrid exist in close proximity to overcrowded council housing and shanty towns dispersed among the swathes of barren wasteland. Corporate speculation and municipal politics are inseparable companions. Domestic violence, behind doors in the cramped confines of urban living conditions, has become a significant political issue. But also neighbourhoods have been transformed by their residents in ways unimaginable for an earlier generation. Examples such as these are pertinent to the film discussed here, for *Carne trémula* proves to be an ironic rather than a celebratory reflection on the transitional period. It is a film that plays on the historical charge running through its 'place'.

Elsewhere I have written of travel that it is a conjunction of unstable time and place (Marsh 2002) and other critics have observed the centrality of movement in this film (Morgan-Tamosunas [2002], Smith [1998]). I hope to demonstrate that in *Carne trémula* 'movement' within the city provides the connective material that links place and gender, urban space and the human body, the public sphere and the private. Importantly, such connections are produced within a teleological framework. Although Paul Julian Smith has labelled this movie Almodóvar's discovery of modernism, it is more than that; the movement of its characters suggests a means by which, for once in Almodóvar, political agency might be located.

Synopsis

Loosely based on a Ruth Rendell novel of the same name, *Carne trémula* follows Víctor Plaza (Liberto Rabal), wrongly imprisoned for shooting David (Javier Bardem), a policeman, and leaving him paralysed and wheelchair-bound. In spite of his injuries David goes on to become a successful paraplegic basketball player and contributes to Spain's medal-winning performance at the 1992 paralympics held in Barcelona. Six years later, on his release from jail where he has long harboured plans to avenge himself, Víctor chances upon Elena (Francesca Neri), a reformed drug-addict in whose apartment the original firearms incident occurred and who is now married to David. David's former partner in the police force is Sancho (Pepe Sancho), a violent drunk, who orchestrated the original shooting in revenge for the affair that David was having at the time with his wife Clara (Angela Molina). Víctor eventually ends up with Elena, having previously prepared for his conquest by means of an affair with Clara.

History

It is this kind of complicated and choral love story, often expressed as high farce, that constitutes the parodic melodrama for which Almodóvar has become famous. Nonetheless the historical discourse within which *Carne trémula* is framed (and, as we will see, it is a skewed one) distinguishes it from his previous films. Beginning in prologue with the official written declaration (and accompanying radio broadcast) purporting to announce a State of Emergency, the film's commencement is signalled by the words 'Madrid, January 1970' superimposed on the screen. Outside on the street workmen are taking down the Christmas decorations. This is the night of Víctor's birth. Just as the movie's historical specificity is impressed upon us so too is its precise location: Víctor is a character indelibly associated with Madrid. His birth – which as Smith and Morgan-Tamosunas have both pointed out is a parody of the nativity scene – occurs on a moving bus at the dead of night in deserted streets and the scene is crowded with references to the city. The formidable and forthright brothel keeper, Doña Centro (Pilar Bardem), who accompanies Víctor's prostitute mother Isabel (Penelope Cruz) says, 'You were in a hurry to get to Madrid'. And then at the moment they pass what is probably the city's most emblematic monument and one of its historical gates, La Puerta de Alcalá,[3] she adds, 'Look Víctor, Madrid'. Seized upon by the local authorities in a black and white parody of Francoist NO-DO (Noticiarios y Documentales) newsreel Víctor is named 'adoptive son of the city' by the unelected city mayor. Not to be outdone, the municipal public transport company awards him a lifetime bus pass ensuring him 'a life upon wheels'. La Puerta de Alcalá is the cinematic linking device that transports us twenty years ahead in time to see Víctor, now a pizza delivery boy on his motorbike encircling the monument. In this way the monumental space of Madrid is put to temporal effect and, importantly, we are being made aware that there are two parallel times running through this film.

Smith's 1998 review of the film in *Sight and Sound* was entitled 'Absolute Precision', a reference to the advertisement for watches that is stamped across the bus upon which Víctor is born. However, historical reference in this film, in spite of its assertions of accurate realism, is far from precise. Such claims are founded upon the documentation (the on-screen reproduction of the original decree declaring the State of Emergency) and in the genuine radio broadcast blaring out in Doña Centro's living room that features the voice of Manuel Fraga Iribarne, the Francoist Minister of Information and Tourism. The opening sequence is fraught with exacting verisimilitude and yet the year is wrong. Almodóvar is mistaken. The State of Emergency to which the radio announcement refers ran from January to March of the previous year, 1969, before it was discontinued. Fraga himself had been forced to resign in October of that year, three months prior to the on-screen events. One can only speculate as to the reasons why Almodóvar chose 1970, but it is intriguing that his one contribution to analysis of national teleology should be factually flawed.

Place and space

Much of *Carne trémula* is filmed on or around Madrid's central thorough-fare, the Paseo de la Castellana, which runs in a straight line from the south to the north of the city. This is a street notable for its clashing styles of architecture that in many ways reflect the aesthetic of postmodernism. La Castellana (and its various extensions[4]) commences at the Puerta de Atocha, the railway station redesigned by the most celebrated architect of the democratic period, Rafael Moneo. Further north it passes the area known as Nuevos Ministerios, constructed in the immediate post-war period and modelled on Mussolini's Rome – and adorned with the city's only remaining public statue of Franco – before it reaches AZCA, Madrid's business zone of office blocks and garish skyscrapers; La Torre de Picasso, the city's tallest building to one side, and the Santiago Bernabeu football stadium (home to Real Madrid) to the other. At its northern end La Castellana is crowned by that most postmodern celebration of excess, the impossibly inclined KIO Towers (so named because of their original owners the Kuwaiti Investment Office) and rebaptized La Puerta de Europa by its new proprietors, the local bank La Caja Madrid.

Víctor lives close to the base of La Puerta de Europa. While the construction of the KIO Towers provided one of the most resounding financial scandals of the many that plagued the Socialist government at the time this film was being made, the contrasting urban landscape in its shadow is equally striking. Víctor inhabits a shack in La Ventilla, the shanty town whose desolation is remarked upon by Clara, Sancho's wife, and the woman destined to become Víctor's lover. 'My God!' she exclaims, the first time she sees the area, 'It is like Sarajevo'. Almodóvar is as knowingly flippant about contemporaneous history as he is with that of the past. Indeed, Víctor refers in terms that are both historically accurate and ironic to the future building project that once filming was over would lead to the disappearance of the shanties around La Ventilla: 'Apparently they are going to call it the Prince of Asturias' he tells Clara.[5]

If La Castellana represents the eclecticism of postmodern architecture, its modernistic counterpart (both stylistically and historically) is the La Gran Vía-Calle Alcalá intersection that runs perpendicular to it. Interestingly, Víctor is linked to both arenas. At the moment of his birth, his mother looks up through the window of the bus to glimpse the statue of the angel perched on the dome of one of the city's best-known early twentieth-century constructions, the Metrópolis building situated at the confluence of the two streets. This is a site in the city's topography which Luis Fernández Cifuentes describes as a 'key point of convergence and divergence for the urban stroller's gaze' (Fernández Cifuentes, 1999: 116). Víctor survives in the temporary, make-shift hovel that was his mother's home, distinguished by what Michel de Certeau has described as an 'unmoored' quality that lacks 'any fixed position' (1984: 86). He either moves as an in-between figure – with the aid of his bus pass – within the spaces of two of Madrid's architectural periods or lingers at its gates (such as Alcalá or Europa). In this itinerant way he insinuates himself tactically into the places of the film's more powerful characters. In counterpoint to the rigidities of the La Gran Vía-Castellana axis, Víctor encircles the city. At one point early in the film he spends an evening sitting on the circle line bus – 'el circular' – that circumnavigates the city centre.

While this is indisputably Almodóvar's male movie, its exploration of heterosexual masculinity is intimately linked to the political configurations of the time and space of the city of Madrid. David and Sancho are representatives of their hybrid times and, perhaps significantly, both are identified by what they consume. Sancho is a whisky-swilling violent hangover from Francoist law enforcement. David, on the other hand, is the sensitive hashish-smoking *new man* – a prototype for the 1990s – who believes in dialogue with criminals and comes to understand when his wife leaves him for Víctor. Writing before *Carne trémula* was made, D'Lugo (1995: 129) had already detected a 'generational cleavage … at the center of [Almodóvar's] films'. Here, though, it achieves 'living' representation, rather than rupture. D'Lugo looks to Foucault and the 'construction of a "new past"' (Ibid.: 129). However, Almodóvar does not break with the past – indeed, in this film he disavows discontinuity – instead he seeks to produce a kind of simultaneity that emerges in the seemingly immobile forms of monuments and masculinities; in doing so he destabilizes (or displaces) both of them.

The very first sequence in which the policemen are introduced is linked to engendered geography and the history of a struggle for recognition within Madrid urban space. The two men drive slowly through Chueca, Madrid's gay district and one of the areas of the city centre to have undergone the most radical demographic and social changes in the last decade. The history of Chueca is an example of the historical mediation of space by opposition. In Chueca the dichotomy between urban geography and chronological history is a manifest falsehood. It is a lived space from which dominant prejudice – nurtured and promoted by Church and State – has been evicted.

Víctor is a victim of the initial rivalry between Sancho and David. He not only lives provisionally in-between the two towers of La Puerta de Europa, he also operates in-between the times of the two rival policemen and, significantly, he cuckolds both of them; Víctor infiltrates their masculine space. Perhaps germane to this is Malcolm Compitello's observation that popularly La Puerta de Europa has been irreverently nicknamed by Madrid wags – as a phallic symbol – *'las entrepiernas'* (the crotch) (Compitello 1999: 209). Víctor is also marked by time. His birth coincided with the beginning of the end of the Francoist regime and he came of age in democracy. However, Víctor misses out on 1992 – he is languishing in jail – a year commonly agreed on as being of major significance in Spain's contemporary narrative. 1992 was the year that saw Spain's full entry into the European Community, the Seville World Fair, the Barcelona Olympics and Madrid named European Cultural Capital.

For a film that is intimately connected with the city of Madrid and movement through it, its characters – with the significant exception of Víctor – travel (off-screen) beyond its borders to a remarkable extent. Global space radiates out from the city of Madrid and vice versa. Elena is Italian. Sancho and Clara visit Portugal on holiday in an effort to repair their ailing marriage. David constantly travels away from the city on tour with his basketball team. Indeed the very first images of him following the shooting are at the Barcelona Paralympics in 1992. The night Elena and Víctor first sleep together he is away playing in Seville and returns the following morning by taxi. The very end of the film finds him writing

Elena a postcard from Miami where he has decided to spend that year's Christmas holidays. As we have already seen it is also a film that is keenly aware of current international affairs.

If place is marked in the city's buildings and street names, lived space is produced by movement. Víctor's 'domain' is an itinerant zone forged by movement and provisionality. From the moment of his birth on a bus to the final sequence in which his own son is born in a moving vehicle he is associated with movement. Both Smith and Morgan-Tamosunas have commented on the symbolism of circular movement and, indeed, the image of the circle itself. The circle, in the form of a target, constitutes the design of the carpet in Elena's home in Alonso Martínez (the residential area home to the city's liberal bourgeoisie). Similarly, David revolves in circles in his wheelchair on the basketball court. The circle provides a stark and mobile contrast to the vertical rigidity of the city buildings. Morgan-Tamosunas has observed the images of circularity are counterpoised with symbols of entrapment 'the prison like bars of the lift shaft through which David and Elenas exchange of looks is lensed at the moment he is shot early in the film, the claustrophobic framing of Víctor's prison cell, repeated shots of David framed by the basketball net' (Morgan-Tamosunas: 188). These contrasting images recall Certeau's formula of 'space as practiced place' (1984: 117), in which walkers elude the rigidities of urban planners; everyday practice (such as 'moving about') in Certeau's urban poetics avoids both the Foucauldian discursive matrix and commodification.

The example of the KIO Towers is symptomatic: places are engendered and marked by sexuality. The bridge that Víctor crosses before entering Elena's house is a well-known sexualized space. The area beneath its structure (it stretches across the Castellana) is an open-air sculpture park – the centrepiece of which is a hanging, poised Chillida, a pendulum of static movement – but perhaps more pertinently it is a favoured gathering spot for the city's transvestite prostitutes. Like Víctor himself, bridges are connecting points between places. Víctor is in-between David and Sancho and forms a kind of bridge. Certeau has written: 'the *bridge* is ambiguous everywhere: it alternately welds together and opposes insularities' (1984: 128).

The ambiguity expressed through architecture is suggestive of an in-between quality, of that between birth and death. Víctor, on his release from gaol, visits his mother's grave in the Almudena cemetery, located on the city's eastern fringes and the most important of the city's several graveyards. This is a cemetery that ricochets around Spanish cinematic history. As I have written elsewhere, it was the setting for key sequences

Gender & the City of Madrid in Carne trémula

in Marco Ferreri's *El cochecito* (1960) and in Fernando León de Aranoa's second movie *Barrio* (Marsh: 2004). Fortuitously, his visit coincides with the burial of Elena's father. The sequence is emotionally charged, not so much by death as by the inexorable presence of the family. Elena's Italian family is stereotyped in mafia-style code (Almodóvar has learned something from Coppola); Víctor goes to pay his respects to his own dead mother. The occasion gives rise to his meeting with Clara. Appropriately for a family scene, Almodóvar includes his own brother Agustín as a grave digger. Families, films, nations and cities have spatial histories. We see a photo of Isabel, Víctor's mother on the niche where she rests. Indeed, the symbolism is potent and pertinent: a grave digger quite literally carves out a space in the earth to be filled. Filled, moreover, with a body. As I will demonstrate later, the relationship between the city and the human body is relevant to this film.

Private and Public Space

The idea of the circle is historically intrinsic to travel. George Van Den Abbeele uses the term *oikos* (Greek for 'home') to describe narrative trajectory. '[O]ikas is most easily understood' he says, 'as that point from which the voyage begins and to which it circles back at the end' (1992: xviii). And as much as it is a film about movement, *Carne trémula* is a film about 'home'. *Domos* (the Latin translation of 'oikos'), meanwhile, contains an echo of 'domain', of domination as well as domestication. Giuliana Bruno notes, however, that 'circularity' is distinctive of the male voyage (Odysseus is the classical example); it is men who depart and return (as in psychoanalysis to the womb – and the term *metropolis* derives from the Greek for 'mother-city'). Women, according to Bruno, are nomadic and their journeys are not defined by the possibility of return; the experience of voyage is one of dislocation not nostalgia (Bruno: 86–8). In this vein, it is noteworthy that Clara abandons her marital home (before she is hunted down and killed by Sancho) not knowing where she is going. Elena is an immigrant, living in a state of dislocation. Víctor, ironically the movie's 'unmoored' character is bound by the city in which he was born and within which he sets about making a home.

The private and the public dichotomy has already been transgressed in the movie's prologue. Víctor's birth is not only seized upon 'politically' in the public sphere when the state functionaries seek to make mileage out of the event by publicizing it with their appearance on national television, but the event of his birth itself occurs not in the privacy of an enclosed unit, such as a house or a hospital ward, but in a public bus almost in the open air. The 'public' nature of such a private act makes Víctor a creature of open space and the object of public surveillance. It is an established pattern that governs the way he is treated but also the way he behaves. Throughout the film he trespasses and others trespass upon him. Aptly provisional, security at Víctor's ramshackle home is limited to a flimsy padlock.

The notion of Víctor's physical vulnerability is bolstered by the impingement upon his intimacy by means of espionage. David, the fashionably empathetic representative of a new Spanish masculinity, places Víctor under surveillance. His voyeuristic camera captures Clara and Víctor in the private space that constitutes the site of both their love-making and their home-making (both activities prove to be dress rehearsals for what Víctor will eventually do with Elena). These are the photos that will be used by the possessive David to provoke Sancho into taking action and lead to Clara's death in a neat set-play exemplary of the generational collaboration – or negotiation – that brought democracy to Spain with no public settling of accounts with the past.

Privacy, moreover, is historically patriarchal and corporeal. Its political associations concern sovereignty, family and property. Nancy Duncan has written that the 'linkage between individual, family and group autonomy and privatization, localization and other exclusionary spatial strategies is one of the most important and interesting aspects of political geography' (1996: 128). The households in *Carne trémula* are like sieves. People are forever encroaching onto other people's property, either physically or by means of surveillance techniques. Perhaps unsurprisingly, the arena for Clara and Sancho's melodramatic final shoot-out is not their own home, where they have previously waged their matrimonial battles, but Víctor's living room. It is in this venue that we are regaled with Víctor's full-frontal nude scene – he leaps out of the shower to extinguish a fire on the stove. Indeed, even Almodóvar's movie camera intrudes upon the intimate environment of his own home.

Home is a concept played upon throughout the film. While Clara helps Víctor make his dwelling more comfortable by passing him second-hand furniture and carpets, the entrance to the home she shares with Sancho is garnished with a doormat stamped with an ironic message; 'Bienvenido' ('Welcome') it proclaims. Contested private space becomes exemplified the afternoon Clara announces to Sancho that she wants to separate following Víctor's declaration that he no longer wishes to continue their affair. She has forgotten that it is their wedding anniversary. The oppressive domestic space of Clara and Sancho's household is made wry in this sequence. There is an evident inversion of conventional gender roles with Sancho cooking in the kitchen and Clara sprawled on the sofa, 'like a bloke' in the words of her husband.[6] There is also an ironic reflection on the function of time in the self-conscious reference to the significant date of the wedding anniversary. There is a kind of 'monumentality' in the calendar of marriage here, in that anniversaries – like the statues that adorn the city's streets and squares – are commemorations in the shared and private imaginary. The laxity that we have already seen with regard to the historical facts of public dates comes to be imbued with private significance. The personal and historical ordering of time intertwines with the domestic and national spatial narratives.

While classical feminist theory holds that space is heterogeneous, public space is traditionally gendered masculine and private space is feminine (Duncan 1996: 127–45). Víctor is, generally, more associated with a stereotypical 'feminine' space than an orthodox masculine one as befits his in-between nature. While lacking the comforts, he is more at home in his particular domestic sphere than Clara is in hers and he has a 'caring' profession as a volunteer at the orphanage.

The connection between the private and public spheres is often made via use of the television screen. That the photographic image, once more, should provide such a link is important. There is both a connection between voyeurism and surveillance as well as between the tactile and the territorial. Moreover, to use Bruno's words, such a space constitutes 'the place where a tactile eye and a visual touch develop' (2002: 253). This is the zone where the five principal characters converge. At significant moments throughout the movie people watch television. There is an interestingly two-way dimension to this and one that is often expressed through the body. While television acts as a public window – a peephole – for private acts, it also provides a conduit – a literal channel – through which access is obtained to the public world from the intimate circumstances of domesticity. During the struggle between Víctor and Elena, Buñuel's *Ensayo de un crimen* (*The Criminal Life of Archibaldo de la Cruz*) is being broadcast on the television. However, shortly before Víctor's arrival at Elena's apartment, we see the 1970 (*sic*) State of Emergency mimicked in a 1990 televised news broadcast by an item detailing the very contemporaneous crisis in hospital waiting lists, a direct consequence of the then Socialist Government's cuts in public services. A timely reminder – in view of the current amnesia – that neoliberal economic policies were first implemented in Spain by a government purporting to be of the Left. The use of the television screen, nonetheless, is not always a question of political irony. Víctor is assaulted by David who punches him in the crotch in his own home before the two of them bond around a goal scored by an Atlético de Madrid footballer against the traditional city rivals, Barcelona, transmitted live on the blaring TV. Following this sequence we see the contrasting urban space of the higher reaches of La Castellana, and, in similar contrast, the different mobility of the two men. Víctor who exercises the freedom of the dispossessed on the streets and in public transport and David, spying on him, who has a car but who is confined – owing to his paralysis – within its claustrophobic space and that of his own body. David and Víctor are both marked by spatio-corporeal configurations that stretch from the body outward to the city and to the world. This in fact comes to mark a kind of colonization. Víctor marks out his territory, in movement through the city of Madrid, with his own body. Víctor (whose name conjures up images of both victor and victim), shares with David an obsession with developing and attuning his bodily possibilities. Both men do so from a position of castration (symbolic and real) marked by different kinds of paralysis: Víctor from prison, David from his wheelchair. Both though are prisoners of their bodily images. Liberto Rabal – who provides the film with its only full nude – has Marlon Brando's thick sensual lips and there is a parodic echo of Brando on his Harley Davidson in *The Wild One* in the adult Víctor's very first appearance in the movie on his moped circling La Puerta de Alcalá delivering pizzas. The body of Javier Bardem, meanwhile, receives ironic treatment. At the time the film was made he was primarily identified with the macho roles he had played in 1990s' Bigas Luna films. While in *Jamón jamón* (Bigas Luna, 1993) his bulging crotch served to advertise male underwear on billboards, his wheelchair image on a giant poster is the first thing Víctor sees on stepping out of jail onto the street in *Carne trémula*.

The film's major sex sequence, when Elena and Víctor first spend the night together, is filmed as an act of exploration and territorial conquest. This character is not called Víctor for nothing. There is an element of cartography in its erotic mapmaking of the human body as – to use Bruno's words – an 'intimate terrain' (2002: 254). The two bodies are 'discovered' (in the sense of uncovered) in use and a relation is established between erotics and arquitectonics, between structures of urban space and the surface of the human body. Likewise, 'circulation', the activity largely practised by Víctor – on foot, motorcycle or bus – throughout the film also connects to the human body: the circulation of the bloodstream. In this way the vertebrae of public and private spaces are laid bare; their internal anatomies are revealed in an inversion of cityscape and bodyscape, like an x-ray image; both the body and the city are turned inside out.

Knowledge and Narrative

It is both his freedom of movement and his in-between quality that defines Víctor. And both link him to the structures of the city. Víctor's in-between condition gives the clue to much of Almodóvar's work. Many commentators on Almodóvar have observed its recycled, makeshift quality – like Víctor's shack – its feel of *bricolage*. This is, in part, due to the director's association with the Rastro, the city's open-air fleamarket and one of the principal spaces of the *Movida* – the exuberant explosion of cultural activity of the late 1970s and early 1980s – whose best-known ambassador is Almodóvar himself. Linked to this distinctive feature of the Rastro is the fact that the market is a space of transaction where things are exchanged and used goods bought, and it is a scenario – amid the seething crowds – of fortuitous encounters. Although the Rastro does not feature in this film, its influence is reproduced in the persistence of second-hand information, accidental meetings, the use of photographic and television imagery to spread skewed knowledge, the misinterpretations and the mistakes.

Indeed, it returns us to the notion of 'mistake'. Without wishing to suggest that Almodóvar deliberately chose to incorrectly date the commencement of this film, his cavalier attitude to precision is reflected in Víctor himself. Amid the mass of papers glued into Víctor's scrapbook bible we catch a glimpse of Elena's name *misspelt* as Helena, as if she were that most potent mythological figure of the static-mobile interplay – once more featuring Odysseus – Helen of Troy. Part of this Rastro-like *bricolage* is in the use Almodóvar makes of his sources. The clearest example of Almodóvar's quotations from other filmic texts here is in the use he makes of Buñuel's *Ensayo de un crimen*. The Buñuel film, like *Carne trémula*, is a brilliantly droll parody of the Hollywood crime thriller. It also deals with similar issues of male jealousy, kitsch religion and architecture. Almodóvar's relationship with this text as well as other national and international sources is parodic, a space within which reverberate an entire gamut of influences, urban, literary and cinematic. Víctor's prison bible proves a symbol of the entire film. It is his scrapbook and photo album into which he has pasted the fragments of his patchwork life. The bible is a space in miniature, suggestive of the director's own method. More than postmodern *mise en scène*, Madrid for Almodóvar

Steven Marsh

is a palimpsest. Such intertexuality once more returns us to the subjects of movement and history. The word 'movement' chimes loudly within a parodic space in-between two historically specific configurations: the *Movida* and the Francoist *Movimiento*. The two times of the movie are reproduced in the actors. Javier Bardem's real mother Pilar Bardem plays Doña Centro. One of Buñuel's favourite actors and close friend Francisco Rabal (who has also acted in a previous Almodóvar film) is Liberto's grandfather. Angela Molina first appeared in a Buñuel film (see Smith 1984). The doubling is generational and historical but it is also spatial. 'Centro' means centre, 'Plaza' – Víctor's surname – means square. These are characters associated with public arenas. The idea that history can be measured in spatial terms is further reinforced in this film by the symbolic presence of very real articulating junctures. At the commencement of Víctor's internal journey through Madrid, a short walk beyond the far reaches of the bridge that links Elena's apartment on Eduardo Dato Street to the Barrio de Salamanca is the *Residencia de Estudiantes*, the famed student residency where Federico García Lorca, Salvador Dali and Buñuel first met in the 1920s. The bridge itself is a matter of metres away from the Rubén Darío underground station. The Nicaraguan poet Darío is by consensus viewed as one of the most significant representatives of the 'modernist' movement in Hispanic letters. Once more the high cultural artistic referents of modernism converge around and beneath the bridge that traverses the city's principal claim to postmodernity.

While the bridge symbolically connects and separates, so do other kinds of threshold. If the city's architectonics are gendered, other spatial articulations suggest a corporeal urban structure. Víctor moves in the orbit – he lingers – of the city gates. Renaming the KIO Towers as La Puerta de Europa is a matter of ideologically recasting them as modern equivalents of a tradition of historical city gates in the vein of the existing Puerta de Alcalá, Puerta de Toledo and Puerta de Hierro and a clear attempt to link (in the historical narrative of the nation) the city's architecture to Spain's entry into the European Union (often viewed – together with Almodóvar himself – as synonymous with Spain's democratic arrival). These gates are circulatory channels in the city's corporeal framework – Víctor climbs on the bus at the Puerta de Europa and circles the Puerta de Alcalá on his moped – and we have seen that these are monuments imbued with gender implications. Such symbolism also connects the private and public spheres. David is shot in the doorway – the threshold – of Elena's home. The doormat stamped with the word 'Bienvenido' at the entrance to Clara and Sancho's home is an ironic reflection on thresholds. David struggles frustratedly to remove himself backward in his wheelchair, stumbling out of the door of Víctor's home and down the steps, from the site where he has both thumped him in the balls and bonded with him in a masculine set-piece. And at the very end of the film Clara and Sancho lie dying from a perspective shot from the doorway of Víctor's home.

The film ends as it began, at Christmas with a birth in a vehicle on the streets of central Madrid. It is a perfect end for a Hollywood-style romantic comedy but, à la Buñuel, it comes with a twist, for Almodóvar never loses his ironic eye. As Elena begins to give birth in the car, Víctor addresses his son and recalls the night he was born on the bus nearby and says: 'The people were indoors shitting themselves with fear. Fortunately, my son, we haven't felt that fear for a long time now'. I interpret this apparently schmalzy ending as ironic in the vein of what has gone before. This time contemporaneous history itself, the narrative of the nation in the form of the Transition to democracy, is subjected to parody. Víctor, after all, only went to jail during a government led by Felipe González. Pointedly, although the sequence echoes the film's prologue when Víctor's own mother went into labour in the brothel – prior to finding the bus – what is recalled by Elena's gasps are those of Víctor's mother sheering against the radio broadcast that announces the suspension of civil rights and the State of Emergency, delivered in the distinctive, and eminently recognizable, tones of erstwhile Francoist Minister of Information and the *current* President of the Regional Autonomy of Galicia as well as the founder of the party that until recently held national office, Manuel Fraga Iribarne.[7] The disembodied presence of Fraga in *Carne trémula*, whose cadence chimes in the nation's memory, conflates and contrasts with today's woeful figure. Fraga is well-known for his difficulties with mobility (both figuratively and literally), his decaying physique and the noticeable incoherence that age has wrought upon his speech. Just as Víctor is a character in-between buildings, genders and the generational constructions of masculinity, in the historical narration Fraga is also an in-between character. Often labelled today as zombie-like – in-between life and death – in *Carne trémula* he is a spectral voice from the archive. His continued participation in political life is like that of a ghost haunting the contemporary nation. In spite of the errors of fact the continuities with the dictatorship – the persistent failure of Spain to fully come to terms with its past – are brought sharply back into focus.

Steven Marsh

Notes

1. Elorza was writing in the aftermath of two controversies concerning the politics of Spanish cinema that erupted early in 2003. First, Almodóvar's *Hable con ella* had been nominated for the Oscar for Best Original Screenplay (an award that he eventually won) having previously been overlooked by the Spanish Academy of Cinematic Art which selected the radical socialist film, *Los lunes al sol* (Fernando León de Aranoa) as the country's representative to compete in the category of Best Foreign-Language Film. Likewise, the right-wing press and elements within the government had sought to vilify the Academy (and a number of actors who, it was suggested by the newspaper *La Razón*, were less inclined to criticize the Basque separatist group ETA, among them the star of the film discussed here, Javier Bardem) following that year's Goya awards in which almost all the recipients of prizes condemned the Spanish government's involvement in the US-UK planned invasion of Iraq. It should be mentioned, however, that the following week Almodóvar headed the huge Madrid anti-war demonstration and spoke at the final rally together with the female star of *Hable con ella* Leonor Watling and veteran actor and director, Fernando Fernán Gómez.
2. As Smith has observed, such an epithet is very much 'a backhanded compliment' (1994: 2) but it is also one that the film-maker himself has done little to disavow.
3. *La puerta de Alcalá* is also the title of a well-known song recorded and performed by Ana Belén and Víctor Manuel. This song was used by the regional government of Madrid in the year 2002–2003 to promote the city as part of its campaign to attract tourism.
4. La Castellana really commences at the Plaza de Colón but in fact the same street under the names of the Paseo de Recoletos and the Paseo del Prado continues further south.
5. In fact when the area was bulldozed and rebuilt several years later, the main thoroughfare through the district was eventually called 'Avenida de Asturias'. The error is once more illustrative. I have written elsewhere on the relationship between street names and the Transition, as well as on the relation of both with the monarchy (Marsh: 2003).
6. Sancho is a character who engenders food. At this point he is cooking 'bull's tail with brandy' (a dish resonant with machismo). On the occasion of the initial shooting he threatens Víctor and says he intends

'making an omelette out of your balls'. (The Spanish word *huevos* [eggs] is the equivalent in slang to the English *balls*).
7. The relevance of the convergence between the public and the private spheres could not be better illustrated than when, in 2002, precisely at a moment when the country was convulsed by Spain's record figures for domestic violence, Fraga was filmed on national television responding to a woman in the city of Pontevedra who had heckled him, with the words 'If it were not for the fact that you are a woman, I would punch you out'. At the time of writing the woman has been charged and is awaiting trial for having insulted Fraga.

References

Allinson, Mark (2001), *A Spanish Labyrinth: The Films of Pedro Almodóvar*, London: I.B. Tauris.
Bruno, Giuliana (2002), *Atlas of Emotion: Journeys in Art, Architecture, and Film*, New York: Verso.
Certeau, Michel de (1984 [1980]), *The Practice of Everyday Life*, trans. Steven Rendall, Berkeley and Los Angeles: University of California Press.
Clarke, David B. (ed.) (1997), *The Cinematic City*, London and New York: Routledge.
Compitello, Malcolm (1999), 'From Planning to Design: The Culture of Flexible Accumulation in Post-Cambio Madrid', *Arizona Journal of Hispanic Cultural Studies*, 3: 199–219.
D'Lugo, Marvin (1995), 'Almodóvar's City of Desire', in Barbara Morris and Kathleen Vernon (eds), *Post-Franco, Postmodern: The Films of Pedro Almodóvar*, Westport CT: Greenwood.
Duncan, Nancy (ed.) (1996), *BodySpace: Destabilizing Geographies of Gender and Sexuality*, London and New York: Routledge.
Elorza, Antonio (2003), 'El sexo de los ángeles', *El País*, 19 February: 14.
Fernández Cifuentes, Luis (1999), 'The City as Stage: Rebuilding Metropolis after the Colonial Wars', *Arizona Journal of Hispanic Cultural Studies*, 3: 105–27.
Marsh, Steven (2002), *Comedy and the Weakening of the State: An Ideological Approach to Popular Spanish Cinema 1942–1962*, PhD thesis, University of London.
—— (2003), 'Insinuating Spaces: Memories of a Madrid Neighbourhood during the Spanish Transition', in Paul Gready (ed.), *Political Transition: Politics and Cultures*, London: Pluto.

——(2004), 'Tracks, Traces and Commonplaces: Fernando León de Aranoa's *Barrio* (1998) and the Layered Landscape of Everyday Life in Contemporary Madrid', *New Cinemas*, 1(3).

Morgan-Tamosunas, Rikki (2002), 'Narrative, Desire and Critical Discourse in Pedro Almodóvar's *Carne trémula* (1997)', *Journal of Iberian and Latin American Studies*, 8(2): 185–99.

Morris, Barbara and Vernon, Kathleen (eds) (1995), *Post-Franco, Postmodern: The Films of Pedro Almodóvar*, Westport CT: Greenwood.

Preston, Paul (1993), *Franco: A Biography* London: HarperCollins.

Smith, Paul Julian (1994) *Desire Unlimited: The Cinema of Pedro Almodóvar*, London and New York: Verso.

——(1998), 'Absolute Precision', *Sight and Sound*, 8(4), April: 6–9.

Ugarte, Michael (2001), 'Madrid: From "Años de Hambre" to Years of Desire', in *Iberian Cities*, New York and London: Routledge.

Van Den Abbeele, George (1992), *Travel as Metaphor*, Minneapolis: University of Minnesota Press.

5

Madness, Queenship and Womanhood in Orduña's *Locura de amor* (1948) and Aranda's *Juana la loca* (2001)

Celia Martin Pérez

Juan de Orduña's *Locura de amor* (1948) and Vicente Aranda's *Juana la loca* (2001) are both films that tell the story of the Spanish Queen, Juana I of Castile (1479–1555), who allegedly went mad because of her obsessive love for her Flemish husband, Felipe 'The Handsome'. These two cinematic representations deal with gender issues of queenship and romantic madness, posed as conflictual, since the first links woman to the public sphere, while the second associates her with the private world of emotions. The construction of womanhood as seen through the character of Juana, therefore, becomes a complicated matter. My intention in this chapter is to look at how these two issues are dealt with in each film and thereby show how notions of womanhood were affected by the historical circumstances from which they emerged.

Although Orduña's film was produced by CIFESA, the film company that seemingly acted as an ideological mouthpiece of the Francoist regime in the decade following the 1936–1939 Civil War (Font 1976: 107), it can also be seen as subverting the regime's reactionary discourses on the social role of women in the domestic or private sphere. On the other hand, in spite of the contemporary director's allegedly 'feminist' intentions to vindicate her as a woman – Aranda believes her to have been 'ahead of her time' (*El País*, 22 November 2000: 50) – the portrayal of Juana's madness and queenship in the more recent film can be read as reinforcing the traditional association of woman with nature. In this way Aranda might be seen as supporting the undermining notion that women 'have not made the transition from animality to culture, because they are still tied to nature through their sexuality and fertility' (Turner 1996: 199).

In drawing this initial comparison between the different approaches to the figure of Juana, it is important to note that both Orduña and Aranda based their films on Manuel Tamayo y Baús's play *Locura de amor* (1855), as did Ricard de Baños, who directed the very first cinematic version of Juana's story in 1909. The Tamayo y Baús play contains an important subplot to Juana's mad love for Felipe: an account of the power struggle within the Spanish court. On one side there are the Flemish and their Spanish allies, supportive of Felipe as sole ruler of Castile, who accuse Juana of being mentally unfit so as to remove her from public sight. The opposing faction, however, is made up of those Spanish loyalists who support and defend the Queen.

While this subplot arguably looms larger than the romantic drama in Orduña's film, in Aranda's version 'the political intrigues that surrounded her reign [Juana's] are overshadowed by the love that Juana feels for Felipe' (Sánchez 2001: 41). Furthermore, it would appear that for Orduña, Tamayo's secondary storyline could be used to explain Spain's contemporaneous international isolation. In February 1946 Spain had been refused entry into the United Nations and the following December the UN had called for the withdrawal of accredited ambassadors to Madrid. Orduña's emphasis on a group of 'good' Spaniards acting in defence of their Castilian Queen against a 'corrupt' foreign force in cahoots with self-serving and anti-patriotic Spanish 'traitors', would serve, thus, to legitimize Spain's geopolitical situation in the popular imagination. Angel Fernández Castellano suggests that *Locura de amor* is blatantly about 'goodies' and 'baddies' 'Felipe bad, Juana good' (1976: 52). Felipe the 'bad' foreigner, Juana the 'good' Spaniard. An illustrative example of the constant attempts of the period to manipulate public opinion into believing the ill-intentions of foreign powers is the headline in the Madrid daily newspaper *El Alcázar* on 8 October 1948, the same year *Locura de amor* was premiered, which read: 'Sinister Anti-Spanish Manoeuvring by Britain's Labour Government'. This was a reference to the announcement by the British Foreign Office of a pact between Spanish monarchists and socialists in exile. Orduña's emphasis on the political implications of Tamayo's play, while apparently ideologically coherent with the Regime, also served to heighten Juana's function as a political figure.

Aranda's film, meanwhile, would seem to owe little to contemporary, or even past, political issues despite the director's insistence that the movie exposes the Regime's own claims. '[A]s opposed to what Franco would have us believe that the Catholic Kings sought to maintain the unity of Spain, it is very clear that Fernando the Catholic following Isabel's death did all in his power to divide the kingdom' (Reviriego 2001: 40). Although *Juana la loca* does contain a scene depicting a meeting between Juana's father (Fernando the Catholic) and Felipe, in which the former gives his approval to imprison Juana, it is passed over fleetingly and is so contrived within the context of the narrative that it appears to be little more than a token riposte to Francoist historical discourse. Aranda's willingness to gloss over the political plot of the story is made more explicit in his use of a voice-over narration which, as he has explained, serves to introduce important facts mostly in relation to politics (Reviriego 2001: 40). The employment of voice-over to outline the main political events diminishes their importance, factual as they are, and locates them at a tangent to the narrative. Its purpose is merely, as the director himself has noted, to help with plot transitions (Reviriego 2001: 41). In essence, this depoliticization minimizes Juana's role as a public figure. In Aranda's film she is rarely shown as operating within the political arena.

The different treatments of Juana as a political entity are obvious from her very first appearance in each of the two films. Both productions start from the same point and function in flashback as Juana, nearing the end of her life, is seen in confinement at the castle of Tordesillas, to which she has been taken after Felipe's death, accused of madness. At the very beginning of *Locura de amor*, Juana's regal status can be deduced by the presentation of her at court, seated upon a throne and surrounded by courtiers. Further reference to Juana's royal status is conveyed by a horseman who asks for direction with the words: 'Where is Queen Juana's castle?' The same horseman also announces the arrival of Juana's son, Emperor Carlos I, who has come to visit her, in an apparently symbolic reference to an endorsement of Juana's contribution to the creation of the Spanish Empire.

Similarly, Juana's story is told to Carlos I by Alvar, a captain in the Spanish army, who commences his narration with the death of Isabel the Catholic, Juana's mother. This narration consists of a single shot that focuses on a painstaking recreation of the nineteenth-century painting by Eduardo Rosales *El testamento de Isabel la Católica* (1864). This work aimed, in Rosales's words, to show how 'the greatest Queen, the pride of Spain, concerned herself with the welfare of her people with the love of a mother' (Díez 1992: 214). Introducing Juana's story with the 'live' reproduction of this painting has the effect of establishing Juana's credentials as a Queen and associating her with a positively constructed cultural myth of queenship. During Francoism, Isabel the Catholic was regarded as Queen *par excellence*, a point highlighted in the film by Captain Alvar who refers to her as 'the greatest Queen'. She was viewed by elements within the Regime as the consummate defender of

Celia Martín Pérez

the Catholic faith, a central plank of Francoist ideology. She was also regarded as the founding 'mother' of the Spanish Empire, who provided financial support for Spain's American adventure.[1] It should also be added that, via widespread dissemination of reproductions of Rosales's painting during the Francoist period, the myth of Isabel the Catholic as the nation's finest Queen was firmly established in the popular Spanish psyche. This was especially evident in schoolbooks, of which *Historia de España* is exemplary. In this text a picture of Isabel is accompanied by the explanation that in 1504 'the most sublime Queen that History has known placidly gave up her spirit to God' (Edelvives 1949: 66).

The Rosales painting is also re-staged in *Juana la loca* as if to convince us that Aranda also sought to legitimize Juana's status as a Queen. This might, though, be better interpreted as a homage to Orduña together with the reproduction of another painting that is recreated in both films, the nineteenth-century Francisco Pradilla y Ortiz's painting *Juana la loca* (1878). This is perhaps the best explanation for such intertextualization, since the presence of such paintings in Aranda's film could not possibly have the same significance, with regard to the historical context of Francoist discourse within the narrative, for present-day audiences. Moreover, the restaged painting of Isabel appears in the middle of Aranda's film, placed between scenes in which Juana's love for Felipe is displayed, thus suggesting that its intention is simply to give additional historical background to the narrative. This is maybe unsurprising as Aranda does not appear to hold Juana's mother in any great esteem: she was, in his view, 'the real mad woman ... a woman trapped by her own megalomania' (Fernández-Santos 2000: 50). Aranda's rejection of Isabel as a political icon is revealed in the film when one of Juana's Flemish enemies denounces her madness as being akin to that of her grandmother (Isabel of Portugal) and that of her fanatical mother. Felipe, in Aranda's view, was therefore obliged to rid Spain of Juana to free Castile from fanaticism and superstition. In contrast, Orduña refers only to Juana's grandmother's madness and makes no pejorative mention of Isabel.

As outlined above, in Orduña's film Juana is first presented as a regal figure. Aranda chooses to introduce her in very different terms. In *Juana la loca*, the Queen first appears alone and in a very dark room, with no sign of a royal entourage, conveying the idea of isolation. Accompanying this visual image we hear a voice-over informing that the woman before us 'was the daughter of ... the wife of ... and the mother of...', before finally adding that she was Queen of Castile and León. In this, Juana's introduction, major importance is given to Juana's private background, emphasizing, ironically in the vein of Francoist patriarchy, her identity

---

Celia Martín Pérez

the Catholic faith, a central plank of Francoist ideology. She was also regarded as the founding 'mother' of the Spanish Empire, who provided financial support for Spain's American adventure.[1] It should also be added that, via widespread dissemination of reproductions of Rosales's painting during the Francoist period, the myth of Isabel the Catholic as the nation's finest Queen was firmly established in the popular Spanish psyche. This was especially evident in schoolbooks, of which *Historia de España* is exemplary. In this text a picture of Isabel is accompanied by the explanation that in 1504 'the most sublime Queen that History has known placidly gave up her spirit to God' (Edelvives 1949: 66).

The Rosales painting is also re-staged in *Juana la loca* as if to convince us that Aranda also sought to legitimize Juana's status as a Queen. This might, though, be better interpreted as a homage to Orduña together with the reproduction of another painting that is recreated in both films, the nineteenth-century Francisco Pradilla y Ortiz's painting *Juana la loca* (1878). This is perhaps the best explanation for such intertextualization, since the presence of such paintings in Aranda's film could not possibly have the same significance, with regard to the historical context of Francoist discourse within the narrative, for present-day audiences. Moreover, the restaged painting of Isabel appears in the middle of Aranda's film, placed between scenes in which Juana's love for Felipe is displayed, thus suggesting that its intention is simply to give additional historical background to the narrative. This is maybe unsurprising as Aranda does not appear to hold Juana's mother in any great esteem: she was, in his view, 'the real mad woman ... a woman trapped by her own megalomania' (Fernández-Santos 2000: 50). Aranda's rejection of Isabel as a political icon is revealed in the film when one of Juana's Flemish enemies denounces her madness as being akin to that of her grandmother (Isabel of Portugal) and that of her fanatical mother. Felipe, in Aranda's view, was therefore obliged to rid Spain of Juana to free Castile from fanaticism and superstition. In contrast, Orduña refers only to Juana's grandmother's madness and makes no pejorative mention of Isabel.

As outlined above, in Orduña's film Juana is first presented as a regal figure. Aranda chooses to introduce her in very different terms. In *Juana la loca*, the Queen first appears alone and in a very dark room, with no sign of a royal entourage, conveying the idea of isolation. Accompanying this visual image we hear a voice-over informing that the woman before us 'was the daughter of ... the wife of ... and the mother of...', before finally adding that she was Queen of Castile and León. In this, Juana's introduction, major importance is given to Juana's private background, emphasizing, ironically in the vein of Francoist patriarchy, her identity as a daughter, wife and mother rather than Queen. This becomes explicit when the elderly Juana reminisces and her thoughts are made audible as she stares at Felipe's picture in her hands and utters the words: 'When I close my eyes he approaches, I feel his skin on my finger tips, I feel his voice in my ears, I perceive the scent of his armpits, my desire arouses...'. Clearly, the intention here is to link Juana directly to her sexuality rather than to offer a 74-year-old woman the opportunity to reflect on her role as a Queen. The voice-over ends the scene with the words, 'they call her Juana the madwoman' thereby establishing Juana as 'mad' from the start.

In Aranda's film, unlike in *Locura de amor*, Juana is labelled 'mad' on numerous occasions and it is Felipe who first uses the term, early in the film, during a scene in which Juana is breastfeeding their new baby daughter. As far as Felipe is concerned Juana is displaying inappropriate behaviour and he scolds her for being 'the only princess that breastfeeds her children', telling her that her 'behaviour is startling everybody'. Juana's justification is that both the baby and she enjoy breastfeeding. The audience, meanwhile, has witnessed the self-gratification, the almost orgasmic experience that Juana derives from breastfeeding prior to Felipe's entrance. In turn, doubt is cast on Juana's motivation for the notion of maternal bonding, compounded at the end of the discussion when Juana uncovers her breasts and offers them to Felipe, saying, 'I am full', thereby lending weight to Felipe's response, 'you are mad'. The idea that Aranda tries to convey in this and other sequences throughout the film, as he explains, is that Juana 'for her time was mad', but 'from a modern perspective, she was not ... Juana was demanding with her emotions ... and had inappropriate tendencies for that period' (Fernández-Santos 2000: 50). Aranda's comments suggest that his attempt is to demonstrate how Juana's behaviour today would be considered as that of a sexually liberated woman rather than a lunatic. However, Aranda goes to such lengths to make this point that the result is the creation of a Juana whose sexuality and 'natural' instincts seem to be all that constitutes her persona to the detriment of her 'cultural' and political image as a Queen.

Another sequence of the Aranda film sees Felipe at the dinner table raising the issue of Juana's improper behaviour as Queen. 'Your conduct shocks me', he says. Juana's response is an unequivocal demand for him to see her as a woman. More than a Queen, she tells Felipe, she desires to be 'your wife, your woman, your whore'. In keeping with his own regal sense of decorum, Felipe's reaction is to tell Juana that she is 'shameless' and 'there is cause indeed for the rumours that you are mad'. As if to confirm such suspicions, Juana then advances toward

Felipe in an agitated manner with a knife clasped in her hand. Yet, as she does so, her response ('mad because my love drives me to madness … mad because I hope to bear your children … madly in love') shows that she understands the reason for her so-called 'madness', that she is an excessively passionate woman. The scene ends with Felipe taking the knife from Juana and throwing them both to the floor. But before leaving the room he pauses and returns to her, raises her skirt, by which we are afforded a view of Juana's already parted legs, and takes her. The scene suggests that Juana's 'madness' is a result of her unfulfilled sexual passion toward her husband. Yet by using 'vulgar' language, threatening Felipe with a knife, and her willingness to copulate with him after he has just abused her, Juana is also portrayed as an impulsive woman who lacks self-control and is incapable of behaving rationally. She has apparently not fully made the transition from animality to reason.

Indeed, Juana's ties to 'nature' are so accentuated in Aranda's film that she is frequently *animalized*. When Juana finds Felipe in bed with a woman whom she has not time to recognize, we see her sniffing animal-like the sheets to find out the identity of her husband's lover. Later, she is again shown behaving similarly, sniffing Inés, one of her ladies-in-waiting and the woman she suspects. As she recognizes the smell of Inés's body she calls to her attendant to 'hold this whore', so as to be able to cut off all her hair. Toward the end of the film when Felipe is dying, Juana is shown kissing and licking the sores on his body, an act commonly associated with animal behaviour.

In relation to Juana's *animalization* in *Juana la loca* it is interesting to see how Aranda portrays her in those scenes in which she requests love-making devoid of feelings of romantic love. An example of this is when Felipe and Juana arrive in Burgos to be crowned. After acknowledging their subjects from the balcony, Juana returns to the room and throws herself onto the bed asking Felipe to caress her stomach to feel the baby. Within seconds she opens her legs indicating to Felipe that she wants to make love. Perhaps the most striking aspect of this 'primal' behaviour – in stark contrast with Juana's regal position – is her giving birth to the future Carlos I in a toilet, an act that takes place in a matter of seconds and without any assistance, medical or otherwise. This scene is particularly illustrative of the point that Juana is animalized. We are witnesses to how, with the blood-splattered baby in her lap, she severs the umbilical cord with her own teeth. Meanwhile, outside the toilet, we have heard one of her ladies-in-waiting commenting that 'her Highness is like a cow', thus stressing the animalization of Juana. This idea of Juana being 'like a cow', alludes to her fertility and her facility to give birth, and is further emphasized by the presentation of Juana as an expectant mother – she is heavily pregnant for much of the film – the recurrent references to her 'generous fertility', and her capacity to give birth. Aranda's animalization of Juana's character, moreover, reinforces her portrayal as a person deviant from the world of reason and politics. Thus the myth of her madness is legitimized.

Turning once more to Orduña's film we see that Juana's madness is – as opposed to that of her depiction in Aranda's movie – directly associated with the world of politics. It is presented as a question of state, which divides the court. As mentioned earlier, to one side there is the group of Castilian traitors in league with Flemish members of the court. This faction is personified principally by the scheming character of Don Filberto de Vere who argues that Juana's mental state is dangerous for Castile, as her inability to reason makes her unfit to govern. In opposition, a group of loyal Castilians defend the Queen from the accusation and assert that her 'excessive' behaviour is not a sign of madness but merely a reaction to her husband's infidelities. The two groups are shown to be so divided on the issue and the situation so serious that twice in the film the possibility of civil war is mooted.[2] The fact that it is the faithful Castilians who are portrayed as the virtuous side of the two groups constantly defending Juana from accusations of insanity facilitates the audience's belief that the charge of madness is erroneous. Exemplary of this is when a supporter of Juana, the Admiral of the Castilian fleet, explains that the diagnosis of the Queen's madness is just a Machiavellian political ploy as 'the king has bribed most court doctors prepared to confirm the absurd madness of the Queen'. Furthermore, it is insinuated earlier on by Alvar, when he begins to tell Juana's story to Carlos, that the allegations of Juana's madness were the consequence of a political conspiracy devised by Don Filberto de Vere, who sought to acquire power for himself should Felipe rule alone as King. And, as Alvar goes on to inform us, de Vere 'had to erase the Queen from Felipe's heart and that of her subjects'. Throughout the film we are privy to de Vere's encouragement and his creation of opportunities for Felipe to be unfaithful to Juana and, likewise, for her to find out in anticipation of her reaction manifested in a jealous rage. Thus it is that her excessive behaviour can be used and cited as 'proof' of madness.

In a scene in which members of the court, including the King and de Vere, go hunting, we hear the latter explaining to the Marqués de Villena that they had to allow Juana to find out about Felipe's love affairs so Juana, then, 'will remind him of his duties as a husband...,
she will suffocate him with her jealousy..., he will hate her.' According

to de Vere's scheme, given the difficulty of proving Felipe's infidelities, it would subsequently be very easy to show Castile that Felipe was being misjudged by his excessively jealous and deluded wife. De Vere demonstrates further deviousness when he substitutes a blank piece of paper for a love letter addressed to Felipe from his lover, which would justify Juana's excessive and jealous behaviour before the court. When Juana makes a fool of herself in front of the court by presenting the blank paper, believing it is the love letter, de Vere takes his cue and says, 'Gentlemen, how much madder do you need her to be?' Although on-screen Juana is discredited as consequence of the cruel trickery, any cinema audience, having seen de Vere intrigue, would believe Juana to be sane. In fact, it is not until the very end of his film that Orduña allows Juana's character to act as she were 'mad'. Just after Felipe's death, and again using a recreation of a nineteenth-century painting, (this time by Lorenzo Vallés, *Demencia de doña Juana de Castilla* (1866)), Juana asks for silence in the presence of her dead husband, as she believes he is not dead but just sleeping.

It is noteworthy that Orduña presents Juana not as a mad woman but as a political figure. Her mad love for Felipe becomes in *this* film (unlike Aranda's) secondary to the political issues, which impregnate the entire film. To this end, I would disagree with Felix Fanes's conventional view that in '*Locura de amor* passion plays the most important role, while politics ... take second place' (1982: 169). In fact, even the 'love' scenes in the film between Juana and Felipe are not without their political overtones. When Juana goes incognito to spy on her husband we see how a romantic affair is interwoven with political matters. Felipe has taken to frequenting a tavern having become besotted with a beautiful 'Moor' called Aldara. To catch Felipe out, Juana pretends to be Aldara, using the darkness of the tavern to conceal her identity, a deception that Felipe soon uncovers. Greatly annoyed, Felipe says to her: 'You are capable of everything except bearing the crown of Castile with dignity. In your madness you have not realized that in order to spy on me you have come down to this loathsome tavern'. Using the same excuse given by Felipe for his secret tryst at the tavern, Juana tells him she had gone there to meet the Duke of Alba on state business, adding, 'I have not come to spy on you, I have come to help you with your business. I would like to tell him myself how much Spain owes you as a King... Do you know that being King is not as simple as it appears to be? Poor soul! So many humiliations to avoid a civil war!' Unconvinced by her story Felipe tells her to 'Be quiet!' to which she responds 'I do not want to! You still have not realized that I am mocking you.'

Although this scene ostensibly deals with the subject of conjugal love and betrayal, it is as much an argument about their public roles as Queen and King. In this sense Juana gets the upper hand. The dialogue shows her outwitting her husband. Even in the film's most romantic scene, in which Juana declares her love for Felipe, the issue of queenship intervenes, when she informs her husband that sometimes she hears her mother Isabel telling her 'to think of your duties and I will think of you, love your people and I will love you ... I want to cry as a Queen and I only cry as a woman in love'. Although this scene might appear to undermine Juana's political function as Queen, given that she is shown putting her love for Felipe before her love for the people, it is still symptomatic of the constant theme of the film: that the romantic cannot be divided or separated from the political. This is illustrated in the final 'love' scene when the dying Felipe apologizes to Juana for his behaviour. Referring to her as a Queen and not as his wife and companion, he talks of 'the loyalty of this Queen whom I never knew how to understand'.

So far I have argued that Aranda's representation of Juana emphasizes her madness by distancing her from reason and marrying her to nature and thereby diminishes her as a Queen. I have also suggested that, in Orduña's film, the audience is constantly reminded of Juana's public status, with the issue of her madness portrayed as a political plot. It is, nonetheless, also important not to ignore the performances of the actresses who played Juana in both films. The interpretations of the two actresses who played the role of Juana have undoubtedly affected readings of the historical character. Aurora Bautista, who plays Juana in Orduña's version, was an unknown theatre actress at the time who became a star as a result of the film. According to Fanes, the movie was 'one of the great all-time successes of Spanish cinema' (1982: 168). Bautista won Best Actress award at the First Festival of Latin American Cinema for her performance in *Locura de amor*. In Aranda's film, Pilar López de Ayala starred as Juana. A young actress with a television background who, like Bautista, was not widely known before taking on the role, López de Ayala was rewarded for her interpretation with the Silver Shell at the San Sebastián Film Festival as well as Goya award for Best Actress, even though the film itself received lukewarm reviews (Boyero 2001: 57; Fernández-Santos 2001: 51). In spite of its disappointing critical reception, *Juana la loca* proved to be an important and enduring commercial success throughout Spain. Yet, while both Orduña and Aranda enjoyed a measure of success for the films in their day, the performances of the actresses could not have been more different. While Bautista's rendition is pure melodramatic excess, López de Ayala gives a more contained performance. Carlos

F. Heredero suggests that this owes to the fact that in Aranda's films 'the acceptance of excess and transgression paradoxically carries with it the relinquishing of accessories, the eradication of visual adornment, decoration and melodramatic rhetoric' (2000: 123). In other words, as Sergi Sánchez has noted, López de Ayala's interpretation of Juana is 'diametrically opposed to the histrionics of Aurora Bautista' (2001: 41). It is not difficult to concur with this view. Throughout *Locura de amor* Bautistas's performance verges on the hysterical, which may lend greater weight to the notion of Juana's madness than could have been drawn from the script. Even López de Ayala herself has commented on her predecessor's performance as being 'madder' than her own. She, in turn, sees herself as 'more Juana' (Marín 2001: 64). In Orduña's film, nonetheless, Bautista's hysterical and excessive performance also comes to empower Juana's character on occasions. This we can see by comparing both films' rendition of what is perhaps the most powerful scene in relation to queenship, the point at which Felipe summons the court to officially declare Juana insane and unfit to govern. At this gathering Juana turns up unexpectedly to defend herself. In Orduña's version of the scene Bautista's hysterical performance is complemented by the *mise-en-scène* which is, as Fanes notes, 'delirious, excessive and grandiloquent' (1982: 169), but which tends to work in favour of Juana's image as Queen. First, Juana's arrival at Burgos Cathedral, where the court is in session, is presented as a great magisterial event. Following the enumeration of Felipe's royal titles, a list which sounds prosaic without musical accompaniment, Juana's entrance is made even more authoritative and dramatic by the camera that follows her from the entrance through a long corridor to the dais where the throne stands. Ceremonial music is played inundating the scene to accompany the litany of Juana's royal titles. After this grand entrance, Juana is seated on the dais above her enemies whom she accuses in 'an absolutely excessive interpretation' (Santos Fontela 1976: 46) of being greedy traitors. The placing of Juana above her enemies, however much it accords with royal protocol, also symbolically emphasizes her superiority, not only as a Queen, but also as a witty and ingenious political foe, a match for any man. She employs irony to expose her enemies declaring, 'we mad women don't know what we are saying', a reference that appeals to her audience, on screen and off. Despite the scene's ending with Juana leaving the Cathedral with her head bowed, having been humiliated by the production of the previously mentioned letter that purported to prove Felipe's infidelity, it is difficult to disagree with Gortari who notes in referring to this scene that it 'has undeniable monarchical grandeur' (1976: 49).

In comparison with the context of Orduña's version, there are some marked differences discernible in the way in which the same scene is constructed by Aranda. In the more recent film Juana's entrance to the Cathedral, although accompanied by the reading of her titles, is not supplemented with music, which to a certain extent diminishes the grandiosity of the moment. In spatial terms there is also little sense given of Juana's regal superiority since during this scene Juana is not placed above her enemies, as in Orduña's film, but addresses them at eye level. Her authority is symbolically lowered. Furthermore, Aranda, in this scene, adds vulnerability to the character by placing great emphasis – through a variety of different camera angles – on Juana's heavily pregnant state, highlighted by Juana resting her arms and hands on her stomach. All in all this scene fails to communicate the grandeur of monarchy[3] and queenship that, helped by Bautista's hysterical but strong performance, Orduña's emotionally charged version of the scene transmits.

In this chapter I have argued that in adapting Juana's story for the screen Orduña and Aranda were faced with having to deal with gender issues of romantic madness and queenship, which consequently affected the way womanhood is constructed within the film. In *Locura de amor* the figure of the woman is clearly associated with the domestic world. Juana is presented as a Francoist model of a diligent wife who has the palace 'lively and joyful so the King does not feel any need to leave it'. She is also portrayed, in keeping with Francoist discourses of womanhood, as a desexualized being, always demurely attired, well groomed and frequently wearing headdresses, in counterpoint to Felipe's sexualized loose-haired lovers. However, Orduña's Juana, as with other female protagonists of post-war historical films is also represented as 'strong and eager' (Fanes 1982: 181), a woman who can be in control and a figure of political weight. Surprisingly, throughout Orduña's film there is no direct reference to Juana's motherhood, a factor that would lend itself to the idealized image of woman as a nurturer, a central role for women in Franco's Spain.

Juana's famed romantic madness, which would have undoubtedly connected her to the world of feelings, is depicted by Orduña as the consequence of a male political conspiracy and her husband's infidelity, showing Juana to be a victim of patriarchy, ironically the fate of many women in Spain of the time. This notion is further supported by the fact that some of Juana's dialogue in the film endorses the Francoist view of women's inferior social position. This point is emphasized by Bautistas's excessive performance that conforms to Peter Brooks's thinking on melodrama. Brooks notes that 'expressive language acts as a carrier or conduit for the return of something repressed, articulating these very terms that cannot be used in normal, repressed psychic circumstances' (Brooks 1976: 42). A good example of this occurs when Juana discovers that Aldara is Felipe's lover and exclaims dramatically: 'How lucky men are that when they fight they fight to the death', thereby underlining the passive and resigned role of women following the model of the Francoist regime. The same can be said of the moment Juana is required by Alvar to defend herself from Felipe's accusations of madness and responds: 'It is useless ... everybody has mocked me. I defended my rights as a woman and they called me mad; they would believe I were mad if I defended my rights as a Queen.' Clearly in this speech Juana is implying that if she is not respected as a woman in the private sphere, then how could she possibly command respect as a Queen. Such lines, heard by cinema audiences, which 'during the late 1940s were predominantly female and lower class: that is, made up of the two social groups who most suffered the effects of Francoist repression' (Labanyi 2000: 165) could be seen from a gender point of view to be subversive, while 'identification with these competent historical heroines must have served for some women as a form of psychological revenge on men for their present disempowerment' (Labanyi 2000: 175). It should be pointed out that these two pieces of dialogue have been conspicuously omitted from Aranda's version. Of course, times have changed between the making of *Locura de amor* and *Juana la loca*, with postmodern and postfeminist critique having affected our perceptions about history and women's role in society. I would suggest, however, that the representation of women in *Juana la loca* can be viewed as possibly reactionary and regressive, in the sense that it returns to old derogatory concepts of womanhood and is very far from being the 'feminist' cinema in which Aranda would claim his films can be located (Vera 1989: 22; Guarner and Besas 1985: 18–19; Vera 1989: 11). Aranda's Juana does not appear to have any other ambition other than sexual gratification.

Aranda's over-sexualization of Juana in the film is best demonstrated when, in talking about the difference between 'the peasants' and 'the aristocrats', Juana poses the question: 'Are not peasant women like us, do they not they have the same thing between their legs as you and I?'. This emphasis on the 'sexualization' of Juana's character could perhaps be explained as forming part of 'the current revival of the practice of demythologising monarchs on screen: the seemingly insatiable public need for seeing royals as all too human' (Cartmell and Hunter 2001: 5). Whether or not Aranda was affected by cultural trends when making this film, the outcome of his representation of Juana is that of an 'uncontrolled' woman who lives and breathes just for sex, which is evidently undermining of her image as a public and *political* figure. To conclude, I should like to draw attention to the fact that *Locura de amor* and *Juana la loca* are just two of the very many cultural interpretations of Juana's story. Recently, Juana has been the subject matter of a number of other representations. That fact alone is suggestive of the continuing fascination with this particular Queen. Included among these are a flamenco show, *Juana la loca* – produced and performed by the renowned dancer Sara Baras – and the play of the same name staged by the theatre group *La novia*. Both productions emerged in the year 2001. A biography *La reina Juana, Gobierno, piedad y dinastía* by Bethany Aram also appeared the same year. Such interest is symptomatic of an ongoing debate currently alive within Spanish society concerning the figure of Juana la Loca. The discussion oscillates between two compelling questions: 'Was Juana really mad?' and 'How much political power did she exercise?' Perhaps such cultural manifestations are pointedly revealing interrogations of the representation of women in public life.

Notes

1. Isabel la Católica was also symbolically important during early Francoism, as the 'new educational system aspired to promote true Catholic womanhood by appealing to Spanish historical traditions' (G. Morcillo 2000: 36), and Isabel was 'chosen' as a female role model. However, as Graham suggests, representations of Isabel, together with those of St Teresa, another Francoist role-model of womanhood, had to be sanitized as she was an empowered model of womanhood (Graham 1995: 184).
2. The mention of civil war in Orduña's film has been inferred by Santos Fontela (1976: 46) to represent the Spanish Civil War 1936–39. However, I believe this reference is more likely to be in connection to the Spanish Carlists Wars (1833–40; 1870–75) which were fought between those who defended Queen Isabel II, daughter of Fernando VII, and those who followed his brother Carlos, who claimed the throne for himself. During this period significant debate about queenship ensued, involving discussions about women's ability to

reign. Indeed in 1948, this historical fact would still be quite fresh in the audiences' minds, with the connection not too difficult to make, as the Carlists, who 'have lasted as an active political force within Spanish politics until now' (Carr 1999: 187), fought on Franco's side during the Spanish Civil War. Ironically, though, the Queen this time is defended by the nationalists.

3. This glorification of the monarchy was one of the ideological contradictions of the film as, throughout more than a decade, Franco's regime fomented antimonarchical propaganda (Payne 1997: 74), since it was seen as a threat to the regime. The fact that the film concerned a female monarch also subverted the regime's ideology, as one of the conditions of Franco accepting a monarchy as a successor to his regime was that the future monarch had to be a male (Payne 1997: 74). Nevertheless, it could be argued, as Carlos Puerto points out, that although in those years 'monarchy was a word that was taboo' the film 'makes a point of showing that monarchy can lead to civil wars' (Puerto 1976: 49).

References

Boyero, Carlos (2001), 'Una inmensa actriz en una película correcta y fría', *El Mundo*, 26 September: 57

Brooks, P. (1976), *The Melodramatic Imagination: Balzac, Henry James, Melodrama and the Mode of Excess*, New Haven: Yale University Press.

Carr, R. (1999), *España 1808–1975*, Barcelona: Ariel.

Cartmell, D. and Hunter, I.Q. (2001), 'Introduction: Retrovisions: Historical Makeovers in Film and Literature', in Deborah Cartmell and Imelda Whelehan (eds), *Retrovisions: Reinventing the Past in Film and Fiction*, London: Pluto.

Díez, J.L. (1992), *La pintura de historia del siglo XIX en España*, Madrid: Madrid Capital Europea de la Cultura.

Edelvives (1949), *Historia de España: Primer grado*, Zaragoza: Editorial Luis Vives.

Fanes, F. (1982), *Cifesa: La antorcha de los éxitos*, Valencia: Institución Alfonso el Magnánimo.

Fernández Castellano, A. (1976), *Revisión del cine español de los años cuarenta*, Segovia: Encuentros de cine en Segovia.

Fernández-Santos, A. (2001), 'Pilar López de Ayala borda una hermosa idea de cordura de la reina Juana la Loca' *El País*, 26 September: 51.

Fernández-Santos, E. (2000), 'Vicente Aranda recrea los engaños y los celos que enloquecieron a Juana de Castilla', *El País*, 22 November.

Font, D. (1976), *Del azul al verde: El cine español durante el franquismo*, Barcelona: Ariel.

Gortari, C. (1976), *Revisión del cine español de los años cuarenta*, Segovia: Encuentros de cine en Segovia.

Graham, H. (1995), 'Gender and the State: Women in the 1940s', in H. Graham and J. Labanyi (eds), *Spanish Cultural Studies: An Introduction*, Oxford: Oxford University Press.

Guarner, J.L. and Besas, P. (1985), *El inquietante cine de Vicente Aranda*, Madrid: Imagfic 85.

Heredero, C.F. (2000), 'La lava y el Iceberg: Lenguaje y estilo en el cine de Vicente Aranda', in Joaquín Canovas (ed.), *Miradas sobre el cine de Vicente Aranda*, Murcia: Universidad de Murcia.

Labanyi, J. (2000), 'Feminizing the Nation: Women, Subordination and Subversion in Post-Civil War Spanish Cinema', in Ulrike Sieglohr (ed.), *Heroines without Heroes*, London: Cassell.

Marín, K. (2001), 'Está bien ser reina por dos semanas' (*El País* 7 October).

Morcillo, A.G. (2000), *True Catholic Womanhood: Gender Ideology in Franco's Spain*, De Kalb: Northern Illinois University Press.

Payne, S.G. (1997), *El primer Franquismo, 1939–1959: los años de la autarquía* (Madrid: Historia 16).

Puerto, C. (1976), *Revisión del cine español de los años cuarenta*, Segovia: Encuentros de cine en Segovia.

Reviriego, C. (2001), 'Protagonistas', *El País Cultural*, 19 September.

Sánchez, S. (2001), 'La pasión de Aranda', *El País Cultural*, 19 September.

Santos Fontela, C. (1976), *Revisión del cine español de los años cuarenta*, Segovia: Encuentros de cine en Segovia.

Turner, B.S. (1996), *The Body & Society*, London: Sage.

Vera, P. (1989), *Vicente Aranda*, Madrid: 1989.

–6–

New Sexual Politics in the Cinema of the Transition to Democracy: de la Iglesia's *El diputado* (1978)

Alejandro Melero Salvador

The years between Franco's death and the consolidation of democracy in Spain were remarkably fruitful for a film industry that had long been weak, to the extent that Spanish cinema launched vigorously into a new era of exploration of novel forms of representation. It was a time of exceptional freedom for all those who had not had the chance to express their beliefs and politics during forty years of authoritarian rule. The unsteady socio-political atmosphere in Spain at the time, together with the burst of cultural experimentation that took place in the decade running from 1975 to 1985, are witnessed in the films of these years, making them a unique testimony to the Spanish transition to democracy.

This chapter aims to explore the representation of new sexual politics in a number of films of this period, paying special attention to popular films ignored at the time (and today) by traditional criticism which are, nevertheless, important testimonies of those years. After examining the situation of homosexuality in Spanish society and film history, I will focus on Eloy de la Iglesia's *El diputado* (1978) as representative of a new cinema interested in portraying those that had rarely found a place in Spanish film-making (Republicans, communists, homosexuals). I shall argue that de la Iglesia took advantage of a film industry and audience deeply interested in the representation of explicit sex and eroticism in order to develop a wider exploration of sexuality. My analysis will refer to both Michel Foucault's and Leo Barnessi's theories on the representation of gay sex.

Homosexuality and Francoism

The study of the situation of homosexuals under Francoism is a difficult task because, added to the difficulty of studying the repression of the silenced victims of fascism is the silence caused by an issue which can still be considered a taboo. Queer theorists and critics such as Paul Julian Smith 'note and regret that there are no historical studies for Spanish-speaking nations comparable to those which exist for Britain and the United States' (Smith and Bergmann 1995: 1), a situation that becomes especially evident when we approach the field of film studies. When, in the late 1990s, Spanish television made a documentary about homosexuality under Francoism, they found it was very difficult to gain access to official information as well as to victims' testimony.[1] They did, however, find some people who had suffered torture and abuse prepared to talk, as well as documented information on the concentration camp where they were imprisoned.

Homosexuality remained illegal until 1979 (four years after the death of the dictator), and even after democratic government was installed individuals could still be prosecuted and imprisoned as they had been before. In the official encyclopaedia dealing with social, economic and political issues in Franco's Spain during the 1970s, homosexuality is included as a 'crime' together with 'adultery' or 'drug-taking'. In this official document Spaniards are told how 'Spanish society must face the challenge of deviant behaviour that is presumably going to increase considerably' (Fraga Iribarne and Fuentes, 1972–74: 961).

Despite small liberal concessions introduced during the Second Republic in the 1930s, including the legalization of divorce, the onset and the duration of the dictatorship ensured that the values promoted by Catholicism were strictly preserved, given the active role of the Catholic Church in the regime. Decades later, post-Stonewall gay liberation movements left no mark on this backward and isolated nation. Smith comments on how, while by the 1960s, 'gay-liberation began to flourish in Britain and the United States, "homosexual centers" were established in Madrid: penal camps in which deviants were subjected to solitary confinement and minute medical examination' (Smith and Bergmann 1995: 10).

We should not think that homophobic political attitudes died with Franco, as this chapter's analysis of *El diputado* will show. The homophobic discourse of Francoism was maintained during the transition to democracy and, even after the transition years, when democracy was consolidated, the official attitude toward sexual minorities remained unchanged. Issues such as divorce or abortion were already publicly discussed and sometimes tolerated but sexual difference continued to be a taboo subject.

Despite this, it is generally admitted that during the years of the transition a 'homosexual identity' was created. In 1977 a number of gay and lesbian associations flourished all over Spain, such as 'Dignity' in Barcelona or 'COGAM' in Madrid (Perriam, 393–5). It was a time of political vindication: the communist party was visible and would become legal the following year; feminism had a voice and claimed equality for women, for whom the law still required their husbands' permission to open a bank account. Divorce, still illegal, was a highly discussed issue together with that of abortion. Magazines of the time brazenly discussed scandalous issues like pre-marital sex or virginity. And homosexuals were not going to miss the opportunity of making themselves heard for the first time in history.

It was obviously not easy for gays to defend their ideas in Spain's fledgling democracy. The magazine *Guardiana* published a survey in 1975 in which 80 per cent of the participants were against the decriminalization of homosexuality. The vast majority of Spanish society seemed opposed to homosexual liberation, as did the country's politicians; thus, gay associations such as the Gay Liberation Front of Catalonia would have to wait another five years to be legalized.

Homosexuality and Spanish Cinema

The history of Spanish gay films remains largely undocumented and cannot be understood in isolation from this peculiar historical context. However, any historian who intends writing a Vito Russo-like analysis (trying, like an archaeologist, to find hints of homosexuality in 'officially' straight films) would probably find that there are not many differences in the representation of sexual minorities between Spanish cinema and that of Hollywood. Thus, the stereotypical representation of lesbians as threatening and predatory vampires that Russo finds in films such as Roger Vadim's *Blood of Roses* (1960) or Joseph Larraz's *Vampyres* (1974) also crops up in Spanish horror films such as Jesús Franco's *The Vampires* (1970) or *Female Vampires* (1973). These films follow Russo's maxim that 'the essence of homosexuality as a predatory weakness permeates the depiction of gay characters in horror films' (Russo, 1981: 49). Other horror films presenting scary lesbians are Vicente Aranda's *Las crueles* (1969) and *La novia ensangrentada* (1972), which Martín-Márquez sees as examples of how 'lesbianism perhaps first surfaced onscreen during the late Franco years, tellingly, in horror movies' (1999: 247). Russo's history of the representation of homosexuality on-screen ends with an obituary to some of the gay characters whose sexuality led them to death as a punishment for their perversion. Some Spanish films could also belong to this list, such as *Diferente* (José María Delgado, 1962) or *Silvia ama a Raquel* (Diego Santillán, 1979).

There are, however, a number of meaningful differences between Spanish and American representations of homosexuality in films. First of all, it cannot be forgotten that the longer and stronger Spanish censorship system ensured that all sequences with lesbianism and male homosexuality were strictly forbidden, to the ridiculous extent of banning such films as *Death in Venice* (Luchino Visconti, 1971) and *Some Like it Hot* (Billy Wilder, 1959). About this latter film, José María García Escudero, the then General Director of Cinematography, declared that it had to be 'prohibited ... if only to continue our clamp-down on poofs' (Hopewell 1986: 66).

This situation would slowly change in the early 1970s, when a swell of gay issues emerged in several mainstream films. During the first years of this decade some of the most popular comedies included, if not homosexual characters, quite often comic situations based on the confusions created by cross-dressing in an atmosphere of sexual ambiguity. Therefore, in comedies such as *La tía de Carlos en minifalda* (Augusto Fenollar 1967) or Fernando Fernán-Gómez's *Crimen imperfecto* (1970), the climax is reached when well-known stars are obliged to impersonate female characters. In *Fraude matrimonial* (Ignacio Iquino 1976) a bourgeois gay leaves his fiancée on their wedding day and runs away with his gay and very camp friends, a fact presented as an attack on the supreme Francoist institution, the (traditional) family. In *Mi hijo no es lo que parece* (Angelino Fons 1973) homosexuality is presented as an illness that can be cured by a 'proper woman'. The movie tells the story of a mother who is dramatically worried because she suspects that her son is homosexual and is having a sexual relationship with his best friend. She, thus, sets about doing her best to cure her son's illness and aims to find the proper woman to marry him. The seemingly unending list of comedies dealing with these questions include notorious titles like Mariano Ozores's *Ellas los prefieren ... locas* (1976), in which actor José Sacristán plays a man pretending to be gay in order to secure his wife's forgiveness for his infidelities, *El y él* (Eduardo Manzanos 1980), *Gay Club* (Ramón Fernández 1980), and *Haz la loca ... no la guerra* (José Truchado 1978).

The 'highpoint' of this tendency was the extremely popular comedy *No desearás al vecino del quinto* (Fernández 1970), a comedy that proved to be an extraordinary commercial success, 'in no small measure due to its patently sexual comic style' (D'Lugo 1997: 18). The popularity of this film is still recalled by older generations and it was to hold the record as the country's biggest box-office hit for the following three decades. It tells the story of a gynaecologist, Pedro, and his neighbour Anton, a dressmaker, who live in Toledo. Pedro's clinic is not very successful because, despite his talent as a gynaecologist, men do not trust their women to visit such a good-looking doctor. On the other hand, Anton is very successful because he pretends to be a homosexual and women are not afraid to be naked in front of him ('in front of you, we don't mind. You are not a real man', they say). Anton is actually a highly promiscuous straight man who has a clandestine flat in Madrid, where he often goes for the kind of sexual encounter he cannot have in Toledo, where everyone thinks he is a sissy dressmaker. Anton's active sexual life is compared to Pedro's, who still lives with his mother Rosario and has been engaged to the beautiful and virginal Jacinta for twelve years. When Pedro discovers Anton's strategy, he does not hesitate to join him in his lascivious life in Madrid. However, Jacinta, worried that her fiancée spends too much time away from her, decides to go to Madrid and investigate Pedro's new life. Rosario and Jacinta are shocked to discover Pedro's apparent homosexuality ('my poor son, he was so innocent,' says his mother). The rumour spreads all over Toledo and Pedro's clinic becomes very popular. Jacinta does not care about her fiancé's revived profession and devotes her time to fretting about Pedro's 'sinful' life. She decides, as a consequence, to seduce him back in order to prove that 'he is a man'. Eventually, Pedro gets married and Anton goes back to his wife and five children, whom we had not heard of before. Anton's wife becomes his secretary and Jacinta becomes a nurse at Pedro's clinic, so that they can always watch over their hypersexual husbands.

This improbable plot that ignores the fact that Anton could have been arrested for his presumed tendency did not prevent the enormous success of *No desearás al vecino del quinto*. Such popularity was crucial to the proliferation of these 'camp comedies' and would determine the stereotypical image of the homosexual in Spanish popular cinema in years to come. This tendency would last more than a decade and even in the 1980s we find films such as *Capullito de Alhelí* (Ozores, 1983), about two homosexuals who meet on the day the democracy suffered a coup d'état in 1981, fearing that all the social improvements they had experienced were at risk.

Interestingly enough, while popular comedies could and did make use of homosexuality as a dramatic convention, a more serious analysis or representation of it was strictly banned in other genres. The representation of sexual minorities seemed to be only suitable for comedies in which the sexual perversion could be cured (*Mi hijo no es lo que parece*) or the result of a lie (*No desearás al vecino del quinto, Ellas los prefieren ... locas*). De la Iglesia remembers how 'although the criteria for censorship was not clear at all [in 1977], it was clear that homosexuality could not be dealt with, just like any other "sexual aberration", but you could use ridiculous effeminate characters' (Corporate Author, 1996: 131). Only after Franco's death did homosexuality become an issue in genres beyond comedy. As Stephen Tropiano has demonstrated, this 'unprecedented popularity of gay-themed films by a mass audience during Spain's democratic transitional period (1975–78)' was due in part to the ability of many film-makers to make of this polemic issue a mainstream interest. Tropiano remarks that 'de la Iglesia's ability to link homosexuality as a marginalized form of sexuality to current socio-political issues' helped to popularize 'a subject matter that had been virtually absent from Spanish cinema until the early 1970s' (in Kinder 1997: 158).

A complete analysis of homosexuality on-screen in the 1970s would also require an examination of the avant-garde and underground films made at that time, including Almodóvar's early short films such as *Sexo va, sexo viene* (1977), about transsexualism. In Barcelona, a group of film-makers known as 'Cinco Cucas' were specialized in gay films, quite often with a clearly provocative, as well as didactic, intention. With their films, 'Cinco Cucas' sought 'to say that there are homosexuals everywhere, in all professions and social classes' and that 'the world of the homosexual is despised because not enough is known about it' (Contel 1979: 56).

Sex and Spanish Cinema

The 'boom of the homosexual', as Marsha Kinder (1997: 436) puts it, can only be explained with reference to the special circumstances of Spanish cinema of the time and the outburst of movies characterized by the *destape* ('uncovering') phenomenon. Officially initiated by Jorge Grau's *La trastienda* (1976), which was the first film to show full female nudity on-screen, *destape* was based on the proliferation of explicit images of sex, normally with no narrative intention and no justification in the plot. It created its own star-system and recruited its own directors, some of whom had made their names in early post-war cinema, such as Ignacio Iquino, who went from titles like *Alma de Dios* (1941) to others like *Aborto criminal* (1973) or *Chicas de alquiler* (1974). Study of the *destape* tendency reveals many aspects of Spanish society of the time.

Under Franco, Spanish spectators had already pressed for an end to rigid film censorship, particularly with regard to sex. This can be seen in a curiously pre-*destape* phenomenon, which saw large numbers of Spaniards make short trips across the border to France to see forbidden films. Augusto M. Torres has explained this peculiar fashion as follows:

> In the early 1970s censorship disappears from most European countries, with successes like ... *Last Tango in Paris* (1972) or *La Grande Abbufata* (1973). However, in Spain, censorship not only does not disappear but also becomes even harder... These productions, and many others, become very popular in Spain as notorious erotic films, and also because of their prohibitions. Many Spaniards were tempted to go to Southern France where such films were exhibited with subtitles in Spanish. Travel agencies organised short trips during weekends and bank holidays, first of all in French cities and later in Portugal as well, after the Carnation Revolution. The so-called 'cinematography weekends' were advertised in film magazines and the main newspapers. They allowed people to get access to up to three or four forbidden (in Spain but not in France or Portugal) films a day at affordable prices (1997: 283).

Today's public would doubtless find it amusing that 110,000 people had seen *Last Tango in Paris* in Perpignan, a city with a population of only 100,000. But it should not be forgotten that these curious anecdotes were representative of the situation that Spanish spectators found themselves in and of their anxiety to see new forms of representation of sexual issues in cinema.

Once Franco was dead and censorship became more relaxed, this anxiety was transformed into figures, and pseudo- or semi-erotic films boomed in Spain. In the last week of April 1978, the top ten box-office movies in Spain included three *Emmanuelles* (*Emmanuelle* [1], *Emmanuelle 2* [5], *Black Emmanuelle* [8]), *Last Tango in Paris* (4), and *Story of O* (6). Pseudo-pornography was fashionable and became one more sign of the direction Spanish democracy was taking. In Hopewell's words, 'as Spain's politicisation peaked, there was even an attempt to pass off a burgeoning pornography trade as a mark of democratic tolerance' (1986: 161).

Analyses of the *destape* phenomenon have been widely debated and theorists have applied various social, economic and political readings to it. Robert Graham sees it as 'a natural reaction to years of accumulated repression' (1984: 274). Hopewell, however, attributes it to 'economic

Alejandro Melero Salvador

interests' (1986: 79) while critics such as Barry Jordan and Rikki Morgan-Tamosunas find other political implications in this phenomenon, considering *destape* a 'diversionary strategy to deflect attention away from growing political tensions' (1998: 113). This explanation of *destape* is shared by many other theorists. After new norms of censorship were put into practice in February 1975 – which in turn permitted the presence of sex on screen – Carlos Saura, the most internationally respected Spanish film-maker of his generation, complained that there was little difference to the previous censorship regulations, with one exception. The one novelty – Item 9 – allowed for the exhibition of the nude body but only on the condition that it did not arouse the passions of the normal spectator. The *apertura* had been sidetracked into a *destape* – 'opening' became an 'uncovering'. Or, as *Posible* deftly put it: 'sex yes, politics no' (Hopewell: 1986: 96). This 'sex yes, politics no' positioning, however, would be seen as unworkable and film-makers like de la Iglesia would use sex in order to explore politics and study the repression and sexual politics of minorities under Franco. No matter what explanation theorists find for the upsurge of explicit images of sex, the fact is it would determine a large part of the film production of the time and for years to come.

Within a very short time, sex alone would prove insufficient and more morbid and extreme representations were produced. From 1976, just a few months after Franco had died, a vast number of films would deal with issues such as incestuous relationships (Borau's *Furtivos*, 1975), the sexual life of priests (De la Iglesia's *El sacerdote*, 1977) and nuns (Grau's *Cartas de amor a una monja*, 1978), paedophilia (Giménez-Rico's *Retrato de familia* [1976], *El sacerdote*) or bestiality (De la Iglesia's *La criatura* in 1977 and Bigas Luna's *Caniche*, 1979). Such representations tended to be very explicit and it certainly blurred the limits between eroticism and pornography. The Madrid daily newspaper *Diario 16* was ironic about the fact – only a few months after Franco's death – when it remarked that a number of Spanish films could not be shown abroad 'due to their explicit sex' (Corporate Author 1996: 60). As de la Iglesia himself comments, this was due to a temporary 'legal gap' (Corporate Author 1996: 140) in the already weak and very much despised code of censorship. De la Iglesia seems proud to state that 'a film like *El diputado* would not be possible today' (Corporate Author 1996: 140). It is only within this context that the existence of *El diputado* can be understood. Casimiro Torreiro shares de la Iglesia's nostalgia for this period of exceptional freedom. According to him, 'the unstable but irreversible process of democratic normalisation that Spain experienced since 1977, together with Spanish society's interest in forgetting Francoism, produced a considerable creative liberation that, in the case of film-making, caused many different approaches and proposals, and possibly the moment of bigger thematic and formal wideness in the whole history of Spanish films' (in Gubern 1995: 381–2).

El diputado

El diputado tells the story of Roberto Orbea, a member of the Communist Party whose political career is determined by his homosexuality. Roberto is married to Carmen, who is perfectly aware of her husband's sexual inclination. When Roberto is imprisoned in the latter days of Francoism he meets Ness, a male prostitute who convinces Roberto to return to the homosexuality he thought forgotten. Through Ness, Roberto meets Juanito, a very young boy with whom Roberto starts a relationship. Juanito and Roberto regularly meet in Roberto's clandestine flat that used to be a refuge for communists under Francoism, and Roberto very soon falls in love with Juanito. In the meantime, the Communist Party is legalized and Roberto is elected as a member of parliament in the first democratic elections. But the still powerful fascists will not miss the chance to use Roberto's sexuality as a weapon against his promising career. An influential group of right-wingers led by Carrés tempts Juanito with money in order to get scandalous pictures of Roberto and his young lover. Juanito accepts Carrés's offer but, eventually, falls in love with Roberto and, what is more, rediscovers his own homosexuality. As Juanito becomes more and more involved in politics Carmen feels she is losing Roberto and virtually adopts Juanito as a member of their family. There are rumours that Roberto is going to be elected secretary of the party but the fascists have other plans for him. Ness, paid by the fascists ('it was easy for you to buy me, and also for them') tells Roberto to go to his clandestine flat where he finds Juanito's dead body. The following day, while tears run down his face, Roberto prepares to explain everything to his comrades when the police arrest him.

The whole film is laden with references to people and events of the time. There is mention of well-known leftist musicians and film-makers and allusions to crucial episodes of the transition, such as the trial of ETA terrorists (in which Roberto figures as a lawyer) or to the killing of five leftist lawyers in Madrid in 1977. There is even a fake documentary in which we see Roberto, as a member of parliament, in the congress with the most relevant politicians of the time. The fascist characters of the film may have been very familiar to those who saw the film when it first came out. One character plays an Argentine journalist who is intriguingly similar to the notorious Jorge Cesarzky.[2] The allusions to real facts create a sense of veracity and immediacy that, at the same time, contribute to outdate the film. For this reason today's spectators, even in Spain, may have difficulties in following all the events and names mentioned in the film. De la Iglesia himself admits that his 'films are not applicable for today. They were made at a time when many things were happening, very hurried moments' (Corporate Author 1996: 134); he also considers that 'praise [of the homosexual] seems excessive today' (Corporate Author 1996: 113). It must, however, also be admitted that his films 'represent a crucially important contribution to the de-demonization of homosexuality' (Jordan and Morgan-Tamosunas, 1998: 148) and that, 'if such vindication of homosexuality is dated today, it is so precisely because films like *El diputado*' were made (de la Iglesia in Corporate Author 1996: 133).

It would be a mistake to ignore the fact that films like *El diputado* were seen by large audiences, and normally shown in neighbourhood cinemas. As D'Lugo puts it, his 'films were clearly an effort to address a popular audience in a direct and unpretentious style on a series of topical social themes that had been proscribed by the now-defunct censorship system' (1997: 168). And de la Iglesia did succeed in reaching a mass public. His movies transpired to be the most successful of their day and their popularity would endure, as is attested to by the fact that, ten years after it was made, fifteen million viewers saw *El diputado* when it was aired on Spanish national television (De Stefano, 1986: 65).

In order to get the larger possible audience, de la Iglesia has never shrunk from resorting to formula. Sex and *destape*, mixed with other forms of scandal, are not rare in his films. Whether they like it or not, most critics agree that de la Iglesia believed 'that the presentation of sexual perversion was one way to drag Spanish audiences out of their chronic stupor' (Hopewell 1986: 112). De la Iglesia might be included in the list of those film-makers who, aware of the 'sex yes, politics no' policy, used sex to explore politics. This could be done because there was 'a unique moment during the transition to democracy when the topic of homosexuality and the mass audience coincided in Spanish cinema' (Smith 1992: 129).

Nevertheless, even though he was one of the most commercially successful Spanish directors of the time, his work seems to have been forgotten today. Precisely because of this commercialism, films such as *El diputado* were ignored by critics when they were made. Smith has noticed how 'to read the accumulated press files in the Filmoteca is to be exposed to an extraordinary catalogue of abuse, some of which is clearly homophobic' (1992: 130). Thirty years after they were made, de la Iglesia's films offer new readings and serve as useful testimonies of their time.

The explicit representation of gay sex provided by films like *El diputado* challenges both Leo Barnessi's classic essay 'Is the rectum a grave?', which explained social homophobia on the grounds of anxieties surrounding sex between men and Foucault's opposite view on the subject. According to the latter,

> imagining a sexual act that does not conform to the law or to nature, that's not what upsets people. But that individuals might begin to love each other, that's the problem. That goes against the grain of social institutions: they are already crisscrossed by emotional intensities which both hold them in place and fill them with turmoil – look at the army, where love between men is endlessly solicited and stigmatized. The institutional regulations cannot approve such [emotional] relations [between men], with their multiple intensities, variable colorations, imperceptible movements, and changing forms – relations that produce a short circuit and introduce love where there ought to be law, regularity, and custom. (Halperin, 1995: 98)

According to Foucault, it is homosexual love and not sex that threatens to destabilize society. In the context of Spanish society, love is traditionally linked to family and religion, and opposed to lust. When this (homosexual) lust turns into love, this new loving relationship between men can destabilize the traditional domination of heterosexual models. This is the threat de la Iglesia's film presents: in *El diputado*, individuals (two men) begin to love each other while they practice sex that spectators can explicitly spy on. By introducing both gay sex and gay love, de la Iglesia challenges thus one of the most vivid polemics for queer theorists.

El diputado is not de la Iglesia's first film to introduce homosexual characters. He had done so several times previously in his earlier films, *La semana del asesino* (1971), *Juego de amor prohibido* (1975) and, especially, *Los placeres ocultos* (1975). These films, made under the strictest censorship, presented quite explicit images of sex and positive representations of gay characters, like the supportive neighbour in *La semana del asesino* or the gay activist in *Los placeres ocultos*. However, all those films were made under Francoism, albeit at the very end of it, and freedom of speech was severely restricted. *El diputado* presents a novelty in that it was made in democracy at a time of hitherto unknown creative freedom. De la Iglesia makes the most of this freedom to criticize the former regime while also criticizing his own immediate present. *El diputado* is not only critical of Francoism and its legacy, it also 'attacks the hypocrisy of a Spanish democracy which parades its liberties but rejects homosexuals' (Hopewell 1986: 222). De la Iglesia, a militant in the Communist Party himself, is critical of the Right, but also of his comrades as he exposes leftist prejudice toward homosexuality. Thus, 'a contrast is drawn between the continuing clandestinity of homosexuality and the new political freedoms in the immediate post dictatorship period' (Jordan and Morgan-Tamosunas, 1998: 149). In *El diputado* we find the disenchantment of homosexuals who, despite the shift to democracy, have experienced very few improvements in their situation. This criticism toward the disappointment of democracy is a constant in de la Iglesia's films, which tend to 'make clear that democracy is no better than the former regime because power remains in the same hands' (Hopewell 1986: 234).

Roberto has spent all his life fighting the regime and living clandestinely as a communist. Once Franco dies and democracy is established, Roberto sees that there is no great difference in his life and that, as a homosexual, clandestinity is still necessary. When he goes to the secret apartment where the communists used to hide and meet, Roberto realizes how underground his life remains: 'I still need this place for certain aspects of my life; I still need the secrecy', he says.

As a militant and 'the first prominent Spanish intellectual to publicly declare his homosexuality' (De Stefano 1986: 58–9), it is not surprising that de la Iglesia's treatment of homosexuality is 'consistent with the political agenda of the Spanish homosexual rights movements to demonstrate how homosexual desire continues to be constructed and controlled by patriarchal capitalism and the legacy of Spanish fascism' (Tropiano in Kinder 1997: 164). Many things had improved in the new Spain but for sexual minorities the oppression had not diminished or, as Smith says, 'in the new democratic Spain, styles may change, but patriarchal structures (fatherhood, police, army) remain the same' (1992: 160). This disappointing fact has been studied by Dieter Ingenschay, who applied Foucault's theories on homophobia in the Spanish context:

> In his first volume of the *History of Sexuality* Michel Foucault analyses power, its social repartition and its effects over the despotise of sexuality. According to Foucault, power does not strictly mean official regulation but the sum of forces that rule the techniques and strategies of the forms of sexual desire (chapter 4, 2). Homophobia remained a part of the social forces after

the end of the Third Reich and after Franco's regime. In the Spanish context this means that the official Catholicism and chauvinism kept control over the dispositive of sexuality and that therefore homophobia could not disappear with the death of the dictator. (in Resina 2000: 171–2)

El diputado is the narration of this theory by means of documentary techniques. Spectators are shown black and white pictures of the lifestyles of homosexuals during Francoism: clandestinity and marginalization, photographs of shabby places that homosexuals used to frequent and prisons. As the film develops, we see that the same marginalization remains to the extent that it ruins Roberto's and Juanito's lives. De la Iglesia tells his spectators that as far as power is controlled by a 'phallocratic' (Halperin 1995: 89) – to use Foucault's term – society (whether under Franco or under democracy), there is no hope for people like Roberto:

You know, I wanted to go down in history and instead I will have to suffer it. I have not been very lucky, have I? ... I know very well what you mean, Carmen, it's very easy: in a few years, those who still remember me, will say: 'yes, sure, Roberto Orbea, that faggot who wanted to be a politician, a funny guy, an irresponsible'. You will leave, fed up with all this game and sacrificing the best years of your life for nothing, or almost nothing, just to get some affection and the gratefulness of a person who is a failure. Juanito, logically, will leave as well. He will find someone younger or a woman to live a lie with and be happy. And 'normal', above all normal, this is all what it is about. As far as myself, maybe I will end up being one of those sissy old men that frequent public toilets, write obscene graffiti on the doors of the loos and sit in the last rows of double-bill cinemas, spend their afternoons playing pools or at the gates of schools... But, of course, I can also go back to the theoretical stuff, to the precise analysis of a precise reality, and, maybe, who knows, I get convinced that the best way to make history is like this, suffering it. Let others take control of the power, those who do not mind lying and hiding as far as they get power. But not me, I am tired of lies and hiding.

Critics like José Enrique Monterde have noticed 'the didactic intention of the film when it deals with the problem [of homosexuality]' (1978: 62–3) and de la Iglesia himself admits that *El diputado* 'treats homosexuality didactically' (cited in De Stefano 1986: 58). Indeed he had already done this in his earlier films, which tend to lecture the Spanish spectator on the possibilities of different sexualities. Thus, in *Los placeres ocultos*, the main characters discuss homosexuality in the following terms:

Miguel: isn't it natural?
Eduardo: nature is as nature does
Miguel: but, if there was a shot that would cure you, wouldn't you take it, even if it cost a million dollars?
Eduardo: not even if it were free.

De la Iglesia poses the questions that Spanish people of the period never had the chance to ask about diverse sexualities and also provides the answers he considers people should learn. This is a strategy used also in *El diputado*, as some critics have noticed. Téllez draws attention to a particular technique:

> from time to time, one of the characters pretends to address another and, looking into the camera, expresses one of the salient points about the transition. In this coarse, Brechtian way, political analysis is made to predominate over the plot which is merely a vehicle for it. The audience is directly addressed, invoked as a countershot to the close-up. (cited in Smith 1992: 151)

Such didacticism should not be understood as pamphleteering or as cheap propaganda for gay liberation. De la Iglesia is able to insert his political messages within the plot of the film, without making his political reflections intrusive. This extract from Roberto's speech at the trial is a good example of this:

> Your Honour, to try to hide the social, political and moral reasons that determine a man's behaviour is against any kind of justice. It is, therefore, a compulsory duty to listen to the accused.

This speech refers to the terrorists that Roberto is defending, but it also refers to his own homosexuality, which will be judged later in the film. The same technique applies to the following sentence: 'legal or illegal ... we have always been present in the life of this country'.

Although this line refers to how communists have been part of Spain even during Francoism, it undoubtedly also applies to homosexuals. *El diputado* teaches Spaniards that homosexuals do exist, and they exist at all levels of society. Alexander Walker remarks how 'it states graphically but with persuasive plausibility the presence of a large homosexual sub-life in a long repressed section of Spanish urban life' (Walker, 1979).

Later, de la Iglesia would extend the topic of homosexuality to make connections in other films with nationalism and sexual repression. The 1970s, however, are notable for being a period when Spanish film-making was able to open up to different explorations of sexualities. These films were the first in a long line of Spanish movies representing sexual minorities onscreen. In many cases, they enabled cinema-goers to see positive representations of homosexuals for the first time in their lives and provided a different image to that of the popular stereotype depicted in *No desearás al vecino del quinto*. These films, thereby, deserve to be remembered by today's scholars and recognized as testimonies of a time not so far away from our own.

Notes

1. For further details on this point see Ingenschay (in Resina: 2000: 158).
2. For more details see Torreiro (Corporate Author 1996: 38).

References

Barnessi, Leo (1986), 'Is the Rectum a grave?', in Douglas Crip (ed.), *AIDS: Cultural Analysis, Cultural Activism*, Cambridge MA: MIT Press.

Contel, Raul (1979), 'Cine de Homosexuales', *Cinema 2002*, 56, October.

Corporate Author (1983), *Historia de la Transición: 10 años que cambiaron España, 1973–83*, Diario 16.

Corporate Author (1996), *Conocer a Eloy de la Iglesia*, San Sebastián: Filmoteca Vasca.

Corporate Author (1996), *Historia de la democracia: La aventura de la libertad*, El mundo.

De Stefano, George (1986), *Film Comment*, May–June.

D'Lugo, Marvin (1997), *Guide to the Cinema of Spain*, Westport CT and London: Greenwood.

Fernandez, Ramón (2003), interviewed in the DVD edition of 'No desearás al vecino del quinto', *El País*.

Fraga Iribarne, Manuel and Velarde Fuentes, Juan (eds) (1972–74), *La España de los años 70,* Madrid: Moneda y Crédito.

García Escudero, José María (1978) *La primera apertura: Diario de un director general*, Barcelona: Planta.

Alejandro Melero Salvador

Graham, Helen and Labanyi, Jo (eds.) (1995), *Spanish Cultural Studies: An Introduction: The Struggle for Modernity*, Oxford: Oxford University Press.

Graham, Robert (1984), *Spain: Change of a Nation*, London: Joseph.

Gubern, Román (ed.) (1995), *Historia del cine español*, Madrid: Cátedra, D.L.

Halperin, David M. (1995), *Saint Foucault: Towards a Gay Hagiography*, New York and Oxford: Oxford University Press.

Hopewell, John (1986), *Out of the Past: Spanish Cinema after Franco*, London: British Film Institute.

——(1989), *El cine español después de Franco 1973–1988*, Madrid: Arquero.

Jordan, Barry and Morgan-Tamosunas, Rikki (eds) (1998), *Contemporary Spanish Cinema*, Manchester: Manchester University Press.

Kinder, Marsha (ed.) (1997), *Refiguring Spain,* Durham NC and London: Duke University Press.

Martín-Márquez, Susan (1999), *Feminist Discourse and Spanish Cinema*, Oxford: Oxford University Press.

Monterde, José Enrique (1978), 'Crítica a el Diputado', *Dirigido Por*, 59.

Perriam, Chris (2001), 'Not writing straight, but not writing queer: popular Castilian "gay" fiction', in Jo Labanyi (ed.), *Constructing Identity in Twentieth-century Spain: Theoretical Debates and Cultural Practice*, Oxford: Oxford University Press.

Resina, Joan Ramón (ed.) (2000), *Disremembering the Dictatorship: The Politics of Memory in the Spanish Transition to Democracy*, Amsterdam and Atlanta GA: Rodopi.

Russo, Vito (1981 [1987]), *The Celluloid Closet*, New York: Harper and Row.

Smith, Paul Julian (1992), *Laws of Desire: Questions of Homosexuality in Spanish Writing and Film, 1960–1990*, Oxford: Clarendon.

Smith, Paul Julian and Bergmann, Emilie L. (eds) (1995), *Entiendes? Queer Readings, Hispanic Writing*, Durham NC: Duke University Press.

Téllez, J. (1979), 'El Diputado', *Contracampo*, April.

Torres, Augusto M. (1997), *El cine español en 119 películas*, Madrid: Alianza Editorial.

Walker, Alexander (1979), 'When the sex mixes with politics', *Evening Standard*, 6 December.

7

Borderline Men: Gender, Place and Power in Representations of Moroccans in Recent Spanish Cinema
Parvati Nair

Four Moroccan men share a dank flat in Barcelona's immigrant quarter, the *Raval*. The living room of the flat, furnished in Moroccan style, has low sofas and a few scattered, embroidered cushions in a make-shift effort to recreate a feeling of 'home'. The Moroccans share plates of *cous-cous*, and sing in Arabic to the accompaniment of traditional instruments, such as the *darbouka*. Nevertheless, the traces of immigrant displacement are all too obvious: the flat is depressingly dark, the walls are thin, the neighbours hostile. The men are engaged in diverse kinds of work, all on the margins of Barcelona's ample, bourgeois society; yet, through their very social invisibility, the lives of the immigrants are inextricably woven into the fabric of the latter. One of them, the wealthiest and apparently most 'successful', is a pimp and drug dealer, another works in a restaurant, while yet another trudges the streets as a hawker of Moroccan carpets. For each and every one of them, the reality of their existences does not match the expectations that led, in the first place, to their presence in Barcelona. 'Nothing is as I imagined it,' says the protagonist of Llorenç Soler's film, *Saíd*, in a sweep of immense despair; neither his flat-mates, nor the city, nor, indeed, his own existence as a fugitive from the law had featured in the northward dream he had had of life in Europe, beyond the Straits of Gibraltar.

Some twenty years on since the start of substantial immigration flows into and through Spain, the sights and sounds of cultural difference have now become largely commonplace, though not necessarily acceptable, to visitors and residents of Barcelona and other urban centres in Spain. Increasingly, cultural productions, in particular the media, focus on the problematic posed by ethnic minority groups, as do local and regional authorities, who have established multicultural practices in education and other areas of public life. Since the start of the 1990s, a substantial number of film-makers have also turned their lens onto the all too thorny question of immigration and cultural identity in contemporary Spain. Prominent among them are Montxo Armendáriz (*Las cartas de Alou*, 1990), Imanol Uribe (*Bwana*, 1996), Llorenç Soler (*Saíd*, 1999) and, more recently, Chus Gutiérrez (*Poniente*, 2002), to name but a few. Many of these films have focused principally on the social and cultural experiences of ethnically diverse, immigrant men, although, in fact, sizeable immigrant communities comprising men, women and children, particularly among Moroccans, have for some time been a feature of Spain's demographic patterns. A notable exception is, of course Icíar Bollaín, whose film *Flores de otro mundo* (1999), co-scripted with the writer Julio Llamazares, explores the experience of Latin American women in Spain as they encounter autochthonous men. The predominant gender focus of most film-makers, however, almost certainly reflects social realities: the majority of first-generation immigrants to Spain continue to be male, although in recent years, the numbers of women arriving transnationally have risen significantly. Indeed, perhaps one of the most sensitive of the many issues relating to immigration in Spain is that of family reunion, as twists in the law benefit the state by allowing a constant working population of immigrants, who nevertheless are not granted permanent rights and hence are unable to bring their families over or indeed to reside in Spain with any sense of permanence. Coming as they often do from those parts of the Third World where patriarchy continues to dominate and where the male takes on the role of breadwinner, it is not surprising that the vast majority of such immigrants be male.

This chapter will focus on the intersections of place, gender and ethnicity in representations of immigrant Moroccan men in two recent films: Soler's aforementioned *Saíd* and José Luís Guerín's documentary, *En construcción* (2001). *Saíd* is, as Soler has repeatedly stated in the wake of the considerable acclaim with which the film was received, a documentary-style fiction, based on the novel *L'aventura de Saïd* by Josep Lorman (1995). Indeed, as the latest film in the director's career, it draws upon his considerable experience in documentary film-making. *Saíd*, the film, explores the attempts made by a young Moroccan who arrives in Spain illegally and sets about finding a footing in Barcelona. The film, in so doing, exposes issues of racial violence and the disjuncture of cultural and economic difference. *En construcción* is a documentary that offers viewers an open-ended narrative of fundamental and irrevocable change experienced by a working-class neighbourhood in terms of its urban and human landscape when plans for urban reconstruction are set in motion. Thus, through skilful editing of extensive hours of filming, the recording of a real demolition and rebuilding process in Barcelona's *Barrio Xino* is turned into a filmic construct that reveals identity in the context of globalization to be reflexive, fraught with risk, traversed by impermanence, and inconclusive. *En construcción* provides a kaleidoscopic view of a neighbourhood in its last moments; as such, this is not a film about immigrants per se, although the interaction between locals and immigrants plays an important part in this film's narrative. Nevertheless, and despite the many other equally interesting and thought-provoking characters that the film explores, for the purposes of this chapter I shall focus on the figure of the Moroccan, Abdel Aziz el Mountassir. Given the shifting landscape that surrounds all the characters in this film and the migrancy that is thus forced upon them, the immigrant, by dint of his ethnicity and his social marginality, doubly epitomizes the displacement experienced by those whose social location is at the edges of capitalist expansion. Furthermore, he is able, from this borderline position, to bring to his context a sense of reflexivity that unsettles the complacency of those who lack this perspective of alterity.

My aim is to problematize the question of representing the 'other' in these two films, by analysing the contextual means of place and ethnicity through which each of them offers a portrayal of the male immigrant. I shall argue that while these films, each in its own way, clearly open a space for immigrant representation – indeed positively give a 'platform' to an otherwise unvoiced aspect of contemporary Moroccan-Spanish cultural experience – the categories of gender, place and ethnicity are seen to be both mutually implicated and traversed by complex mechanisms of social domination and subordination. In recent years, theorists have looked for ways of forging links between notions of gender and conceptualizations of other aspects of identity, such as history, class and race. Despite increasingly fluid imaginations of gender, such as those put forward by queer theory, which locate gender in a nexus that is socially and historically constructed, there is still a reliance on ease of access to such dimensions. In other words, gender, a key form of private and public definition or empowerment – indeed, perhaps, an aspect of identity that bridges the private with the public – relies on historical and social location in order to be acknowledged. The question then arises as to what happens to gender in the context of migrancy? Can the gendering of the migrant be understood in the same terms as those applied to him or to her prior to the experience of migration? Does the scattering of history and cultural memory, the experience of dislocation and the subsequent disempowerment of the immigrant in the social sphere have an impact

Parvati Nair

on the performance of gender? How can gender be imagined when it is lived and played out on the shifting fault lines that separate First World from Third? *Saíd* and *En construcción* both deal with the question of social disempowerment for the immigrant. Gender, in this context, is subsumed in the larger panorama of social marginality and historical rupture. To analyse gender in such terms, then, is also to take into account the insecurities and the fluxes of the borderline where the figure of the immigrant is located. These films thus offer portraits of post-colonial subjectivity, which are nevertheless determined by where, how and by whom they are seen. Such post-colonial representations are weighted with the metaphorical and historical experience of displacement, relocation and mobility. While film theory, and in particular feminist film theory, deals with issues of difference, there has as yet been little attempt to merge post-colonial critique with gender critique in the context of film analysis. This analysis is located, therefore, in the overlap of these three theoretical frameworks, whereby a consideration of gender, place and power will serve to uncover the geopolitical implications of attempting to represent Moroccan men as 'others' who are also part of the here and now, in the heart of the Western metropolis.[1] My questioning of these cinematic representations of immigrant men, therefore, aims to explore the extent to which they both subvert and extend a historically Europeanized 'way of seeing' the non-European other. To what extent, then, does the portrayal of the Moroccan function as an act of troping, whereby his body becomes the signifier of alterity and hence the marker of the border that defines Spain? To what extent, also, does the Moroccan disturb preconceptions of such boundaries through his own borderline ambivalence?

It is useful here to turn to the concept of Third Cinema, which seeks out a theoretical and practical delineation of film-making that offers an alternative to the dominant models existing in the First World. Both gender theory and film theory emerged in the First World and both theoretical fields evolved in their early years largely around ahistorical, psychoanalytic categories, such as 'desire', 'the gaze' or 'the female spectator'. As such, they offer broad parameters that do not always encompass the specificities of location, in particular when these fall outside of the historical and political boundaries within which these concepts were developed (Shohat 2003). The socio-cultural and economic hegemony of the First World, where these concepts arose, thus does not always facilitate their translation or translocation to other historical, spatial and temporal mappings. Thus, important conjunctures and contradictions of history, class and culture are overlooked, as are the complexities of post-colonial engagements with mechanisms of power. Third Cinema, in this context, needs to be differentiated from Third Worldist Cinema, which forges a vision of the post-colonial nation often in accordance with the received models of Western or European nationalism. Instead, Third Cinema is an attempt to stage the post-colonial experience, not as new nation building, but as one of displacement, mobility and marginality. It is a cinema of the dissonant, the diasporic, the transitional. It explores those spaces of poverty on the underside of Western hegemony and it follows the ravages of globalization's unremorseful sweep. As such, it underlines a politics of gender, race and identity understood in terms of migrancy. Those fixed categories, which denote situated fields of knowledge, are thereby unsettled, deconstructed and deferred in the transitional context of migrancy.

Robert Stam, a leading theorist of Third Cinema, marks out three related aspects of the aesthetics of such films: hybridity, chronotopic multiplicity and the redeeming of detritus (Stam 2003). Hybridity, for Stam, is 'a conjunctural play of identification' (2003: 32), symptomatic of colonial and post-colonial experience. Hybridity confounds the binary opposition of self and other through an ambivalent and often indeterminate play of identity that takes place at the borders of difference. Questions of power thus become hard to isolate, as apparent acts of surrender can also denote strategies of resistance. Chronotopic multiplicity, according to Stam, is a palimpsestic temporality, a multiplicity of time and location, as seen in artistic texts that refer to plural and contradictory temporal moments. Stam goes on to describe the redemption of detritus as the transmogrification of waste into art, a further feature of the aesthetics of bricolage, whereby what is low or discarded is drawn into a social overturning, thus attempting to trigger consequent shifts in balances of power. It reveals a strategy of the dispossessed and forces a negotiation with the negated. It throws light onto histories of discontinuities and lends voice to the many forced silences that accompany strategies of domination.

Saíd and *En construcción* both reveal all three of these aspects, as we shall see. Hybrid experiences of cultural identity combine with the social marginality of the characters concerned in order to highlight the precarious counter-time of their status as strangers. In this experience of alienation, where identity is neither situated nor recognized, the immigrant subject lives the transforming experience of disempowerment. Gender, a key aspect of the way in which power is performed and lived, is at stake here, as all facets of identity are veiled by the fact of legal and economic marginality. Thus, while the immigrant engages in the hybrid act of reinventing the displaced self, he also simultaneously experiences the multiplicities of time and place that accompany the migratory experience, whereby the memory of a former located, gendered and defined self interferes with the fluid, mobile and unreliable present. In this fractured present, an imagination of the future becomes impossible. Disempowerment plays itself out at numerous levels, from the experience of social discrimination to the denial of stable spatial and temporal fields from within which identity can be performed. Thus, all aspects of social interrelation, gender included, become muted.

Both Soler and Guerín are notable for the social engagement of their creative work, reflected most strongly by their long experience – prior to making their respective films – in documentaries. The genre of the documentary targets, of course, the faithful recording of social and cultural realities. In its active disengagement from the seduction and evasiveness of fiction, the documentary sets out to explore, inform and offer insights into aspects of such realities that would otherwise go unnoticed. In this sense, the genre of the documentary must be viewed in opposition to more popular and hegemonic film genres. By being, per se, a marginal genre, the documentary eschews the mainstream, making itself an ideal form of cinema for the representations of marginal identities. Furthermore, by its very definition, the documentary can support more innovatory means of film-making, or it can project unusual perspectives. The documentary, for both Soler and Guerín, focuses on the margins of Barcelona's bourgeois society, whereby new geographical, ethnographic and social territories are explored. If the documentary is itself on the borderlines of cinema, then its focus here is also what lies on the borders of the mainstream. As a result, these films expose imbalances in power, thus revealing strategies of domination. The borderline of capitalist society, here, is a site of selective privilege and marginalization, a marker of power that underlines social hierarchies in accordance with differentiations of class, nationality and ethnicity.[2] In this context, it should be borne in mind that neither director is an immigrant. Precisely because of this, it is a specific position of political and moral empathy with the 'outsider' that leads to their focusing upon issues related to immigration, social disempowerment and identity. Both call upon their prior experience in making documentaries, though for different ends. The difference between Soler and Guerín is that while the former constructs a film of fiction as social realism, Guerín uses the documentary mode in order to deconstruct identity as an inconclusive and contingent construct. Furthermore, identity seen as construct is foregrounded by the carefully edited 'filmic text', so that the conscious exposure of the film-making process leads the viewer toward a fluid, documentary narrative that questions the demarcations of genre, as well as any claims to authenticity. The strength of these films, both of which have received considerable acclaim from members of the Moroccan immigrant community in the *Raval* in Barcelona, doubtlessly lies in their ability to evoke, though in very different ways, the real-life experiences of many Moroccans in Spain. This point was stressed by both Samir El Quichiri, the actor playing the part of Ahmet in this film[3] and the Moroccan singer and actress Chahrazad in interviews that I had separately with each of them in Barcelona in 2002. Nevertheless each of these film-makers positions himself on different sides of the boundary between fiction and documentary. While Soler avails himself of fiction in order to create a realist 'text' that mirrors the experiences of countless Moroccans in Spain in capturing key experiences of dislocation, Guerín's work uses lived experience in order to construct an inconclusive, but deeply moving, exploration of displacement. For Soler, as we shall see, Saíd's story is framed by the clear-cut aim of representing the discrimination suffered by immigrants. The result is a forceful, if somewhat closed, representation of social realities. *En construcción*, on the other hand, is as much a detailed and rigorous 'documentary' of popular experience as it is an open-ended questioning of the process of transition for a neighbourhood composed of socio-cultural diversity. The film dwells on the characters who make up the locality and reveals the mettle with which disadvantaged people live life against the grain of capitalist expansion. At the same time, the film never moves beyond what can be seen or recorded: there is never any mention of what will happen to the residents of this area once the process of change is complete. Viewers of both films, therefore, will find themselves presented with two quite different treatments of similar issues relating to Moroccans in Spain.

Immigration into Spain has grown in tandem with Spain's own involvement in globalization and its active membership of Western hegemony. The establishment of Moroccan communities around Spain with its subsequent cultural consequences for both host and immigrant communities can only be considered in the light of Spain's long-standing and complex colonial relation with Morocco. Furthermore, the cultural memory of Islamic rule in Spain in medieval times, with all its linguistic, cultural and architectural legacies that exist to this day, together with that of the subsequent expulsion of Moors, has left an important legacy on the discourses that surround contemporary Spanish-Moroccan relations. This in turn affects the ways in which Moroccans are represented in Spanish culture. Two predominant stereotypes that colour the popular imaginary are visions of the Moor as exotic and orientalized, a fetishistic marker of what lies beyond the Christian boundaries of Spain and visions of him as the marginal who lurks on the outskirts of society and threatens to somehow soil or destabilize the latter. Either way, the Moroccan serves to define the contours of Spanishness by providing a figure of alterity, which in turn is availed of in order to confirm self-identity. The Moroccan, more often than not referred to in common parlance as *el moro*, is, moreover, that familiar 'other' whose very proximity leads to a double rejection: that more generally accorded to economically disadvantaged immigrants, especially Muslims, around Europe, combined with the historically specific animosity of centuries – an animosity, it should be added, that has not prevented a convoluted mutual implication over time.[4] In the context of contemporary globalization, as represented in these films, the geographical proximity of Spain and Morocco – as seen in the opening scenes of *Saíd*, when the protagonist crosses illicitly into Spain on a raft – underlines their close physical relation as well as the fact that in this blurred line of contact lies also the boundary that separates Europe from its economically disadvantaged 'other'.

The complexities of the borderline extend well beyond the physical demarcations of Spain versus its poorer neighbour to the south. The borderline in lived practice asserts itself in the daily encounter with alterity; it demarcates the safe from the unsafe, the legal from the illegal, the rich from the poor. The presence of the immigrant as 'other' turns the Western metropolis into a borderline space: here the expansion of capitalism and the engagement with globalized enterprise run up against otherness through the embodied presence of the migrant, as the city invites and seeks to consume the disempowered in the name of its own empowerment. In this way, city spaces become marked with the signs and traces of alterity. Place, in both of these films, is inextricably tied to the representations of social class, gender and ethnicity. The immigrant male is situated in the back streets of Barcelona, whereby the liminality of the immigrant is heightened by the perceived economic marginality of the setting. The *Raval* and the *Barrio Xino* are that part of Barcelona traditionally relegated to those who have fallen short of Catalonia's long-standing affluence. Equally, these parts often house those by dint of whose labour such affluence is made possible. Barcelona, long the destination of internal migrants from other parts of Spain, most importantly Andalusia, now attracts a growing multi-ethnic immigrant population, whose presence underlines the city's own stature as one of the more economically desirable capitals of Europe. Nevertheless, as immigrants, the Moroccans inhabit that part of the city that houses the disadvantaged – a location that marks concerns of class and race that will inevitably inflect the ways in which gender is imagined and performed. At once in the heart of the Western metropolis and disempowered by the centrality of that location for reasons of ethnicity, cultural memory and economic vulnerability, the Moroccans live out the immigrant experience of inhabiting the double time of cultural incommensurability. Ironically, therefore, it is precisely when immigrants attempt to enter hegemonic domains, such as the urban capitals of Western Europe, that they find the greatest resistance to their integration. The result is an existence that is ambivalent, troubling, contradictory.

Both films are thus as much about the city and its inhabitants as they are about immigrant experience, in the sense that the city serves as the locus of difference. Cinematic fascination with urban settings is nothing new; no doubt, it owes much to the mobility and multiplicity of sounds and sights that make up the city, a mobility and multiplicity that is matched, in fact, by cinema as a cultural form that relies on movement, sound and sight. Thus, an easy partnership arises between form and content, as one of the most significant cultural media of late modernity couples with a major form of cultural organization pertaining to the latter, the metropolis (Shiel and Fitzmaurice 2001: 1). An important aspect of the focus of this alliance in these films is one of the key socio-cultural phenomena of late modernity, the growing flows of global labour migration from south to north. The result is a cartography of power within urban settings, whereby difference, be this cultural, economic or political, is both delineated and left open, via the inconclusiveness of all representation, to imaginative challenge.

'*Saíd*', I was told by Samir El Quichiri in the course of my interview with him, 'is a story that many of us here in the Raval have lived. Like him, many people here crossed into Spain on a *patera* (raft) and many risked their lives by doing so. Many Moroccans come here thinking they will have a good life, but then they see what it is like to live without friends, without family, without acceptance by society, without papers, without jobs, then they know what it is to be an outsider' (interview, 2002). Having crossed the Straits of Gibraltar, Saíd also finds himself uprooted from his native village of Xauen in the Rif Mountains of Morocco to the cosmopolitan environment of Barcelona. Experiencing rejection and scorn in the city, he further becomes the victim of violence both from his supposed 'friend' and mentor Husein and from local racist gangs. Husein is himself an ambivalent character, altered by the experience of migration. His apparent success in Barcelona receives much praise from his relatives at 'home', but it is based on a life-style of which he is ashamed, that of a pimp. Eventually, he claims to have genuinely fallen in love but finds it impossible to extricate himself from his contexts. Thus, he resorts to violence, a move that will undoubtedly lead him to yet more marginalization. While Saíd distances himself from Husein once he learns the truth about him, Saíd too is affected by the impossibility to make choices in life. This is seen most explicitly in the failure of his relationship with Ana, the Catalan journalist. Ana, well intentioned, if somewhat naive, has embarked on a study of Moroccan immigrants in Barcelona, and interviews Saíd in order to 'document' his story of migration and in order to learn more about the conditions of life faced by Moroccans in Barcelona. Despite her obvious political and moral empathy with the Moroccans, the objectification implicit in her documentary effort is laden with insinuations of difference. Indeed, it is precisely as she attempts to 'document' that the differences between her, as a well-to-do Catalan, and 'them' as illicit Moroccans, come most to the fore. Thus, the documentary comes face to face with its limitations precisely as it approximates the subject of documentation. Even in those moments when Ana risks her own well-being for the sake of the Moroccan men, she avails herself of a safety-net provided by her bourgeois background and status that will never be available to them. While feelings of love develop between Saíd and Ana, they are nevertheless held back by vast gaps in social class, ethnicity, religion and levels of education. The chasm between Saíd – as a poor, illicit, immigrant male, whose presence in Barcelona must ultimately depend upon evasion from the authorities, and hence social invisibility – and Ana – as the educated, articulate, privileged daughter of bourgeois parents becomes larger as the film progresses. In contrast to conventional stereotypes of male-dominated heterosexuality, then, it is Ana who makes the move to express her attraction to Saíd and to kiss him. Saíd's response is muted. Eventually, in a bid to protect Ana's safety, he withdraws completely from her as he comes to the realization that there is no future, not merely for this relationship, but also for himself in Spain. As he states to Ahmet, this love is impossible because the differences between him and Ana are so great and so many that they cannot be bridged. Thus, ironically, while Saíd's main reason for leaving Morocco was to become a 'provider' for his mother, whose husband was imprisoned, he is unable to enjoy a sexual or affective relation by the same token. In this sense, gender, a marker of power that finds its most potent expression in terms of relation with an 'other', is muted here because of a larger powerlessness that arises from the context of illicit immigration.

The performance of gender thus alters according to place as well: Morocco is portrayed by Soler in this film as marked by deep gender divisions, which assigns men a public role and confines women to domesticity. Morocco is portrayed by Soler in sharp contrast to the *Raval.* Here, women, such as Husein's mother and sister, sift *cous-cous* grain and chop vegetables in a brightly coloured and idyllic setting where even the motor car is a novelty. In such a context, the man's role is clearly dominant, vibrant, played out most effectively by the role assigned to him as breadwinner and provider. In Spain, however, the immigrant must contain himself in a bid for invisibility, thus stifling expressions of gender. This altered, almost silenced, performance of gender can only be understood in the context of the location of the subject, in other words, in terms of where he is seen to be. The grey tones of the *Raval*, as portrayed by Soler, contrast sharply with the vivid colours of the Rif. In similar vein, the affirmation of gender identity becomes muted, monotonous, almost listless in keeping with the displacement and disempowerment suffered by the subject. Place and gender thus mutually affirm one another. The definitive demise of the relationship between Saíd and Ana also marks the breaking of the immigrant's dream. In this context of transitionality, Saíd must move on, faced as he is with deportation. The film comes full circle, therefore, ending with Saíd in a coach, along with other anonymous, unwanted Moroccan men like himself, being returned 'home'. Nevertheless, given that he is marked by the experience of his troubled year in Barcelona, the Saíd who 'returns', we know, is far removed from the eager young man who had set out.

The circular structure of *Saíd,* whereby the immigrant's story halts at the moment of return, underlines the impossibility of gaining acceptance for cultural permeability and social understanding between Spaniards and Moroccans. Saíd's time in Spain was a 'non-time', a negation of his identity that lived itself out most evidently at an emotional level in terms of his failed embryonic romance with Ana. The viewer of this film is left with a bleak perspective, one that raises a worrying interrogative over the future of the increasing numbers of Moroccan and other immigrants who seek entry into Spain. In some ways, therefore, and despite the strong sense of social criticism that this film effectively conveys, it confirms the inferior alterity assigned to Moroccans as poor, unwanted relatives from across the Straits. For families such as Ana's who are comfortably ensconced in their bourgeois environments, the plight of the Moroccans is a source of annoyance. On the one hand, they acknowledge the discrimination imposed upon immigrants, but equally dismiss any suggestion of moral or ethical responsibility. Within such closed social barriers, the inevitable hybridity resulting from migration, most evident in Saíd's participation in the all-male raï music group 'Baraka', is a troubling reminder of dislocation and loss of a fixed sense of 'home'. Identity, as a result, is governed by social class and is thus largely defined by the empowerment afforded by ease of access to capital. The bourgeois inhabitants of this major European city are thus set apart from those who form the dregs of such a society. In this sense, *Saíd* successfully interrogates the morality, or lack thereof, of Western capitalism. Furthermore, and very importantly, the figure of Saíd as outsider, condemned to exclusion from even the very basic emotional needs and experiences enjoyed by most young people in the West, posits the question as to whether Western-centred imaginations of gender and identity carry any relevance for those who find themselves at once caught up in the capitalist drives of globalization's hegemony and on the shifting, unstable borderlands of the centres of such power. Not only does Saíd find himself uprooted in Spain, but, in a further bitter twist, his marginal position as an illegal immigrant deprives him of an affective or personal life of any quality. Thus, the controlling mechanisms operating through border control extend their grip even on the experience of empowerment at an intimate level that is offered by the performance of gendered relations. Saíd states in the film that by becoming a fugitive from the law, he no longer recognizes himself. Hiding as he does from the eyes of the police, his body becomes captive to the social imaginaries of the alienating West, thus rendering him alien to himself and to his social and cultural past.

Guerín's film, on the other hand, a subtle, cinematic contemplation of identity as construct and process, dwells on the actual reconstruction of the *Raval* area in order to engage with the complex dynamic existing there between old and new, past and present, self and other. *En construcción* successfully exploits the genre of documentary in order to offer a vision of identity as indeed a 'work in progress', to quote the preferred translation of the title into English. Furthermore, difference, as embodied by the Moroccan in Spain, does not present itself here as the neat opposition of self and other, but rather through the blurred half-light of shared, borderline existence. In this sense, what we as viewers are compelled to engage in is the troubling suspension of Derrida's *differance*, a difference that is also a deferral. *En construcción* records the last moments of a neighbourhood, caught in the grip of capitalist expansion, in the throes of being 'regenerated' from its raw, multi-grained social texture into the globalized, uniform tonality of middle-class accommodation. This is a not untypical case of urban expansion, carried out by appropriating and converting the lowly margins of the city. Yet, it is precisely this enforced project enacted in the name of the future, with its accompanying destruction of all that was, which leads to a sense of displacement shared by all those whose lives, regardless of race, gender or ethnicity, cross one another in the space of the *Barrio Xino*. More to the point, people and place alike share the threat of an irrevocable rupture with the past and a scattering of personal and communal histories, as the forces of capital gradually expand their grasp. This fractured temporality is perhaps what is most poignantly displayed in *En construcción*. This film records an instance of social mutation, when new purpose-built flats rise up over the ruins of previously demolished old tenement dwellings. The camera follows the works and the people involved in or affected by this process of construction in the knowledge that this new skyline will irrevocably alter the face of the city. Inevitably, what we thus witness is also the history of a people and a locality in transformation. Yet, the camera never ceases to dwell on repeated acts of demolition, and hence loss. A key event in the construction process is the unexpected discovery of Roman ruins. In palimpsestic mode, therefore, the plans for the future coexist with visions of the past. Furthermore, this archeological discovery confirms the importance of the *Barrio Xino* in ancient times, a place transformed now in the eyes of the locals from urban marginality to the scene of bygone power. Ironically, the residents of the area begin to acquire a much clearer notion of what there was in the past, as opposed to what the future has in store. The result is an unusual exploration through a crevice of spatial and temporal fracture, where the present gives way to other contradictory and coexisting temporalities. In this prolonged moment of existential indecision, the camera familiarizes viewers with a handful of locals. The irony of this documentary, of course, is that these local inhabitants whom the camera traces are 'characters' in the real sense of the word. They are the actors who construct the locality and give it its identity. By equal token, they are the forgotten people of Barcelona, the ones the city wishes to relegate to inconsequence in the urge to acquire a new, globalized, urban face. Yet, it is precisely in this locality of social 'detritus' that the camera lingers, unveiling a wealth of not merely insights and knowledges, but also the spontaneous and individually unique humanity of people just surviving on the edge. By following their movements and by regarding them in the larger context of juxtaposition to one another and the demolition process, both the fluidity and the spontaneity of identity surfaces from the forced 'deconstruction' of the locality.

Within this context, the Moroccan immigrant appears as one more person on the brink, defined not by his marginality or 'otherness', but, in fact, by his defiance of expectations that viewers may have of him as culturally or ethnically different. Indeed, difference in this film does not come in expected forms. In a quote cited in the sleeve of the DVD of *En construcción*, Guerín states that Abdel Aziz el Mountassir, the Moroccan construction worker, is the one of the most well-read people that he knows. Indeed, what Mountassir does is to unsettle both his Spanish co-worker and viewers by challenging any stereotypes about Moroccans. Despite his social status as both immigrant and worker, he reveals a provocative and lively, as well as informed, intellect that unsettles the complacency of his colleague. Thus, with his fiercely Marxist position, he critiques the capitalist system within which he himself is embroiled, viewing it in Marxist terms as a phase in history. He points out with subtlety to his colleague that perhaps the latter's insomnia is symptomatic of an alienation arising from refusal to consider issues of class. He suggests too that important gender differences arise with differences of context: thus, while the Catalan worker makes little effort to 'court' a woman whom he is interested in, the Moroccan must waylay her through deft conversation and other means of enticement. He rightly attributes such different behaviour to questions of place and social context. Mountassir, like other characters in this film (Juani, the prostitute reveals an immensely affectionate and loving nature; her boyfriend, Ivan is a rough, young lad, but shows himself to be emotionally fragile and needy of her love; Atar the sailor is an elderly man that many would consider irrelevant, but he is well versed in numerous languages and has seen much of the world), broaches subconscious stereotypes and brings to light the all too often overlooked socio-cultural wealth and diversity of the 'margin'. Indeed, in comparison to these central figures in the film, the middle-class purchasers who come to survey the new flats seem depressingly flat, levelled by a cosmopolitan monotony that is shaped by capitalism. While Mountassir too is implicated in this process of 'reconstruction', nevertheless it is precisely his double marginality – that arising from his social class combined with that derived from his immigrant status – that affords him a perspective that can sidestep any norms. Interestingly, and in stark contrast to Saíd, Mountassir is in fact empowered by his position as an 'other' – it is from this perspective that he critiques the contexts that he is in. The difference between the two characters, however, is also important to note: Mountassir is clearly educated, while Saíd is not. Knowledge, it would appear, gives him an intellectual stability that does not rely on social or economic continuity.

To return to theories of Third Cinema, *Saíd* and *En construcción* clearly engage in different ways with an aesthetic of marginality and dispossession, thus providing rare imaginations of identity in the context of an economically disempowered and forced migrancy. In such a context, difference cannot be grasped or viewed as situated, but must be considered as permutation, contextual and contingent. In situations of economically disadvantaged migration, where ambivalence and inconclusiveness predominate, discourses and categories of knowledge that have historically been developed in contexts of political hegemony find themselves challenged and even possibly dislocated. Cinema, itself a product of the colonizing West, shifts its locus here to that of the post-colonial. If the fluid medium of cinema is, therefore, to make an intervention in the balance of global power, then perhaps this is most viable through its global appeal as a mass medium, which allows for a reimagining of the concepts through which discourses of knowledge are articulated and propagated. To problematize issues of identity in migrancy is also to challenge discourses of authority and to reveal, thereby, their own dependence on certainty, stability and fixed location. Thus, as seen in both the films considered here, the vulnerability of immigrant subjectivity leads not merely to experiences of disempowerment; they can also lead to a deconstruction of established power structures, as seen in the example of Abdel Aziz el Mountassir, the Moroccan construction worker in *En construcción*, and thus force a renegotiation of social and cultural hierarchies. To consider gender in such a light is to bear in mind that the performance of gender, like the performance of other aspects of identity, is to engage in the play of power. In this light, the intersections of gender, place and power in the context of immigrant identity in these two films underline the assertion of the margin, not solely as that which has been delineated by the centre, but, indeed, as the disconcerting force of a post-colonial counter-narrative. This margin is also the border that traverses the spaces and times of the immigrant, one that exposes the unspoken and unsettling imagination of incomplete hegemonies and unconquered – indeed, perhaps unconquerable – arenas of power.

Notes

1. I have explored questions of displacement and cultural memory in the context of migration from Morocco to Spain in my article 'Albums of

no return: ethnicity, displacement and recognition in photographs of North African immigrants in contemporary Spain' (Nair 2000).
2. A compelling analysis of immigration to Spain is to be found in *El peaje de la vida* (Goytisolo and Naïr 2000).
3. My forthcoming chapter 'Voicing Risk: migration, transgression and relocation in Spanish-Moroccan raï' (Nair 2004) focuses on the music of Samir El Quichiri in Barcelona. The music heard in *Saíd* is typical of Spanish-Moroccan raï.
4. An excellent study of the image of the Moroccan in Spanish culture is *La imagen del magrebí en España* (Martín Corrales 2002).

References

Goytisolo, J. and S. Naïr (2000), *El peaje de la vida*, Madrid: Aguilar.

Lorman, J. (1995), *L'aventura de Saïd*, Barcelona: Cruïlla.

Martín Corrales, E. (2002), *La imagen del magrebí en España*, Barcelona: Edicions Bellaterra.

Nair, P (2000), 'Albums of no return: ethnicity, displacement and recognition in photographs of North African immigrants in contemporary Spain', *Journal of Spanish Cultural Studies*, 1(1), 59–73.

——(forthcoming in 2004), 'Voicing Risk: migration, transgression and relocation in Spanish-Moroccan raï', in I.D. Biddle and V.N.M. Knights (eds), *Popular Music and Nationalisms*, London: Ashgate.

Shiel, M. and T. Fitzmaurice (eds) (2001), *Cinema and the City*, Oxford and Malden: Blackwell.

Shohat, E. (2000), 'Gender and Culture of Empire: Toward a Feminist Ethnography of the Cinema' in R. Stam and T. Miller (eds), *Film and Theory: An Anthology*, Oxford and Malden: Blackwell.

Shohat, Ella (2003), 'Post-Third-Worldist culture: gender, nation and the cinema', in Anthony R. Guneratne and Wimal Dissanayake (eds), *Rethinking Third Cinema*, London: Routledge.

Shohat, Ella and Robert Stam (2000), *Unthinking Eurocentrism*, London: Routledge.

Stam, R. (2003), 'Beyond Third Cinema: the aesthetics of hybridity', in A.R. Guneratne and W. Dissanayake (eds), *Rethinking Third Cinema*, London: Routledge.

Interviews

Chahrazad, Barcelona, April 2002.
Samir El Quichiri, Barcelona, April 2002.

8

A Psychoanalysis of *La mujer más fea del mundo* (1999)

Eva Parrondo Coppel

To my friend Céline Bel

According to the film critic José Luis Martínez Montalbán (2000), *La mujer más fea del mundo* (1999), scripted by Nacho Baerna and directed by Miguel Bardem, 'can be taken as the prototype of contemporary Spanish cinema' (p. 398). Produced with significant financial backing,[1] it counted on prestigious names in both technical and artistic areas,[2] and was released on the wave of a major publicity campaign addressed specifically to a youth audience: the film was promoted as a 'science-fiction *noir* thriller'.

In spite of its alleged 'prototypical' Spanish qualities, the film bears the hallmarks of a 1990s Hollywood production. Bearing in mind that Hollywood cinema is part of the Spanish cinematic context,[3] I will argue in psychoanalytical terms that *La mujer más fea del mundo* can be seen as 'a *science-fictional* prototype' in which the circuit of symbolic exchange between cinemas[4] is restored on the basis of an antagonistic reciprocity (Baudrillard 1985: 102). Contrary to 1990s multinational *noir* films, but in line with 1940s Hollywood romantic *noir* films,[5] this Hollywood film *made in Spain* displays a happy-ending scenario of heterosexual love. It could be argued that, after a series of murderous/erotic wish-fulfilment revenge scenarios, the *classical* happy-ending scenario of love – in which 'the miracle of the Other stretching his or her hand out to me' (Zizek 1997: 192) is displayed – functions in *La mujer más fea del mundo* as a means to establish an inter-textual dialogue with different endings in other 1990s *noir* thrillers with 'female avenger'.[6]

1. *La mujer más fea del mundo* announces from the outset (before the film's title credits appear on screen) that it is going to deal with the Real dimension of the body, that is, with the body as 'living flesh' *driven* to

death. The film opens with the steadily increasing sound of boiling. A fade-in introduces the spectator to a formless, organic, and yellowish image that resembles a 'volcanic brain'. The words, 'Madrid. 1 January 1982. The Miraculous clinic. 1:00 a.m.' superimposed on-screen inform us of the location, the date, and the hour of the birth of Lola Otero, the female character that is to occupy the position of the movie's protagonist. Following the cinematic conventions of 1970s horror movies, which often shape the science-fiction genre, the film leads the spectator, by identification with the character of the nurse that initiates the action of an unsettling camera, to witness 'the horror' that the sight of the female body provokes in the (female) other. The construction of 'sexual difference' (girl = pink blanket, 'prettiness,' the mythical name of 'the beautiful Otero')[7] does not integrate *the sight* of the (off-screen) Real body: the sequence ends with a low-angled medium close-up of the nurse screaming while covering up her ears. The camera approaches her face and finally 'enters' her open mouth. Fade-out to black.

The fade-out to black, which ends the film's pre-title sequence, can be seen to constitute the narrative, traumatic *originary* point ('lethal' *jouissance*) which 'cannot be positively *signified*' but only '*shown*, in a negative gesture, as the inherent failure of symbolization' (Zizek 1997: 217; see also Copjec 1994: 123). For the fade-out to black not only functions as an internal textual limit (the Real of the body is excluded from the field of representation) but also as a sign of violent textual rupture[8] from which meaning originates (Zizek 1997: 161): there is a fade-in to a full-screen 'volcanic brain' from which the film's title emerges, like silvered mercury. The camera approaches the word 'ugly' (*fea*), and the word disappears like silvered dust. Ugliness, then, is not only the film's initial missing representation (fade-out to black) but also the film's 'originally repressed' representation (Zizek 1989: 159).

After the film's title, it follows a long shot of a *Blade Runner*-type city with the similarly silvered lettering announcing: 'Madrid. Federal District. New Year's Eve 2010. 23:45 p.m.', while the 'exotic'/masculine *pasodoble* 'Patricia' is heard in the soundtrack.[9] The wide-screen film/TV image of *an explosion* (long shot of the deliberate crash of two spaceships in a science-fiction film shown on a TV set) *wakes* Lieutenant Arribas. The reverse shot of a close-up of him is a full-screen TV clock striking twelve. A female TV presenter is heard saying: 'Happy 2011! Greetings to you, your family, and all your nearest and dearest who are sharing this special moment with you. Nobody can feel alone on a night like this. [The Lieutenant begins to cough and leaves] Today is the first day of our lives. Be happy!'

Psychoanalysis of La mujer más fea del mundo

Lola Otero and Lieutenant Arribas are portrayed as a 'noir couple': the two characters are inextricably entwined both through a 'scenario of traumatic birth/life' and through a forthcoming (but already *in* the present of the narrative) 'scenario of death'. This conflict is made apparent in the film's poster (see www.culturalianet.com/art/ver.php?art=1967). Whereas the 'I only want to be loved' (at the bottom of the poster) defines the motivation of the female protagonist's actions, the female character's image (Lola Otero is *dressed to kill* [Brian de Palma, 1980] as a *Matrix femme fatale* while addressing a challenging look to the spectator from its high position) not only announces the film's criminal scenarios but it also qualifies them as ambiguous, as 'psycho-logical'. Although in the film's poster the beautiful Lola wears black, has dark glasses on, and holds a machine gun, the notion that a hidden and dark monster-woman kills to be loved is displaced onto and condensed in her monster-shaped, threatening shadow.

2. In order to work through, that is, in order to offer a 'fictional solution', both to the science-fictional/traumatic Real dimension of the body (the female protagonist's monstrous body, the male character's weak body) and to an impersonal ever-present time ('today is the first day of our lives'), *La mujer más fea del mundo* sets out a series of *noir* scenarios in which 'the scenario of traumatic life' collapses into the 'scenario of violent death'. The second sequence of the film, in fact, opens with 'a home' where old people are celebrating a New Year's Eve party and with a long shot of *Lola's menacing shadow* approaching the building. A series of travelling shots from her subjective viewpoint along the empty corridors are cut with shots of the party where a 'dirty old man'[10] is taking a polaroid of an elderly beautiful lady he is attracted to, Ms. Lidia, as she is about to leave the party to go to her bedroom. The intruder, *disguised as* a nun (with the attire of Mother Theresa of Calcutta), attacks Ms. Lidia, pushes her onto her bed, and stabs her to death.[11] The criminal scenario that triggers the Lieutenant's narrative, the trajectory of his investigation is, therefore, narrated in a highly ambiguous way: 'Mother Theresa of Calcutta' stabs a beautiful old lady *on her bed*, after a scene in which this woman has been flirting with a 'dirty old man'. In addition, the scene of the crime is also constructed as a sexual/love scene: apart from the sentence 'new year, new *life*' *written in blood* on the wall (the 'Mother' is *in* the scene of the crime) and a group of candles, Ms. Lidia's corpse is covered with *semen* (later in the film it turns out to be wax), so the 'male lover' is also *in* the scene of the crime.

In a similar fashion to the portrayal of the 'dirty old man', the Lieutenant is also portrayed as *dominated by* 'the scopic drive'. That is to say he is depicted as *driven* by pleasure in looking (Copjec 1993: 182) in relation to (a) the criminal's image and (b) the criminal's text, from the beginning of his investigation, that is, from his arrival at the scene of the crime. My reading of the Lieutenant's fascination with the criminal's *image*, connoted as *excessive* by the film's enunciation, finds its basis in one sequence where we see the Lieutenant looking at the security-camera video from the old people's home while using a taken-from-*Blade Runner* computer program that gets a printed close-up of the beautiful female criminal, disguised as 'Mother Theresa'. After getting 'the woman's image', and while 'his pasodoble' is heard in the soundtrack, Arribas is shown removing his hairpiece, his false teeth, and *his fake eye* in his bath-room. The reading that the Lieutenant's fascination with the criminal's text is also connoted as *excessive* by the film's enunciation comes from a brief scene in which we witness Arribas looking at the polaroid of Ms. Lidia taken by her suitor and realizing that Ms. Lidia's heart-shaped brooche *is missing* from its place (she did not wear it at the scene of the crime). Through the Lieutenant 'signifying description of the scene' around this trace that is *not* visible in the scene of the crime, the film's enunciation (1) portrays the Lieutenant as able to *unmask* 'the imaginary unity of the scene as it was staged by the assassin' (Zizek 1991: 53) and (2) highlights Ms. Lidia's brooche as the visual-narrative motif that marks both lack ('the impossible object of the drives') and desire (the 'invisible object' is 'the prohibited object') in this film (Copjec 1993: 175–9).

Following the conventions of 1940s romantic noir films, the Lieutenant's investigation of 'the crime' and of 'the woman' echoes the film's enunciation of its own investigation of 'masculine identity' (see Krutnik 1991). In fact, the scene in which the Lieutenant is contemplating the scene of the motherly, sexually ambiguous, crime gives way to a *Psycho* 'shower scene' in which a close-up of the criminal's menstrual blood initiates a slow vertical pan that follows Lola's *new* 'perfect body' illegally *created* by Dr Werner on the day of her eighteenth birthday. Lola (played by the fashion model Elia Galera) is thus located in the sexually ambiguous narrative position of *jouissance* (see, Cowie 1993: 135–6). Coming to embody the fantasy of the *femme fatale* not only for 'the male spectator' but also for 'the female' insofar as from her (the fe[male] spectator's) point of view, Lola's narrative trajectory is driven by revenge.

Four *subjective* flashbacks motivate Lola's vengeful actions. Whereas Lola's first flashback (after the after-murder/erotic shower scene) defines her as 'the daughter' of a *blind* 'religious mother' (as a child, Lola lives in a nun-governed orphanage) for whom she has always been 'pretty' because she looks at her 'with the eyes of the heart' (the blind 'mother' gives her 'daughter' a crucifix, the beautiful Otero wears it around her neck throughout the film), Lola's second flashback links her present narcissistic/aggressive sexual scenarios – owing to her beauty Lola seduces a narcissistic male lover[12] to her bed and, after 'having fucked him' (this scene remains ellided), despises him and expels him from her flat – to a re-*active* rejection of men. In the present of the narrative, before the second flashback takes place, 'the most beautiful woman in the world' *is* in a bar *looking at herself* disguised as a nun on the TV news (she is watching the video of herself recorded by the security camera at the old people's home) when 'the most beautiful man in the world' approaches her, gives her a cigarette and tells her: 'Do you know what I was thinking of while *I was looking at you*? I was thinking that as a child you must have been a *very pretty girl*'. A metaphorical close-up of Lola's *lit match* is accompanied by the words 'ugly, ugly!!' on the soundtrack. These words function as the soundbridge to a flash-back scenario of rejection and abandonment: a boy who loses in 'the match game', refuses to kiss the monstrous Lola and convinces the other children to leave her alone.

Lola's third flashback (after a scene in which Lola visits her blind 'mother' and tells her she is not married because she has not found 'a man who truly loves her', that is, a man *who loves her with the eyes of the heart*) locates her in a self-enclosed, and narcissistic Cinderella scenario, organized according to 'the pleasure principle'. The monstrous little Lola, alone in the girls' bedroom, wishes to become 'the most beautiful woman on earth'.[13] This 'all-fulfilling scenario', however, is defined by the film's enunciation as 'impossible'. The Other sex ('the ferocious wolf') enters the girls' bedroom and the scenario of enjoyment shifts into a scenario of violence: a group of male adolescents rape 'Cinderella' (off-screen). This scenario of rape, which is associated with 'the taboo of virginity' (the third flashback is introduced by a long shot of the statue of 'The Virgin of the Immaculate Heart of Maria'[14] and is ended by a close-up of the Cinderella hand-mirror broken on the floor of the girls' bedroom) retroactively deepens in Lola's exaggerated hostility against men in the present of the narrative, a hostility, that is, which *exceeds* the 'normal hostility' that always mediates the relationships between the sexes (Freud 1917 [1918]).

The film, however, motivates Lola's present murderous/sexually aggressive scenarios not only via a *past* scenario of male rape (the Real/traumatic encounter with the other sex: third flashback) but also via a *present* female Gothic romance film scenario.[15] The scenario of male rejection (second flashback) returns *in* the present of the narrative via a soundbridge of thunderclaps and a dissolve to a close-up of a fairy-tale Quasimodo mask that is in Lola's bedroom. The motif of 'the Quasimodo mask' in the *mise en scène* of the ellided sexual/aggressive encounter between Lola and 'the most beautiful man in the world' stands for *the repressed* (Lola's *disguised* hostility against men) *in* the present of the narrative: Lola murders women. The mask motif, moreover, in the *mise en scène* of the present of the narrative not only announces that men are *seen* by Lola/the fe[male] spectator as 'hiding' a *dark* side ('the most beautiful man in the world' steals Ms. Lidia's 'brooch' from her handbag, while Lola is having 'an after-sex/after-murder shower' off-screen) but also that *the return of the repressed* comes from *the future* (Lacan, 1953– 54: 239). Indeed, Lola's fourth and last *subjective* flashback displays the repressed/disguised conflation between the film's murderous scenarios and a female Gothic Oedipal scenario: Lola's attachment to/dependence on her lost Gothic lover[16] (Luis Casanova)/science-fictional 'father' (Dr Werner). Lola's fourth flashback takes place in a scene in which she is buying a pair of high-heeled shoes to hide a machine-gun with which she intends to kill the next Miss Spain. A close-up of the Cinderella shoes[17] that are being promoted in the shop leads to another close-up of a similar pair of shoes being worn by Lola the night of her eighteenth birthday (New Year's Eve 1999). In a masked ball, the 'charming' millionaire Luis *Casanova* wearing the 'Quasimodo mask' seduces Lola by dancing with her and assuring her that he could fall in love with 'the ugliest woman in the world' because 'if her heart is beautiful, I wouldn't mind her face'. The film constructs Lola's *masked* ball as a wonderful but impossible dream in which spatial dichotomies (inside/outside) collapse. A circular travelling shot of the couple dancing inside the ballroom dissolves into a similar shot of them dancing outside the ballroom in a *Manderley* scenario[18]. The sequence also constructs Lola's encounter with Casanova as one of atemporal fusion: while the off-screen clock strikes twelve, another circular shot encloses Luis and Lola looking at each other's eyes. Another series of dissolves expands Luis's action of removing Lola's mask in order to kiss her, so that their wishes can come true: as they kiss in a close-up, the camera pans vertically up to the fireworks in the sky, a Hollywood convention to represent 'the ecstasy of passion' (see for instance *To Catch a Thief* [Alfred Hitchcock, 1955]).

However, after twelve o'clock, Lola's *wonderful dream* to be truly loved by 'the golden bachelor, heir of one of the biggest fortunes in the country, a successful businessman, a sportsman, and a *bonviveur*' (as he is defined later in the film by Dr Werner) is constructed as 'prohibited'

Psychoanalysis of La mujer más fea del mundo

by the film's enunciation (Metz 1977: 87). Because Lola stays at 'the enchanted ball' after midnight, Prince Charming throws up and leaves. The disgust associated with Lola's third and fourth flashbacks (the scenario of Cinderella's *rape* ends with a close-up of Lola's 'fake' mirror on the floor, the scenario of Cinderella's *enchanted ball* ends with a close-up of the two masks on the floor: the vomit between them) returns *in* the present of the narrative: Lola coldly subjects another male lover to *her* Quasimodo mask (Lola's lover has doubts about his virility).

3. In order to work through Lola's 'impossible/prohibited dream' of being truly loved by Casanova, the third narrative segment of the film displays a series of scenarios constructed according to 'reality principles' relevant to both Lieutenant Arribas (Lola's 'pursuer') and Dr Werner (Lola's 'creator'). In contrast to the collapse of spatial difference between 'outside' and 'inside' that occurs in the *masked*-ball dance featuring Cinderella and Quasimodo, this third narrative segment introduces a clear-cut construction of spatial dichotomies (exterior/interior). A long shot that shows 'the exterior' of the Federal cyber-library, where the Lieutenant goes to discover more about Lola, is followed by a long shot of 'the circular' library interior. After a fade-out to black, the next sequence commences with a repetition of the spatial distinction between 'exterior' (long shot of the exterior of Dr Werner's clinic) and 'interior' (long shot of Dr Werner in his office).

This formal structure (exterior-interior/fade-out to black/exterior-interior) establishes a connection between Lieutenant Arribas and Dr Werner. Such a link, moreover, is also represented at the level of the narrative. On the one hand, inside the library – the locus of the scopic-epistemological drive – the lieutenant watches a sentimental television programme about 'The beautiful Otero: A fairy tale' delivered in voice-over by Dr Werner. On the other hand, inside his private clinic – the locus of the death drive – Dr Werner is threatened by 'his beautiful doll', gun in hand, who steals 'the beauty injections' from him. It can be noted, then, that the two male characters are linked through their *fantasy* view of Lola. Arribas becomes increasingly obsessed with the female killer's video-camera/TV image because of Dr Werner's tele/vision story of Lola as a revengeful *black widow*. In Dr Werner's story, at the funeral of Luis Casanova and his wife (a recent Miss Spain) who have been killed in a car accident while on honeymoon in Monaco, Lola announces to the press that she 'will never forget what that *bitch* has done to me'.

However, contrary to Dr Werner's illegal 'morphogenetic experiments' with patients – he was expelled from the University after his creation of

Eva Parrondo Coppel

Lola and continues to protect 'his beautiful criminal doll' – the Lieutenant
remains on the side of the (judicial) law. He arrives at the clinic just in
time both to arrest Dr Werner (as an accomplice in Lola's murders) and to
rescue the scientist from Lola's gun. Meanwhile he also *misses* Lola who
runs away disguised as a nurse with dark glasses. The woman who runs
away in disguise exacerbates the transgressive sexual tension between
the members of the *noir* 'couple' and decreases the probability that they
can overcome their complicated relationship with the (symbolic) Law.
Yet, soon after she is gone, the Lieutenant is able to send back to Lola
'the true significance' of her message – I *am deceiving you* (Zizek 1991:
57) – by hardening his pursuit of her. In fact, while a *Bullitt* – of *Steve*
McQueen fame – type of music is heard on the soundtrack, the Lieutenant,
together with his police crew, literally *drives* to Lola's apartment. As he
goes upstairs and walks through a series of long and winding corridors,
we hear a *heart beating* drum, getting louder as the Lieutenant 'forces'
his way into Lola's place, the cause of his anxiety.[19]

As a deeper, slower sound encroaches on the soundtrack, Arribas
moves into Lola's hall and looks around *the empty* place. Lola's absence
from 'her place' motivates both the Lieutenant's order to 'search and
arrest Lola Otero' and a series of *suspense* travellings shots that follow
Arribas as he scrutinizes Lola's things (her lighted candles, her veils,
a collection of burned Barbie dolls, a photograph of Mother Theresa,
photographs of herself in women's magazines, and a snap of her as a child
– the face deleted – with her blind 'mother'). Meanwhile, the soundtrack
changes tone to introduce a sharper music (double bass and cellos, with
brief intrusions of *Legend* [Ridley Scott, 1985] 'romantic violins').[20] As
in Preminger's *Laura*, the Lieutenant's *excessive* trajectory regarding
the investigation of the crime/the woman provokes 'an experience of
death' (Zizek 1989: 68). While Lola kills *the double* of the Other Woman
who 'stole' Luis Casanova from her (Lola disguises herself as one of
the organizers of the forthcoming Miss Spain context, picks 'Miss
Cantabria' up at the airport, kills her, and buries her in a military area),
the Lieutenant edits a loop of close-ups of Lola Otero (from Dr Werner's
TV programme), in which she addresses him using the words *she used
to say* to the now dead Casanova: 'I love you. I'll never forget you. You
are the man of my life'. The series of frontal-mirror shot/reverse-shots
between the male character's narcissistic/dead look and the female
character's all-loving/vertiginous image *drives* the Lieutenant/spectator
to *fall* into a 'visual spiral' and into a brief *subjective* wide-angled
'nightmare sequence'. In this sequence, a provocative Lola sitting on a
table, wearing a white, light, evening dress, and her eighteenth-birthday

mask, repeats the sentence, 'I love you. You are the man of my life'. Shots of her are rapidly cross-cut with shots of Dr Werner and Sergeant Pelayo, the Lieutenant's Watsonian companion,[21] also repeating Lola's phrases to the Lieutenant.[22] The nightmare ends with a wide-angled medium close-up shot of Lola laughing hysterically while a candle is burning in the background.

This wide-angled nightmare sequence can be seen as the final visual scenario 'placed in the service of a defence against the [scopic-epistemological] drive' (Copjec 1993: 192). After the artificial loop of close-ups of Lola looking at Arribas (as the dead Casanova) and telling him that she loves him and that he is the man of her life, the Other's difference returns in an uncanny way. The emergence of 'a non-symbolized fantasmatic surplus' (Zizek 1993: 220) *in* reality (Lola's laugh soundbridges the nightmare and 'reality') announces that the Lieutenant is close to 'the dark chamber where the death drive ends' (Turim 1989: 180). He is close to 'symbolic castration'. In fact when the Lieutenant abruptly wakes up from 'his nightmare' he loses his fake eye, which falls on the *original* polaroids of 'the scene of the motherly-sexual crime', including a close-up of Lola disguised as Mother Theresa and another with the sentence 'new year, new life' written in blood on the wall. A medium close-up of the Lieutenant covering his one-eyed face with his hands, fades out to black via a cross-shaped fade.

4. The camera fades in to a cross-shaped close-up of Lola *disguised* as '*the dead* Miss Cantabria', as she enters the all-white, hyper-futuristic building where both the Miss Spain contest and 'the encounter with the Law' are to be held. Inside the 'police-room', the Lieutenant's *excessive* relationship with the female character is replaced by a more tame relationship. Unlike his team of policemen, who look at women like a voracious spaceship crew, Arribas is portrayed not only as reluctant to be seduced by appearances (he refuses to look at the female models' photographs) but also as 'the weak embodiment of the Law' of desire: he 'prohibits' his policemen scopic *jouissance*. 'Have you all gone stupid? Have you lost your judgement? [he coughs]. This is not a game [he coughs again]. I remind you that you are on duty and that we are in a murder case. So I don't want any more nonsense'. The lieutenant's tame position regarding the female character is further related to the Law in the next sequence. A long shot of the sepulchral exterior of the Federal Prison is followed by a scene inside the prison in which the Lieutenant interrogates Dr Werner about Lola's heart. 'She is not bad, Lieutenant,' says the scientist, 'She has had bad luck, that's all. Nobody has ever truly loved her. Nobody. Do you know what it must feel like?'

Eva Parrondo Coppel

The fantasy scenario of violent confrontation between the female psycho-killer and 'the weak embodiment of the Law' to be held at the Miss Spain building is initiated by a series of cross-cut medium close-ups of Lola and the Lieutenant loading their *equal* weapons. In fashion similar to that of 1990s multinational *noir* thrillers involving 'female avengers', the confrontation between the woman and the Law is explicitly related to 1970s feminism (Read 2000: 3–13). On the one hand, the furious, cross-eyed, 1970s feminist leader that remains outside the building is mistaken for Lola – she even looks like Lola in the Lieutenant's *nightmare* – when she attempts to illegally enter the building disguised as a nun with the intention of stabbing any 'top model'/'bitch' with a knife. On the other hand, Lola is mistaken for the 1970s feminist leader, as she is defined as 'an intellectual doll' by one of the male members of the judging panel.[23] By relating Lola's murder of her main rival for the Miss Spain crown – the competitive, clever, and galactic/femenine 'Miss Barcelona/Miss *Photogenic*' – to the feminist leader, the film's enunciation unmasks the 1970s feminist fantasy of solidarity between women (see Read 2000: 194). By locating Lola's murder of Dr Werner in the men's toilet (after helping him pee, she strangles him), the film's enunciation unmasks the 1970s masculine fantasy of women's excessive hostility against women (Dr Werner's televised fairy-tale/revenge story of Lola). Additionally, the film's enunciation connotes Lola's sadistic killing of her science-fiction creator/lustful 'father' (she kills him after a scene in which he looks at her with desire and 'recognizes' her because of the crucifix given to her by her blind 'mother') as both the dead-end of the fashion model's vengeful feminist trajectory (she kills a man) and the beginning of her 'monstrous feminine destiny'.

5. The previously mentioned scene in which Lola kills 'her creator' in the men's toilet not only ends with the image of *La Pietá* but also gives way to a television reality-show of Lola's *orgasmic* mutation from top-model to female monster. 'I'm ugly!' she tells the Lieutenant, 'I have always been ugly! Don't you see it?' Then she shoots at a huge TV screen-mirror, while watched by a large group of diegetic spectators gathered in Madrid's central square La Plaza de España (the Square of Spain). At this science-fictional point where the film mobilizes the visible (Kuhn 1990: 6) – the televised spectacle of the female protagonist's Real monstrous body – the film also mobilizes the origin of meaning. By depicting a visible monstrous Lola *choosing* not to become 'the uncanny embodiment' of non-sensical *jouissance* (the embodiment of that which should have remained hidden: the death drive),[24] the film's enunciation

celebrates the ideology of individual freedom against the ideology of individual fate: Lola is portrayed *choosing* to substitute 'the impossible object of the drives' (the top model's TV *image* and the Miss Spain crown with Ms. Lidia's heart-shaped jewel stamped in its centre: Lola liberates her hostess, 'Miss Las Palmas') for 'the object of a symbolic prohibition': her active machine gun with which she *injures* Arribas in one leg.

The female character's *new position* of desire, mediated by the embodiment of the Law – both by removing his 'mask' (his hairpiece, his fake eye, and his false teeth) and in his recognition of Lola ('I know how you feel, Lola'), the Lieutenant approaches 'the female monster' – triggers 'the birth of female subjectivity'. Out of love for a truthful *Quasimodo* (Arribas resembles the mask) 'the ugliest woman in the world' lays down her *jouissance*/weapon and in a *miraculous* transformation lets the hopeless but brave male Other hug in a *wonderful*/circular but *tamed* TV embrace.

6. By 'giving body' to a limit (the *vertiginous* embrace between Lola and Casanova in the fourth flashback), this fairy-tale, happy-ending TV-style scenario announces the narrative presence of the symbolic Law of desire. After a fade-out to black, then a series of shots of different newspaper headlines (the spectator is informed of the 250-year jail sentence handed down to 'the beautiful Lola Otero') dissolve into a scene in which Arribas (with an eye patch and the help of a stick) enters the Police building to *lay down* his Lieutenant's 'identity' card and gun.

A long shot of Arribas leaving 'the interior' of the Police building dissolves into a long shot of 'the exterior' of the Federal Prison (New Year's Eve, 2011) and, while the 'exotic'/feminine *bolero* 'Lamento gitano' is heard on the soundtrack,[25] Arribas approaches Lola's cell. The cell is constructed as the space of desire: time is measured ('visiting time'), Lola's *image* is improved by a broken mirror, there is a couple united on the basis of their common lack (Zizek 1989: 171–2). A series of shot/reverse shots symbolically differentiate between 'the crippled, one-eyed man' and 'the monster woman'[26] while 'the man' *gives a ring* to 'the woman' as a birth-night present. Lola switches the radio on. In modern Spanish fashion, they eat the twelve grapes together in time with the chimes of the clock heralding in the new year.[27] The film ends with a close-up of Lola smiling with happiness while the radio presenter's female voice can be heard saying: 'We, the family of channel 10, hope that your last year's wishes have come true and that the year 2012 sees your wishes fulfilled and brings you love, a lot of love, to you. And remember, *today is the first day of the rest of your life.*' In the right foreground of this final, personal, towards-the-future ending shot, there is an opened bottle of champagne.

Notes

1. This film was produced-distributed by an 'independent company' (Aurum Producciones, SA) with the participation of Canal Plus (España) and TVE.
2. Such as the actor Héctor Alterio, the music composer Juan Bardem, the editor Iván Aledo, or the Art director Alain Bainée.
3. And not a 'foreign cinematic tradition', as argued in nationalist readings of Spanish films (for instance Roberts 1999: 20).
4. *La mujer más fea del mundo* has been shown in various international film festivals. It was nominated for 'best film' in The Catalonian International Film Festival (Sitges, Spain), won the Meliés d'Argent at Fantasporto (Oporto, Portugal, 2000) and the Grand Prix Award at PIFAN (2000).
5. *The Big Sleep* (Howard Hawks, 1944), *Laura* (Otto Preminger, 1944), *Gilda* (Charles Vidor, 1946), or *Dark Passage* (Delmer Daves, 1947).
6. Such as *The Last Seduction* (John Dahl 1993) – a film with a 'progressive feminist' ending scenario: 'the heroine coolly getting away with stealing millions of dollars' (Kaplan 1998: 12; Read 2000: 207), *Batman Returns* (Tim Burton, 1992) – a film with a 'postmodern feminist' ending scenario: the female protagonist has 'renegotiated' its 'feminine identity' with its 'feminist identity' (Read 2000: 198–9) – or *Bound* (The Wachowski Brothers, 1996) – a film with a 'postmodern' happy ending scenario of homosexual love based on a certain 'sameness' that makes lesbians 'better partners in crime' (Straayer 1998: 159–60).
7. Carolina Otero, la Bella Otero (The Beautiful Otero), was born in Pontevedra in 1868 and died in Niza in 1965. After being brutally raped on 6 July 1879 in her village, Caldas de Reyes, she went first to France and then to New York (1890) where she initiated her artistic career as a music-hall dancer to become one of the most desired women in Europe (1891) during the *Belle Époque* (1889–1914). She

made herself up as a legendary 'passionate Spanish woman' (her real name was Agustina) and was famous for wasting her lovers' money at roulette. Among her lovers were the Princes of Wales, Leopold of Belgium, Nicolás II, Alberto of Mónaco, Alfonso XIII, and Maurice Chevalier. When she was 46, having loved no one, la Bella Otero disappeared so as not to be seen aging (Posadas 2001).

8. Thierry Kuntzel notes that 'fade outs are conspicuous signs of rupture, articulation, enunciation; *culminative* with respect to the sequence as a whole' (1980: 11).

9. El pasodoble is a twentieth-century recreation of Spanish popular dance music that is associated not only with tauromachy but also with modern Spanish wedding parties. It can be argued that the film qualifies this music as both masculine (it is first heard in this male-centred narrative sequence to become the male protagonist's musical motif) and exotic (it is heard in a science-fictional context both at the level of the visual [*Blade Runner*] and at the level of the narrative [Spain is represented as a Republic]). It could also be added that the absence of 'woman' from this heterosexual dance-music scenario, functions to qualify 'science-fictional masculinity', embodied by the male character, itself exotic.

10. In the credits, this character is described as 'viejo vicioso'.

11. We see a series of shots of 'the Mother' holding the knife up before directing it down toward Ms. Lidia's body (off-screen) as well as a series of shots of the blood splashing on the wallpaper and on a crucifix hanging on the wall.

12. A narcissistic other is not necessarily from the same sex as the subject (Freud 1914).

13. Lola asks her 'fake' hand-mirror: 'little mirror, little mirror, who is the most beautiful girl in the world?'; and she answers herself with the words: 'You Lola, you are the most beautiful woman on earth.'

14. I would like to thank both my mother, Amelia, and her friend, Candelas, for this piece of information.

15. 1940s Hollywood films included in this category are *Rebecca* (Alfred Hitchcock, 1940), *Suspicion* (Alfred Hitchcock, 1941), *Gaslight* (George Cukor, 1944), *When Strangers Marry/Betrayed* (William Castle, 1944), *Dragonwyck* (Joseph L. Mankiewicz, 1946), *Undercurrent* (Vicente Minnelli, 1946), *The Two Mrs. Carrolls* (Peter Godfrey, 1947), *Secret Beyond the Door* (Fritz Lang, 1948), or *Caught* (Max Ophuls, 1949).

16. In the 1940s Hollywood films mentioned above, the dark side of the protagonist's seductive and fatally attractive male lover becomes

apparent for the protagonist at some point in the film. After a sudden marriage (conventionally after two weeks of dream-like acquaintance) and while in the marital Gothic mansion, the female protagonist comes to know that her husband wants to kill her or drive her insane.

17. See Bruno Bettelheim's analysis of the female's Oedipal scenario in the Cinderella story (Bettelheim 1976).
18. Manderley is the name of the Gothic mansion in *Rebecca*.
19. Anxiety is an 'internal' sign that warns the subject that the fulfilment of the drives is *too* close (Freud 1919–1920 [1920]: 281–2).
20. I would like to express my gratitude to both Miguel Angel Martín and Marcos Monge for their narrative-reading suggestions and musical descriptions of this sequence.
21. Throughout the film this male character embodies tragic-comic 'contemporary gender trouble'. In a fancy-dress party, celebrated the evening Ms. Lidia was murdered, the heterosexual Pelayo falls in love with 'a woman' disguised as a 'female lion tamer' that turns out to be a transvestite.
22. For an analysis of the relationship between the classic detective and his companion in terms of transference, see Slavoj Zizek (1991: 58). For an analysis of the homoerotic relationships between characters in film noir, see Richard Dyer's work (1978).
23. As a finalist of the Miss Spain contest, when she is asked about her ideal of beauty, Lola answers: 'I think that what really counts is the beauty inside oneself. That is why my ideal of beauty is Mother Theresa of Calcutta. She was really beautiful because her beauty was spiritual. I think that all women in the world should resemble her.'
24. Here I am indebted to Vicente Mira for his lecture on Freud's 'The Uncanny' (11 June 2003, Colegio de Psicoanálisis, Madrid).
25. 'El bolero' is a type of popular music that deals with love matters. The first bolero is considered to be *Tristezas* by José 'Pepe' Sánchez (Cuba, 1886).
26. 'between the shot and the backshot the bar that separates the man from the woman is marked out, defining at the same time, in the same axis, at the point of convergence of the two diagonal looks, the place of the third one' (González Requena 1993: 249).
27. The origin of this custom is properly modern. It began in 1909 as a marketing campaign designed by harvesters to sell their grape stocks.

Psychoanalysis of La mujer más fea del mundo

References

Baudrillard, Jean (1985), 'The masses: the implosion of the social in the media', in Stephen Duncombe (ed.), *Cultural Resistance Reader*, London and New York: Verso.

Bettelheim, Bruno (1976), *The Uses of Enchantment: The Meaning and Importance of Fairy Tales*, London: Thames & Hudson.

Copjec, Joan (1993), 'The Phenomenal Nonphenomenal: Private Space in *Film Noir*', in Joan Copjec (ed.), *Shades of Noir*, London: Verso.

——(1994), *Read my Desire: Lacan against the Historicists*, Cambridge MA and London: MIT Press.

Cowie, Elizabeth (1993), 'Film Noir and Women', in Joan Copjec (ed.), *Shades of Noir*, London: Verso.

Dyer, Richard (1978), 'Resistance through charisma: Rita Hayworth and Gilda', in E. Ann Kaplan (ed.), *Women in Film Noir*, London: BFI, 1994.

Freud, Sigmund (1914), 'On Narcissism: An Introduction', in Sigmund Freud, *Papers on Metaphyschology*, Pelican Freud Library 11, Harmondsworth: Penguin, 1984.

——(1917 [1918]), 'The taboo of virginity (Contributions to the psychology of love, III)', in *The Standard Edition of the Complete Psychological Works of Sigmund Freud*, vol. 11, 1953–1966, London: Hogarth.

——(1919–1920 [1920]), 'Beyond the Pleasure Principle', in Sigmund Freud, *Papers on Metapsychology,* Pelican Freud Library 11, Harmondsworth: Penguin, 1984.

González Requena, Jesús (1993), 'Casablanca: The classical film', in *Archivos de la Filmoteca*, 14, June: 238–49.

Kaplan, E. Ann (1998), 'Introduction to New Edition', in *Women in Film Noir*, new edn, London: BFI.

Krutnik, Frank (1991), *In a Lonely Street: Film Noir, Genre, Masculinity*, London and NY: Routledge.

Kuhn, Annette (1990), 'Introduction: Cultural Theory and Science Fiction Cinema', in Annette Kuhn (ed.), *Alien Zone: Cultural Theory and Contemporary Science Fiction Cinema*, London and New York: Verso, 2000.

Kuntzel, Thierry (1980), 'The Film-Work, 2', in *Camera Obscura*, 5. Translated by Nancy Huston, 6–69.

Lacan, Jacques (1953–54), *El Seminario de Jacques Lacan. Libro 1. Los escritos técnicos de Freud*, trans. Rithee Cevasco and Vicente Mira. Barcelona and Buenos Aires: Paidós, 1983.

Eva Parrondo Coppel

Martínez Montalbán, José Luis (2000), 'Cine para leer 1999', Equipo Reseña (ed.), Bilbao: Mensajero.
Metz, Christian (1977). *Psychoanalysis and Cinema: The Imaginary Signifier*, Translated by Celia Britton et al. London: Macmillan, 1990.
Posadas, Carmen (2001), *La Bella Otero*, Barcelona: Planeta.
Read, Jacinda (2000), *The New Avengers: Feminism, Femininity and the Rape-revenge Cycle*, Manchester and New York: Manchester University Press.
Roberts, Stephen (1999), 'In Search of a New Spanish Realism: Bardem's *Calle Mayor* (1956)', in Peter William Evans (ed.), *Spanish Cinema. The Auteurist Tradition*, Oxford and New York: Oxford University Press.
Straayer, Chris (1998), '*Femme Fatale* or Lesbian Femme: *Bound* in Sexual *Différance*', in E. Ann Kaplan (ed.), *Women in Film Noir*, London: BFI.
Turim, Maureen (1989), *Flashbacks in Film: Memory and History*, New York and London: Routledge.
Zizek, Slavoj (1989), *The Sublime Object of Ideology*, London and New York: Verso, 1998.
——(1991), *Looking Awry: An Introduction to Jacques Lacan through Popular Culture*, Cambridge MA: MIT Press, 2000.
——(1993), '"The Thing that Thinks": The Kantian Background of the Noir Subject', in Joan Copjec (ed.), *Shades of Noir*, London: Verso.
——(1997), *The Plague of Fantasies*, London and New York: Verso.

–9–

Gender and Spanish Horror Film
Tatjana Pavlovic

The invisible man

'I'm going to shoot the perfect film. No plot. Only victims.' This line, spoken by Paul Muller, a psychotic film director from the film *Eugénie de Sade* by Spanish director Jess Franco, would immediately be recognized by the director's fans, but most Spaniards would not know them, the film they come from, or even the film-maker. Jesús Franco, better known as Jess Franco, has made low-budget horror, science fiction, thriller, muscle-man epic, and pornographic films since 1957 and is mostly esteemed in obscure film circles outside his native country (especially in the USA and Germany).[1]

During the screening of his movie *El hundimiento de la casa Usher* at Madrid's 'Imagfic' film festival in 1989, the audience booed and then walked out.[2] Still, despite that disastrous encounter with the Spanish public, a few of his fans managed to organize a retrospective of his work in 1991.[3] Although the retrospective screened some of his best work, Franco remains a largely invisible figure in Spanish film history. Even after the dictatorship ended, he remained unknown, among other things because of Pilar Miró's preposterous classification standards for Spanish films.[4] Most of those film-makers who did not meet her standards of 'quality' were ostracized and therefore financially doomed to obscurity. This marginalization is startling (since he has made over 150 films in a career that spans five decades) but also somewhat understandable (since they are exploitation flicks from various genres that might not appeal to most viewers, critics, and an academic audience). It is also comprehensible since Jess Franco made films that 'display sensations that are on the edge of the respectable' and his opus largely focuses on 'pornography, the lowest in cultural esteem and gross-out horror, next to lowest' (Williams, 1999: 267, 269).

Tatjana Pavlovic

In contrast to his family's association with high-brow culture (his relatives include philosopher Julián Marías, musicologist Enrique Franco, writer Javier Marías, and the late film director Ricardo Franco), Jess Franco's sensibility for low-brow culture and a taste for the bizarre was evident very early in his career. During his student years in Madrid he earned extra money by writing horror stories and western serials. These student writings already envisioned the world of eccentric and unconventional characters that would later become his characteristically outlandish cinematic milieu. After a few years studying law and music, he left university to enrol in the Madrid Film School (officially named the IIEC [Instituto de Investigaciones y Experiencias Cinematográficas]) which he never finished either. The friendships formed in IIEC led to the work on the production of *Cómicos* and his first 'serious' engagement with Spanish cinema. He also worked on government-sponsored documentaries such as *Arbol de España*; that as he himself puts it was 'a bizarre and unusual short (film) about the life and miracles of the olive tree' (Freixas 1994: 41). Later, he was hired by a number of 1950 Spanish directors and he performed various odd jobs including script writing, editing, and music scoring.

Franco also had connections with a group that would produce the oppositional film magazine *Objetivo,* whose debates on film culminated in the Salamanca congress, but whose political and aesthetic preoccupations he never shared.[5] Instead, throughout his career Franco indulged three of his most gleeful obsessions: pop art, pornography and horror. By exploiting images of monstrosity and excess and by exploring the connection of pleasure to cinematic experience, he undermined and disturbed official discourse, rather than opposing it in classic leftist fashion. Further, as an exploitation film-maker, he actually explores the extremes of the cinematic medium itself, 'the spectacle of a body caught in the grip of intense sensations' and 'the pleasure and agitation of flesh' (Shaviro 1995; Williams 1999).

The Dread of Difference (Franco and Feminist Film Criticism)

Independent horror director Lawrence Woollsey, pausing for a rest while driving through Florida on a promotional tour for his newest movie, unexpectedly finds inspiration in a small roadside sculpture of an alligator. Always looking to an angle to exploit, Woollsey begins to muse on the title of his next work: 'Manigator ... ali-man; she-gator ... gator-girl'. Then, after a pause, he announces triumphantly: 'Gal-igator'.

The independent horror director Lawrence Woollsey was modelled on self-styled schlockmeister of horror William Castle but the character described could easily have been Jesús Franco himself. The scene described is from *Matinee* (1993), a homage to B horror movies of the 1950s, and it is recounted by Barry Keith Grant in his edited volume on gender and horror film to exemplify the extent to which the horror film is preoccupied with the issues of sexual difference (Grant 1996).

Written almost thirty years ago, Laura Mulvey's essay on visual pleasure in narrative cinema centred on the issue of a dominant male gaze and problematized relations of gender, power, and spectatorship in cinema. As Susan Martín-Márquez suggests, Mulvey's argument has been 'refined, revised, rejected, and recycled by successive waves of feminist film theorists' (1999: 14). Recent scholarship on horror film has focused on elaborating and complicating figurations of gender and the positioning of gender spectatorship, thereby departing from the rigidity of certain assumptions about gender binarism in the horror film. The earlier simplifications are understandable, especially in a genre in which the revered 'pioneers' themselves insisted that 'women in peril work better in the suspense genre' (Brian de Palma); 'I would much prefer to watch beautiful women being murdered than an ugly girl or a man' (Dario Argento); 'I always believe in following the advice of the playwright Sardou. He said "Torture the women"' (Alfred Hitchcock) (Clover 1999: 234).[6]

In the theorization of horror film, Barbara Creed's, Linda Williams's, and Carol Clover's work still holds prominence. Creed has argued for the centrality of articulations of a 'monstrous-feminine' across the horror genre, emphasizing oscillation in possible identifications for both male and female spectators between victim and monster. Linda Williams points to the 'surprising (and at times subversive) affinity between monster and woman, in the sense in which her look at the monster recognizes their similar status within patriarchal structure of seeing' (1996: 18). Clover, meanwhile, points out that the spectatorial experience for the genre's primarily male audience is a 'feminizing' one, requiring a level of identification with feminine figures in distress with emphasis on one's own passivity, humiliation, and penetration. She questions feminist film theory's insistence on the male gaze as sadistic and privileges a masochistic dimension of male voyeurism (a theoretical move deriving from Deleuze's work on masochism [Deleuze: 1991]). Clover has also argued for the crucial importance of fluidity and uncertainty in figuration of gender. She argues 'against the temptation to read body in question as "really" male (masquerading as female) or "really" female (masquerading as male), suggesting instead that the excitement is precisely predicated on the undecideability or both-andness or one-sexness of the construction' (1992: 217).

Jess Franco's work often foregrounds ambiguities of gender and sexuality and suggests the instability of power relations implied by acts of looking and perceiving corresponding to critical positions laid out by Clover, Williams, Creed and other recent feminist re-evaluations of the genre. Franco gave Spanish cinema many interesting female figures and created remarkable and unusual heroines: women detectives, female and lesbian vampires and women killers. He played with the gender conventions of the genres he worked in and times he inhabited. In his horror opus he gave the audience Miss Muerte, a spider woman trapping and killing her victims in her web; Melissa, a bloodthirsty, blind Bird-Woman; cruel and unstoppable Irina, and so on, thus subverting the traditional horror film formula in which 'the killer has over time been variously figured as shark, fog, gorilla, birds, and slime, [and] the victim is eternally and prototypically the damsel' (Clover 1999: 234).

Already his very first feature film *Tenemos 18 años* (1959) cleverly uses the horror genre to reflect upon familial relationships, gender, and the demarcation of limits of womanhood. *Tenemos 18 años* is a girls' road/horror film centring on women's bonding that was an anomaly in the era in which it was filmed. If anything, Spanish screens were saturated by male-bonding films that focused mainly on the rites of passage from boyhood to manhood, marginalizing women into the domestic sphere so crucial to the Francoist ideological project.

The main characters (María José and Pili) undertake the road trip trading the enclosed space of the home for an expansive one of the road, leaving both literarily and metaphorically the site of paternal authority. The film's focus on the father figure culminates in the confrontation with the most captivating imaginary character, the mysterious Lord Marian. María José and Pili's confrontation with Lord Marian blends elements of thriller and horror films, focuses on incestuous fears and desires, and is a 'tale of sex and parents' (Clover 1999: 239). Lord Marian, a surrogate father figure, enables María José and Pili to assert their sexual autonomy and 'deliver themselves into the adult world' (Clover 1999: 239). This encounter enacts the 'parenticidal struggle' in which 'one's parents must be killed and re-killed in the service of sexual autonomy' (Clover 1999: 239). The film's focus on paternal authority could also be read as an implicit reference to Francisco Franco, the dictator, the 'monstrous Father of all Spaniards' (Geist 1983: 38).

While Franco's first feature film explored hybridity of genres (horror, road film, thriller) and created archetypes for many of Franco's future horror monsters (Dr Orloff, Dr Zimmer, Jack the Ripper, Morpho, and so on), *Miss Muerte*, a striking black and white film from 1965 notable for its chiaroscuro lighting and explorations of monstrosity, marks Franco's venture into the classical horror film with its iconography of mad scientists, gothic castles, full-length dresses and cloaks, velvet curtains, magnetic vampires and mute servants.

The two main characters are Irma, the daughter of the late Doctor von Zimmer – a misunderstood medical genius who discovers how to control people's minds – and Nadia, a nightclub singer and performer better known as Miss Muerte. (In her act she is a spider woman who traps and kills her victims in her web.) Irma's obsession lies in avenging her father's death suffered as a result of humiliation and belittlement by his superiors on the Medical Board. Using her father's discovery of mind manipulation, Irma takes control of Nadia and directs her to kill the members of the Medical Board one by one.

Nadia meets Dr Vicas, the first victim, in a train, lures him to her compartment, blinds him and slits his throat with her poisoned fingernails. The second victim, Dr Moroni, dies in a similar way, first blinded and then killed. The murders of the first two members of the medical board send a wave of panic through the city. The last victim, Dr Kallman, locks himself inside his house, but to no avail, meeting the same fate as his colleagues. Meanwhile Nadia's fiancé Dr Philip Fraser (a famous criminologist) unearths the connection between the late Dr von Zimmer's experiments on the human mind and his fiancée's disappearance. He is too late to prevent the last crime but, knowing how to liberate Nadia from the mind-control device, manages to 'save' her from Irma. Franco leaves us with a very ambiguous ending. Even though Nadia's fiancé boasts of knowledge to free Nadia from mind control, they are last seen in an embrace in which Nadia's sharp fingernails are dangerously close to his neck.

Miss Muerte explores female sexuality as monstrous (monster coded as feminine) and illuminates anxieties about uncontrollable female power. The beautiful, sexually active woman is not the victim – she is the killer. At the same time we see Nadia's victims, professional men, coded as powerful and masterful, screaming, fleeing and dying. They are marked by 'abject terror gendered feminine: crying, cowering, screaming, fainting, trembling, begging for mercy' (Clover 1999: 240). The focus shifts from the scientific, voyeuristic gaze of all three men (victims) to their threatened, frightened eyes. The camera closes in on the pleading victim, who looks at Nadia's fingernails as they plunge into his eyes. Ghoulishly, men's sexual approach lines ('you have such extraordinary nails') lead them to their own destruction. Those very nails that magnetize them are the weapons by which their bodies are fragmented, penetrated and destroyed. The nails assault not just the victims, but as Hitchcock expressively put it: 'The slashing... An impression of a knife slashing, [is] as if tearing at the very screen, ripping the film.' Not just the body is to be ruptured, but also the body on the other side of the film and screen: our witnessing body' (quoted in Clover 1999: 242).

Miss Muerte is the horrifying image that intrudes into the 'proper' sphere. This is especially explicit in the case of the last victim, killed in his own domestic domain. If we accept Creed's proposition that 'the function of the monstrous is to bring about an encounter between the symbolic order and that which threatens its stability', Nadia disturbs the symbolic order supported by science, claims to knowledge, and respectable professions (Creed 1999: 253). Nadia's monstrosity is rela-tional to her ability to disturb boundaries between the proper and the improper, the use and abuse of science, acceptable and unacceptable sexuality, and so on.

The ending of *Miss Muerte* is open. The spectators never find out if the poisonous nails of Miss Muerte are about to tease her fiancé's neck or kill him, disposing of yet another male character. Franco, therefore, breaks with the formula for the conventional horror film ending where 'the plot halts and horror ceases. Day breaks, and the community returns to its normal order' (Clover 1999: 240). The horror narrative ends with the restoration of boundaries, but Franco plays with these conventions in a manner that defies conventional expectations. Instead of redrawing the boundaries that threatened the stability of symbolic order, he posits yet another menacing situation.

Although many of Franco's films successfully twisted genre con-ventions, he also created many 'irredeemable' gal-igators, especially after 1973, when his most interesting and innovative features such as blending horror and eroticism were rapidly dissipating into soft porn and, eventually, into hard-core pornography. His films also became less interesting technically and visually as a result of financial constraints that called for faster and faster production, the overuse of zoom, and mediocre actors. Thus, my analysis does not pretend to posit sexploitation/exploitation/horror/B production cinema, such as Franco's, solely as the site of feminist resistance.

However, Jess Franco's films have a significant female following. On the one hand, the attractiveness of his cinema lies in the gender mix of his victims, his hero/ines, and stalkers that open up space for the exploration of the fundamental instability of identifications along lines of gender, sex, and sexual preference. On the other hand, the appeal is clearly due to the films themselves (apart from directorial intentions) and the ability of popular cultures' to recycle, appropriate and put them to divergent and oppositional uses.

Jess Franco's films became a multiple site of female pleasure; offering enjoyment to the female spectator as much as to the male. Female fans seem to enjoy the interesting variations and twists of his sexploitation/ exploitation flicks, such as vampires that suck life out of their victims' penises. This scenario can obviously be read as a predictable male fantasy. But the structure of male fantasy is progressively undone; the victims are killed precisely at the moment of displaying their phallic hardness. Instead of the logical outcome (as in a traditional porn) of visible penile ejaculations as proof of pleasure we see (sadistic) pleasure-in-power and renunciation of love for pure pleasure (see Williams 1989). In hetero-sexual pornography 'it is the female body in the grips of an out-of-control ecstasy that has offered the most sensational sight', thus Franco perverts it giving us the sight of dying, convulsed male body (Williams 1999: 270). As Linda Williams also points out, 'non-sadomasochistic pornography has historically been one of the few types of popular film that has not punished women for actively pursuing their sexual pleasure' (1999: 274).

The lesbian following centres on Franco's lesbian vampires and WIP ('women in prison') genres such as *99 Women*, *Barbed Wire Dolls*, *Visa pour Mourir* and *Jailhouse Wardress* that especially appeal to the gay audience, with their campy legacy of sadistic wardresses, (female) dictators with strong sexual appetites, innocent young women corrupted in jail, cruel lesbian guards, and so on.

Horror Body/The Body of Horror

Besides focusing on the questions of eroticism, voyeurism, violence, power and disempowerment, Franco also explores the connection to bodies, sensations, pleasures, and affects. Horror film significantly and obsessively centres on the body, bodily substances and its crude materiality: skin, muscles, bones, hair, eyes, viscera and so on. The question of the body is marked by ambiguity: on the one hand there is the desire to keep the inside hidden, thus 'we patch and bandage wounds' (Elkins 1999: 111). The history of bandages involves sutures, knots, staples, pins, bolts, clamps, and other devices, all intended to make an airtight closure" (Ibid.: 114). On the other hand there is an 'intense preoccupation with skin and with the possibility of scratching it away, tearing it off, or seeing through it' (Ibid.: 118).

To tear the skin off and to see through it is connected to the desire to know. Penetration of the body was often (if not always) the object of medical inquiry, merging violent intrusion with discourses of knowledge and power. The mind's desire to analyse and the eye's desire to pierce and separate are kindred motions. Franco's innumerable doctor characters examine, re-examine, probe, categorize, and dissect, reminding us of the 'confluence of words for dissection, seeing, and thought' (Ibid.: 127) since 'dissection is an especially powerful tool: literally, it is a medical specialty, with its own terms and techniques distinct from surgery; figuratively, it can stand for any act of systematic analysis, from a tentative "probe" to the "sharpest" critique' (Ibid.: 126).

In Franco's *Awful Dr Orlow*, filmed in 1961, Dr Orloff is a respectable doctor gone mad because of his disfigured daughter and his unsuccessful attempts to reconstruct her face. The madness only intensifies his obsession with body parts (tissue, nerves, membranes) and leads him to flay his victims and tear off their skin. Hence, Dr Orloff is also a peculiar kind of artist (a body artist): with flayed skin he sculpts, refashions and reconstructs. The medical and artistic gaze converge in a surgical fashioning of a face.

In Franco's cinema the doctor with artistic sensibility has a counterpart in the artist with medical curiosity. Tony Sordi, a protagonist of *Blood of the Vampire*, is Dr Orloff's inverted image. He is not an ordinary artist but one that desires 'to paint the flesh' itself. The doctor and the artist share a stubborn relentless desire to see and penetrate everything and to make everything representable. These themes are of course not new, grounded as they are in a Western epistemological framework: its ways of seeing, categorizing, and thinking. The violent inquiry into the body (and violent alterations of body) has always been invested by and with power mechanisms. Moreover the relationship between dissection and dissected, poking and poked and painting and painted adds the element of gender to the matrix of power relations.

But as James Elkins points out, there are 'few pictures of the living body [that] open the skin and reveal what is inside' because 'the inside of the body is a powerful sign of death' (1999: 109). Tony Sordi and Dr Orloff pay with their lives for probing too closely into 'the incomprehensibility of flesh, and its close proximity with the inconceivability of death' (Ibid.: 29). At the end of the film the painted figures surface from the canvas and the dissected rise from the operating table. Putrefied/decomposed creatures revive and take revenge. The creatures are uncanny, half coated in plaster, their human form and gender almost unrecognizable. They are hideous and grotesque in their troubling plasticity, their agonizing groans and grunts and contorted faces. Their 'uncanny' look proceeds directly from 'the uncanniness of the corpse, which trespasses on the place of the living until it is buried' (Ibid.: 134). Thus the films ends with yet another powerful and indispensable subject of horror films: the living dead (zombies), their unproper burials, and their return.

El extraño viaje (1964)

Jess Franco's work stretches from 1957 to the present. He is a marginalized body that disrupts Spanish official cinema throughout his prolific career; the official body of cinema disregarded him but he created his own extraordinary bodies: the pop-art body, the horror body, and the pornographic body. The horror body is mutilated and reconstructed; the science body merges uncontrollably with its surroundings and it is also endlessly enlarged and reshaped; the superhero's body is idealized, the female body becomes an irresistible force of destruction, and so on.

Jess Franco's approach to film-making is one of total immersion, to the point of obsession. Not only are his plots themselves obsessive, but themes echo obsessively from one film to the next. Tim Lucas notes that 'in a sense, Franco's entire oeuvre is a serial composed of recurring actors, characters, songs, and obsessions. You can't see one Franco film until you've seen them all because, without that information, your set of references is incomplete' (in Balbo 1993: 29). Franco's do-it-yourself approach to film-making – in which he not only directs the film, but also acts in it, and photographs and edits it himself – only accentuates this effect further. Franco's first screen appearance was as the childish and idiotic Venancio in Fernando Fernán Gómez's *El extraño viaje*. Franco's brilliant performance in this film is followed by several captivating and absorbing roles in his other films. In *El caso de dos bellezas* Franco is the awkward art-gallery guard Napoleon Bolivard; in *Bésame monstruo* he is a messenger who gets stabbed to death; in *El misterio del castillo rojo* he is a mad scientist who creates a new race of powerful zombies; in *Barbed Wire Dolls* he is slapped to death by his daughter and he dies in slow motion; in *Exorcism and Black Masses* he is a serial killer; in *Cartas boca arriba* he is a pianist and we also hear his voice through loudspeakers at the bus station advertising a Godard film. In *She killed in ecstasy* he is one of the hunted Medical Board members who gets tortured to death; in *El muerto hace las maletas* he is a knife specialist; in *Vals para un asesino* he plays the hippy guru Kookoo who rambles about an imminent apocalypse; and in *Macumba sexual*, Franco is a hotel-keeper who collects stuffed fish and plays Peeping Tom. These eccentric cameos culminate in Franco himself becoming one of his own horror-film characters, the 'monster with the camera'. Howard Vernon recalls that: 'As I used to watch him working, with his camera on his shoulder – for he usually did the camera-work himself – I would get the impression that here was a very strange being indeed, a creature with two heads and three eyes, the inseparable union of the mind and the art of cinema' (in Balbo 1993: 11).

His eccentric cameos are almost overshadowed by Franco's real life. It is often repeated that he indeed was a monster in his profession. Very often he would shoot several films at once and then sell them to several different distributors. Monica Swinn, one of the actresses that often appeared in his films recalls reading a typical Franco script: 'I'd mull over the previous scenes and think to myself, "this can't be the same character"; "how many films am I really making?"' (in Balbo 1993: 223).[7]

Swinn's anecdote reminds us that Jess Franco's career is rooted in a very specific historical moment and is tied to the larger phenomenon of the European co-production boom, in the late 1960s, that indeed relied on 'monstrous' directors capable of shooting several films at the same time. Thus, Jess Franco's opus, conspicuous in his absence, besides probing questions of gender and problematizing boundaries of genres with which he worked, also disturbs the boundaries of national film production. The international production and circulation of Franco's low-budget, cult, trash, B-production, and sexploitation films have transnational implications posing questions about co-productions, market, and movements across national borders. His *in-corporation* might thus bring an interesting angle to existing discourses on Spanish cinema, unsettling notions of national specificity. It can also shed light on the production of national cinema in catering to an elite audience and its insistence on 'aesthetic quality', 'good taste', 'art', and 'culture'. All the above problematics are also accentuated by Jess Franco's status as cult film director since 'the cult movie is a "supertext", lacking fixed limits and favoring boundary crossing or territorial violations' (Smith 1994: 31).[8] His cult followers scattered around the world problematize notions of the local, global, domestic, foreign and their interplay.

A few years ago, during the Paris film festival (after the screening of *Todo sobre mi madre*, 1999) Pedro Almodóvar was asked to select a Spanish film that had had a profound impact on him. Almodóvar chose precisely Fernán Gómez's *El extraño viaje*, which he classified as 'rural terror and cruel *zarzuela*', in his words: 'one of the strangest cult films and one of the most rarely seen in our national cinematography' (quoted in Strauss 2001: 55). Almodóvar points out that the film's importance in Spanish cinema lies in the fact that it stands out conspicuously amid the avalanche of *comedias playeras* or beach comedies that accompanied the economic and tourist boom of the early 1960s.

Besides standing out from dominant film production, *El extraño viaje* also ends with a memorable image: 'the only beach that appears in the film exhibits the corpses of two fat, ugly drunken siblings' (Almodóvar quoted in Strauss 2001: 55). One of the corpses on the beach is precisely that of the character played by Jess Franco. Like this disturbing corpse on the beach Franco functions (in Spanish cinema) as a stain which smears the picture and disturbs its transparency, a stain which blurs the field of vision. It is in Zizek's words a 'detail [that] always contains some surplus which undermines the universal frame' and 'holds the place of certain formal disturbance' (Zizek 1992: 119, 120). He creates the effect of what Lacan calls *the point de capiton* ([the quilting point]): 'a perfectly familiar situation is denatured ... as soon as we add to it a small supplementary feature, a detail that does not belong, that sticks out, is out of place, does not make any sense within the frame...' (Zizek 1991: 88).

Jesús Franco's presence among other more canonical texts and figures complicates neat readings and problematizes notions of sexuality, gender, and the nation. His incorporation (see Marsh 2002 and Martin-Márquez 1999) is conceived as conceptual and theoretical, exploration and experimentation. His figure helps us to rethink, reconceptualize, at times disentangle, and at times complicate the study of Spanish culture from 1950s to the present.

The Two Francos

'Someone told me one day that I was Spain personified: Jesus Christ and *Caudillo*' (Jess Franco, cited in Seguin 1995). Through his fictional alter ego, a psychotic film director, Franco once described his ideal film as containing 'no plot, only victims'. This aesthetic and ideological ideal is the direct opposite of Francisco Franco's conception of national cinema. Jess Franco's rejection of Francoist cinema with its insistence on proper plotting of the nation is marked by the wacky sense of humour seen in his deconstruction of one of Francisco Franco's favourite post-war films, *Los últimos de Filipinas*. He filmed instead *Las últimas de Filipinas*, an elaborate pun that in spite of its apparent simplicity (Jess Franco simply alters the gender of the subject from masculine to feminine), also changes genre (from heroic military epic to pornography) and problematizes, in hitherto unheard of fashion, the exotic and the oriental. Such juxtaposition was Jess Franco's response to the jaded clichés of heroism, death, duty and law. Pornographic sexploitation stands cheek-by-jowl with a heroic genre that profoundly marked the Spanish post-war period. Placing these two texts side by side can produce peculiar angles, illuminate unaccustomed patterns and provoke unexpected configurations.

In multiple ways, Jesús Franco appears as almost the inverted, ironic figure of his namesake, Generalísimo Francisco Franco. The dictator's interest in film-making, to the point of even making an autobiographical movie (*Raza*, 1941), is well known. Jesús Franco's interest in horror, in pornography, and in the pulp imagery of superspies and musclemen, can be seen as an effort to represent all that the Fascist government had officially repressed. His self-portrayals, in figures such as the crazed Catholic priest, might be regarded as an acting out of those aspects of Francisco Franco's life that the official, whitewashed, cinematic version had deliberately left out. Jesús Franco's films enact a return of Fascism's repressed, the playing out of the delirium from which that political order drew its energy, but had to disavow in the name of normality, Catholic morality, and political and familial order.

In addition to all of the above, Francisco Franco could have also been a character in one of Jess Franco's films. Francisco Franco's last years in power and painful death contain all the conventions of the horror film. Various corporeal alterations and bodily fluids marked his end: marble skin, putrefying flesh, blood, saliva, sweat, and tears. Was not the dictator himself 'the body besides itself', 'the spectacle of a body caught in the grip of intense sensation or emotion' (Williams 1999: 269) with his uncontrollable bursting into tears, excessive and unstoppable bleeding and with the tics that accompany Parkinson's disease (endless trembling, shaking, involuntary movement of the eyelids)?

As in Shakespeare's *Richard II* discussed by Zizek 'whereby the king loses the second, sublime body that made him a king', Francisco Franco at the end of his life lost the second, sublime body that made him a dictator. He was 'confronted with the void of his subjectivity outside the symbolic mandate-title "king" (dictator) and is thus forced into a series of theatrical, hysterical outbursts' (Zizek 1991: 9; see also Pavlovic 2003). Franco also became the monstrous, terrifying, horrific, and abject. 'A bloodstained doll' carried on a carpet to one of his last operations:

> Because we couldn't get a cot down around the curve of the staircase we
> carried the body down from the bed in a rug [...] In that makeshift ambulance,
> I would dare to say, we were transporting a human doll, a man wrapped up in
> a rug, bleeding. But that person was the head of state ... that body we were
> carrying was *Generalísimo* Franco (Prego 1995: 294).

His abjection manifested itself, according to Kristeva's definition, as one
that does not 'respect borders, positions, rules', as seen through Franco's
bewilderment and confusion over limits and identities (Kristeva 1982:
4). Franco's lack of respect for borders from the very beginning of his
regime made him appear like some alien, horrific creature that entered
the entrails of Spain. Ernesto Giménez Caballero's notorious statement
in *La Hora* (1948) suggested that the boundary between Franco's body
and that of the entire country was unclear: 'Franco has penetrated the
entrails of Spain to the point at which one can't know any more if Franco
is Spain or Spain is Franco' (quoted in Martín Gaite 1987: 19). Entrails
are one of the essential elements of horror flicks, sources of disgust
and pain; they are often extirpated crudely. He was also a living dead, a
zombie with 'cold and marbled skin' who on the verge of death declared
that his final horrifying wish was to embrace all Spaniards for the last
time 'to shout with them one last time on the threshold of death: "¡Arriba
España!" "!Viva España!"' (Prego 1995: 326).

This (his)story and the story of Spain inscribed by the dictatorship
of Francisco Franco ends with a historical irony enveloping both horror
and pornography. According to Paul Preston the Franco family estate at
Valdefuentes fell into disrepair a matter of five years after the dictator's
death 'Under the management of Franco's oldest grandson, Francisco
Franco Martínez-Bordiu, its prosperity trickled away to nothing and it
became the location for horror and pornographic films' (Preston 1994:
781). Thus history and time have come to 'legitimize' tying together
the dictator and his lesser-known namesake. Francisco Franco and Jess
Franco meet through the abject, 'the place where meaning collapses',
underlining the point that 'social reality is nothing but a fragile, symbolic
cobweb' and pointing to the fragility of the symbolic order that sustained
the Franco dictatorship (Zizek 1991: 17). 'Reality' must be constantly
reinterpreted. To understand it and its intricacies the (his)story of Franco
and Spain needs complicating by the juxtaposition of 'unlikely' figures
and 'looked at awry' since 'a detail of a picture that "gaz'd rightly", that is
straightforwardly, appears as a blurred spot, assumes clear, distinguished
shapes once we look at it "awry", at an angle' (Zizek 1991: 11).

Notes

1. In 1954 he was a screenwriter for *El Coyote* (Joaquín Romero Marchent) and director's assistant on *Cómicos* (Juan Antonio Bardem). He also wrote music scores for *Cómicos*. His first short film was *Arbol de España* in 1957 and first feature film *Tenemos 18 años* in 1959.
2. Carlos Aguilar, a Spanish film critic, recounts this story in his 'Tribute to Jess Franco' (Aguilar 1993: 248).
3. Carlos Aguilar was again a key figure in this homage and without him and a couple of other Spanish enthusiasts of Franco, this retrospective would never have taken place.
4. The Miró Law of 1983 'provided pre-production subventions for those projects deemed good enough to merit official funding' (Martí-Olivella 1997: 217). They were frequently expensive, ponderous, often period literary adaptations, technically proficient but soulless. See Martí-Olivella. Also see Peter Besas who writes that The Miró Law 'lavished funds upon "serious" film-makers' and where "entertainment and commercial became dirty words' (Besas 1997: 247).
5. *Objetivo*, a progressive, left-wing film journal was founded in May of 1953.
6. Clover adds that these statements are all elaborations/variations on Poe's famous statement that 'the most poetical topic in the whole world is the death of a beautiful woman'.
7. This paradox was seen in the films of the period, which were actually shot and edited in two different versions, one for domestic consumption, and one for international export. As Diego Galán observes 'passionate kissing scenes were shot for the external market and only tender smiles for the Spanish spectators' (Galán 1989: 216).
8. Paul Julian Smith is citing J.P. Tellotte's 'Introduction' from *The Cult Film Experience*. Smith uses it in his discussion of Almodóvar's *Labyrinth of Passion*. See Smith's chapter 'Laberinto de pasiones: Cult Film Experiences' in Smith 1994.

References

Aguilar, Carlos (1993), 'Tribute to Jess Franco', in Lucas Balbo (ed.), *Obsession: The Films of Jess Franco*, Berlin: Frank Trebbin.
Almodóvar, Pedro (2001), 'Una sórdida comedia neosurrealista', in Frédéric Strauss (ed.), *Conversaciones con Pedro Almodóvar*, Madrid: Ediciones Akal.

Balbo, Lucas (ed) (1993), *Obsession: The Films of Jess Franco*, Berlin: Frank Trebbin.

Besas, Peter (1997), 'The Financial Structure of Spanish Cinema', in Marsha Kinder (ed.) *Refiguring Spain: Cinema, Media, Representation*, Durham NC: Duke University Press.

Clover, Carol J. (1992), *Men, Women, and Chain Saws: Gender in the Modern Horror Film*, Princeton, Princeton University Press.

—— (1999), 'Her Body, Himself: Gender in the Slasher Film', in Sue Thornham (ed.), *Feminist Film Theory*, New York: New York University Press.

Creed, Barbara (1999), 'Horror and the Monstrous-Feminine: An Imaginary Abjection', in Sue Thornham (ed.), *Feminist Film Theory*, New York: New York University Press.

Deleuze, Gilles (1991), *Masochism: Coldness and Cruelty*. New York: Zone Books.

Elkins, James (1999), *Pictures of the Body: Pain and Metamorphosis*, Stanford: Stanford University Press.

Freixas, Ramón (1994), 'Hablar el cine: El increible nombre mutante', *Archivos de la filmoteca*, Winter: 39–51.

Galán, Diego (1989), 'Cine español, 1950–1961', in Augusto Torres (ed.) *Cine español (1896-1988)*, Madrid: Ministerio de cultura.

Geist, Anthony (1983), 'An Interview with Juan Goytisolo', *TriQuarterly*, 57: 38.

Grant, Barry Keith (ed.) (1996), *The Dread of Difference*, Austin: University of Texas Press.

Heredero, Carlos F. (1993), *Las huellas del tiempo: cine español 1951–61*, Madrid: Filmoteca.

Kristeva, Julia (1982), *Powers of Horror: An Essay on Abjection*, New York: Columbia University Press.

Lucas, Tim (1993), 'Introduction', in Lucas Balbo (ed.), *Obsession: The Films of Jess Franco*, Berlin: Frank Trebbin.

Marsh, Steven (2002), 'Comedy and the Weakening of the State: An Ideological Approach to Spanish Popular Cinema 1942–1964', Doctoral Thesis, University of London.

—— (2003), 'The *Pueblo* Travestied in Fernán Gómez's *El extraño viaje* (1964)', *Hispanic Research Journal*, 4(2), June.

Martí-Olivella, Jaume (1997), 'Regendering Spain's Political Bodies: Nationality and Gender in the Films by Pilar Miró and Arantxa Lazcano', in Marsha Kinder (ed.), *Refiguring Spain: Cinema, Media, Representation*, Durham NC: Duke University Press.

Martín Gaite, Carmen (1987), *Usos amorosos de la postguerra española*, Barcelona: Editorial Anagrama.

Martín-Márquez, Susan (1999), *Feminist Discourse and Spanish Cinema: Sight Unseen*, Oxford: Oxford University Press.

Pavlovic, Tatjana (2003), *Despotic Bodies and Transgressive Bodies. Spanish Culture from Francisco Franco to Jesús Franco*, Albany: State University of New York Press.

Prego, Victoria (1995), *Así se hizo la Transición*, Barcelona: Plaza & Janés Editores.

Preston, Paul (1994), *Franco: a Biography*, New York: Basic.

Seguin, Jean Claude (1995), *Historia del Cine Español*, Madrid: Acento Editorial.

Shaviro, Steven (1995), *The Cinematic Body*, Minneapolis: University of Minnesota Press.

Smith, Paul Julian (1994), *Desire Unlimited: The Cinema of Pedro Almodóvar*, London: Verso.

Strauss, Frédéric (ed.) (2001), *Conversaciones con Pedro Almodóvar*, Madrid: Ediciones Akal.

Williams, Linda (1989), *Hard Core: Power, Pleasure, and the 'Frenzy of the Visible'*, Berkeley: University of California Press.

——(1996), 'When the Woman Looks', in Barry Keith Grant (ed.) *The Dread of Difference*, Austin: University of Texas Press.

——(1999), 'Film Bodies: Gender, Genre and Excess', in Sue Thornham (ed.), *Feminist Film Theory*, New York: New York University Press.

Zizek, Slavoj (1991), *Looking Awry: An Introduction to Jacques Lacan through Popular Culture*, Cambridge, MA: MIT Press.

——(1992), *Enjoy your Symptom*, New York: Routledge.

10

Heterosociality in *Segunda piel* (Gerardo Vera, 2000) and *Sobreviviré* (Alfonso Albacete and David Menkes, 1999): Strong Women, or the Same Old Story?

Chris Perriam

Introduction

Sobreviviré (Alfonso Albacete and David Menkes, 1999) and *Segunda piel* (Gerardo Vera, 1999) took their places at the end of the 1990s in a minor but continuing sub-tradition of modestly successful feature films with gay characters or gay-themed storylines (Fouz-Hernández and Perriam 2000). Both films have the tragic sudden death of a handsome man as narrative pivots, both feature a strong, wronged, and grief-stricken woman, and both explore extremes of loneliness; but their tone and pace are quite different. Albacete and Menkes's *Más que amor, frenesí* (1996) had already made a move toward a post-Almodovarian and problematically queer aesthetic as well as following other leads toward a light, postmodern/popular style (Fouz-Hernández and Perriam 2000: 102–9). *Sobreviviré*'s target audience can be deduced from its middle-brow but conscientious approach to the representation of social problems, its portrait of the moneyed Madrid gay/bohemian scene, its exploitation of and reference to Hollywood romantic comedy, the average age of its cast (men, twenty-something; women, thirty-five plus), and its soundtrack.[1] *Segunda piel*, with its thirty-something cast, its mainly domestic sets, sombre incidental music, and an often rewarding theatricality and earnestness, looks both back to psychologically complex studies of principled and tortured gay males of the 1970s (Smith 1992: 129–203; Perriam 1999) and less far back to the easy tragic mode of US mainstream gay film-making where settings are comfortable and protagonists are if doomed, at least wealthy and handsome.

This chapter follows signs in these films of what Stephen Maddison (2000) terms 'heterosocial dissent' – bondings between heterosexual women and gay men, and women's alignments with gay or queer subject positions in a refusal of patriarchal power relations (71–2, 178–81, 193–7). It looks for signs of reversal of the discourse of homosociality (89 and *passim*) in two films where that discourse is a potent threat to narratives which are in sexual-political terms ostensibly liberal and affirmative (in *Sobreviviré*) or tragically sympathetic (in *Segunda piel*). Its particular focus is on the representation of women characters who find themselves enmeshed in eroticized gay homosociality while also representing – paradoxically by way of camp moments and stereotypical vignettes as much as by way of personal affirmative actions – a mainstream form of new queer dissent.

In both films there is a moment when homosexuality is placed in a context where it is indirectly encouraged to dare to speak its name by the proximity of a musical number – Henry Mancini's 'Moon River' in *Sobreviviré* and Kurt Weill's 'Youkali' in *Segunda piel* – each open, for different reasons and in different degrees, to a camp reading which is facilitated by a narrative and dramatic context of emotional extremity. Both numbers are diegetically associated with the expression by the central wronged woman of strength and self-determination. These moments instantiate the complex practice of gay men acceding to camp pleasures and teetering on the brink of the oppositional and liberatory (Dyer 2002: 21, 51–62; Meyer 1994: 1–18) and the reactionary/complicit or the misogynistic (Britton; Maddison 2000: 90), or flirting with both radical conservatism and aesthetic rebellion (Dyer 2002: 183–4; Maddison 2000: 159; Kleinhans 1994: 194–9). Stereotypical representations of gay experiences, misogynistic homosociality, and vacillating male bisexuality in the two films are problematically deployed to reassert heterosexist normality and the dominance of masculine systems of desire; but Ariadna Gil and Emma Suárez, who play the strong, wronged women at the centre of both films, can be posited as fulfilling the role of classic gay icons who – despite their lack of full star status, and for all that the iconic type risks perpetuating a regime of subordinating, bipolar differentiation along traditional gender borderlines – allow the sporadic participation of the audience in a dynamics of heterosociality which, in Maddison's words, 'resists male homosocial subjectivity' (2000: 12). Moreover, their characters are engaged in surviving the metaphorical or real exclusionary violence of that subjectivity.

Synopses

Sobreviviré. After losing her boyfriend in a car accident while she is pregnant with his child, Marga (Emma Suárez) has to confront life as a bereaved single mother. Made redundant, she takes up occasional work in the local video-hire shop; Rosa (Marta Ibarra), a Cuban expatriate in flight from a wife-beating husband, moves in with her for a time. In the shop Marga is flirted with by Iñaki, ten years younger than she, an artist, and – as he later reveals – more or less gay, and on the rebound. A shared sense of humour, a videotape of *Breakfast at Tiffany's*, and mutual sexual attraction bring them together; but Iñaki is unsure of his sexual preferences. Only at the end of the film, dancing to 'Moon River' at a gay wedding party, is their romance chastely confirmed.

Segunda piel. Diego (Javier Bardem) a more or less out wealthy gay professional falls for Alberto (Jordi Mollà), a closeted married man. He is strung along by Alberto's fundamental lie – his failure to declare his family life or to verbalize until the end the extent of his psycho-sexual problems. Alberto's wife Elena (Ariadna Gil) early on in the film discovers Alberto's infidelity, but only later finds out about his homosexuality. They separate. Living in his own apartment only exacerbates Alberto's inability to commit to Diego and to a new sexual identity. After a tormented monologue forced out of him by Diego's insistent questioning, Alberto races out into the street, mounts his motorcycle, speeds into the main road and into the path of a car. He dies in hospital. Alberto and Elena meet up in the flat and seem to find common ground in their grief.

Strong Women and Resistance

In thinking about these films and their dubious closures (in one, asexual, sentimental romance making it all right; in the other the annihilation of the transgressive, fallen male) it is useful to look at how and why gay men might identify with the characters played by the two well-known actresses who are at least half the main attraction of each film, characters whose heterosexual desires are disrupted by the intervention of men who have sex with men and who can be seen in turn as breaking into the homosocial refuge to which the men they desire keep secretly returning. Emma Suárez's status as a sex symbol for straight men and her career in intense heterosexual dramas (some of them analysed in Allinson 1999; and Perriam 2003: 63–4, 79–80, 84–7) heightens the sexual-politically resistant potential of her character's affair with a gay man, himself played by an icon of youth masculinity, Juan Diego Botto (Perriam 2003: 188–92), as well as that of his own success at winning her affections. Ariadna Gil, who has a similar straight-oriented sexual charge to her public persona and acting career – not least in *Amo tu cama rica* (Emilio Martínez Lázaro, 1991), *Malena es un nombre de tango* (Gerardo Diego, 1996) and *Tranvía a la Malvarrosa* (José Luis García Sánchez, 1996) – brings resonances of a certain queerness from *Belle Époque* (Fernando Trueba, 1992) and her playing of the lesbian Violeta there as well as from *Lágrimas negras* (Ricardo Franco, 1999) and her playing of the disturbed Ana, involved in a violent, eroticized, female homosocial partnership with the drug addict Cinta (Ana Risueño). Her playing of the character Elena in *Segunda piel* again makes use of a trademark provocative, femme/androgynous look which, in tandem with the butch representational style of the film's second strong woman Eva (Cecilia Roth), is part of the film's larger scheme of questioning of gender categories; and her role is used to point up the dysfunctionality of the middle-class heterosexual family unit, men's propensity for denial and betrayal, and the fragility of constructed sexual identities. In both these films, potentially, there is a refusal of dominant paradigms of gendered power relations which is facilitated by the circulation of desire (through bonding) either between women on screen (in *Sobreviviré* between Marga and Rosa), between women audiences and the drama, or between gay male spectators and women on screen.[2]

Sobreviviré's heroic construction of Marga is reinforced by the fact that at one level at least the narrative is under her control. Despite heavy-duty attention from about a third of the way in to Iñaki's (false) dilemma as a gay man who likes women, Marga's is the focalizing role in the film. Her voice-over opens and closes it and intervenes at the moment when the upbeat chorus of the title song is introduced. This happens when she has just been offered the chance of buying into and running the video-hire store. When she announces this to her family at lunch (mother, father, his father, two younger sisters) – in competition with a noisy football match on television – the seriousness of her conversation with her mother about her situation, money, the mortgage, and her child contrasts to the men's noisy cheering of a goal, the grandfather's mindless hurling of the insult 'mariquita' (pouf) at a player (one of his own team, as it turns out), and the father's indifference to her story. In the street, as the song and its upbeat flamenco-style backing start up, the voice-over notes this contrast, and reclaims for Marga her rights over her life: 'If a mere goal could make everything rosy, then I certainly had the right to celebrate having survived what I'd been through'. This moment is one which places her at a critical distance from the heterosexist normativity of characteristically dysfunctional patriarchal family life, positions her as brave loner and yet at one with the majority (the crowd through which she makes her way, in long shot from above), and aligns her with a straightforwardly functional attempt to elicit sympathy from (some) women and (some) gay male viewers, and secondarily from heterosexual male admirers of Suárez in the role of the feisty victim.

This is in fact the second such moment of sentimental and heroic elevation of her: the background to a long empathy section at the hospital after the death of Roberto is the main body of the same song (performed in this instance by Estrella Morente), with verses each opening on the word 'sola' (alone). A later hospital scene, emphasizing her struggle to live as a single mother, also reinforces her bravery and isolation: the voice-over compares her baby son to 'alien', 'and me as Ripley trying to survive in the spaceship' in an allusion to Sigourney Weaver's archetypal strong mother in *Alien³* (David Fincher, 1992). In the waiting room she meets the other strong survivor of the piece, Rosa (Marta Ibarra). Rosa – a tough, vivacious, knocked-about ex-pro with a heart of gold – is set up as a sister in adversity. Over rice and beans in Marga's kitchen she tells her story, spiced by the script with stereotypical Cubanisms. They come to an agreement whereby Rosa looks after the baby in lieu of rent, and this domestic scene is ambivalent in its coding. On the one hand it offers an alternative to the 'role of the happy mother' that Marga's own mother is trying to enforce and to the scenes of suffocating, dysfunctional domesticity in her parents' home. On the other hand, not least through the caricature representation of Rosa, it enfolds both women in the power structures of a men's world. It permits identification, mainly by women, with these two strong women and with their testimony to their positioning within the patriarchal structures that they resist; but the stereotyping which is the film's easiest route to lightness of touch and its target audience's pocket brooks little dissent.

If we look to what Maddison calls the 'heterosocial tendency' – the possible identifications and alliances of straight women with gay men and vice versa – there are similar but less intractable ambiguities. It is worth noting that the title-song sequence, which empoweringly contrasts the domestic interior with the heterogeneity of the urban scene, is immediately followed by the entry of Iñaki into the narrative; and something of that ambivalence concerning empowerment and entrapment follows him in. For, although the film might well be read as one of a series of Spanish films of the late 1990s where gayness is 'integrated'

(Alfeo Álvarez 2000: 145–6), no more of an issue than other emotional and life experiences, Iñaki rather disruptively refuses to be queer. He is marked instead by a stubborn, if denied, middle-of-the-road, old-fashioned gayness. Although he can be identified with by some proto-queer audiences as a figure dissenting from both gay and heterosexual normalizations (as a man who has sex with men but who is strongly attracted to this woman), and although he seems to Marga to be fun and sensitive (Just Gay Enough), his several confessions and simple gestural shows of emotional 'confusion' are not so much his subjective problem as a structural problem, a manifestation of an ideology of regulatory distinctions (straight and gay; men's worlds, women's worlds). These are voiced in the film by the avatars of restrictive hetero- and homosexuality alike. Marga's family, again at table with the television on, watch news reports of the 1998 Madrid Gay Pride march and shots of campaigners for formal recognition in civic registers of non-married, including same-sex, couples (*parejas de hecho*). The father simply utters the word 'maricones' (queers), while her mother engages on a clichéd micro-homily along the lines of 'if I had a son like that…' On the (apparently) other side, the airline steward 'other half' of the gay couple who wed at the end (the conventionally coded '*media naranja*' is the phrase used in the script) has equally clichéd ideas, shared over the in-flight trolley with a stewardess colleague, on the subject of Iñaki's supposed 'conversion', his using Marga as a front, and on the inevitable, essential fixity of gayness. His remarks call up only half humorously a misogynistic gay homosociality which like its straight partner excludes women, and freezes them in safe, distant stereotypes and tokens, while strenuously constructing for itself a sense of its own identity and unassailable sameness.

The construction of Marga as feisty heroine has been briefly explored above; the melodramatic accents in it, and her role as the survivor figure – an example of Maddison's 'tenacious and plucky' women (2000: 9) – make her more than just obliquely open to readings in which gay men's as much as heterosexual women's investments and identifications are to the fore. In a different direction, the generic proximity to sentimental screen romance of this construction of her activates a camp reading of her situation. Walking back with Iñaki one night early in their friendship, she asks him about his work. Explaining that he makes maquettes and sets out of Styrofoam he mentions the example of a reproduction of the display window of Tiffany's, prompting Marga to recall a solitary and wintry visit to New York and her conscious imitation of Audrey Hepburn in *Breakfast at Tiffany's*: however, she notes (as the script takes one of its several dives into cliché), 'faltaba la música' (the music was missing).

In itself this embarrassing moment would be without interest for the audience: but it is queerly framed. The couple are walking back from a one-man show (and from an interlude in a mixed gay/trendy straight bar on the edge of the Chueca district, Madrid's lesbian and gay village) in which an actor has explored bisexuality by simultaneously playing Marilyn Monroe and Truman Capote. Iñaki (as the script again reaches for cliché) notes that life is not like in the movies, and goes on to recall the performance they have seen; as they near her flat, Marga counters by saying that it sounds too perfect and reminds her, rather, of the sort of magazine exercise where one puts together the perfect man – Val Kilmer's lips, Mel Gibson's eyes, John John Kennedy's torso, Antonio Banderas's arse. Iñaki picks up on this last feature jocularly and notes that though Melanie Griffith is far from perfect, she does at least have possession of Banderas's arse. He then moves straight into transferring the habitual awkwardness of what to do when saying goodbye at the door into another awkwardness altogether, that of his own confusion (highlighted by his displacement of his own possible interest in Banderas's arse). To snatches of the 'Moon River' melody on single extra-diegetic guitar he kisses Marga, and picks up on her earlier question 'What is normal?' Leaving it in the air, he walks backward away from her and from the possible moment of confession or decision.

The connections here are with screen idols, impossible dreams come true; some sort of audience is being asked to revel in reflected excess of feeling, in sentimental affiliation. But the unusual absence of the heterosexual male partner puts a potential spin on this: there is a doubly delicious but easily confected irony in the unexpectedly extreme distance at which Marga finds herself from the classic romantic ideal of her mimicry of Hepburn. At the end of the film Marga attends the wedding of her two nice gay friends; for a while she sits sadly by; but when the orchestra, from their modestly glamorous stage, strike up 'Moon River' and the married couple get up to dance, not only does it cue a smoothing out of the political difficulties surrounding the legitization of gay partnerships reported earlier on the news (while, of course, unconsciously prompting others) but it also cues the reappearance after a long and guilty absence of Iñaki. The reassertion of heterosexual-patterned behaviours (the wedding, the style of dance, tuxedos) and Iñaki's apparent second escape from the homosexuality he has temporarily been taking refuge in again, in a sealed-off other life, is all wrapped in the swirling, gooey moves of musical arrangement, swooping camera moves, the reference back to *Breakfast at Tiffany's*, and the emotive not-really-lovers' clinch – in, that is, a far-from-straight confection. These elements seem to open up the possibility of a 'feminist camp' reading of the sort investigated by Pamela Robertson in *Guilty Pleasures* (1996) which 'enables not only gay men, but also heterosexual and lesbian women, and perhaps heterosexual men, to express their discomfort with and alienation from the normative gender and sex roles assigned to them by straight culture' (1996: 10). However, non-resistant readings of the 'Moon River' syndrome here are also more than available: closed-in, clique-y gay readings, that is, of the glamour of classic film and musical; readings of Marga as deluded victim at first whose only relief is in the arms of a man at last. As Maddison points out, following on in a long line of debate (for example the 1980 co-written essay in Dyer 2002: 15–30), 'gay male audiences' camp reading traces' (159) may in fact play into the hands of patriarchy and 'precipitate the celebration of filmic imagery that marks, however sublimely, women's powerlessness in heterosexual relations with men' (159–60).

Although Marga, at the hands of the script-writers, seems not to know whether or not she is dissenting or complying by surviving, there is, it seems to me, potentially a variant of the heterosocial dynamic to be rescued from this film. Iñaki's sense of his own complication and confusion does not only have to be read as banal but might instead be disruptive, calling into question the strict codes of gayness and non-gayness. When he says, prior to the pair's first sexual encounter – and in the context of his own battle to accept himself and have others accept him – 'we've both suffered enough' it is a heterosocial plea, a plea for 'queer sisterhood', and establishes the two of them more surely as potential dissenters than the pairing Marga/Rosa does. Similarly, Marga's slippages – her fallings back into the habits of a homosocially dominated world – do not have to be read as uncorrectable. When they first have sex, Marga's admiration at the size of his cock aligns her with the phallocentric desires activated in the image of the one gay man we do see Iñaki sexually engaged with, in a casual encounter in a clothing store. Through the half-open curtain of the fitting room Iñaki's sexy prey, stripped to his underpants, grabs his substantial crotch and sustains Iñaki's gaze before he approaches. However, not only does his guilt and confusion – which on a generous reading one might attribute to his feelings for Marga – intervene and make him break off his caressing of the pick-up, but the same fitting rooms are later the scene of a passionate kiss between Marga and Iñaki. She comes to represent a certain indirect empowerment by the fact that she too can objectify the penis and have an active role in erotic play in what was earlier a site of gay masquerade and trying on of jeans and desires. It is, lastly, important to remember her closest encounter with Iñaki's 'other' life: in a bar on the edge (appropriately) of the gay district of Chueca she meets his ex, but brushes off his catty competitiveness and defiantly leaves this scene of homosociality – with its cliques of gays and its banter – by simply walking out the door.

Elena, in *Segunda piel*, on the other hand, finds the evidence of male bonding – made damaging because made secretive by Alberto – constantly coming in through the doors of her home to exclude and to trap her. Her discovery of an incriminating hotel invoice in his recently laundered jacket pocket, the later revelation that it is a man whom her husband is seeing, and the recognition of her own abandonment and Alberto's disintegration are all represented in images whose pathos encourages engagement by several sectors of the audience. Her position as the wronged woman, the glamour and associations attaching to the actress who plays her, and her strength in wretchedness, as well as an overtly targeted gay audience, suggest too that we might highlight that particular set of heterosocial identifications which concern Maddison when he asks (2000: 9) 'why has the adoration of strident, emotionally resilient, privileged, tenacious and plucky women become so powerfully understood as a cultural expression of men who sexually desire other men?' and suggests that 'in aligning themselves with gay culture, or with feminism, women ... are undertaking acts of gender dissent ... contesting patriarchal ideas of womanhood ... women who bond with gay men do so as a form of political resistance'. Unlike Marga, though, Elena does not 'bond with gay men' in any obvious sense for most of the film (it is Eva in her bossy friendship with Diego who seems to do this) – she is sexually and emotionally estranged from Alberto even before she knows that he is homosexual; and it is only in the strange, convenient closing moments that she bonds with Diego in their shared grief. In the case of Elena we have to read for heterosociality on the bias, and, as in *Sobreviviré*, again camp becomes an unlikely auxiliary tool for doing so.

At a smart Madrid cabaret – packed, mid-week, with this film's version of the affluent urban classes – a charismatic and exotically made-up black singer in a glittering long dress, picked out by a spot against the quiet low lighting of the venue, performs Weill's poignant song 'Youkali'. The scene matches the lyrics' evocation of a distant utopian island with a perhaps unintentional evocation, in its *mise-en-scène* and the dramatic premise, of the high-class kitsch of late-evening light entertainment of the 1960s and of the strenuously sophisticated sex dramas of the cinema of three or four decades ago. The counterpoint of Elena's desperate attempt, in the context of her painful discovery of his infidelity, to open up a frank discussion with Alberto about their failed sex life, amid the improbable mid-week display of rather passé glamour plus melancholy lyric theme, makes this a moment which is at once grave and impossible to take seriously. The classy glitz supplies a sentimental substitute for several lacks in both the listeners and does so ironically. It is quietly and poignantly laughable that the elaboration of a fantasy of bitter-sweet, romantic solitude should be set up as a possibly cathartic or therapeutic background to the tense emotional exchange which underpins the evening the couple are spending together. It is precisely because Alberto has got himself lost in his own fantasy island but cannot, as it were, sing about it that the two are so distanced and so harmed. It is grimly true that the dazzling, fluid, feminine sexiness on stage is something that once Elena might have herself performed but has now had frozen out of her; just as it is true that Alberto is encased in a rigidity which is in large part due to a misconception of his own duty to masculinity and in particular, to patrilinearity. (He sticks at his job as an aviation engineer because that was his father's job before him.) Above all it is embarrassingly noticeable that Alberto in particular is out of place here; the flagrant exoticism of the musical fantasy exaggerates his stiffness and conventional look. He is markedly unable to recognize his gay masculinity in part because of an inability to engage with camp pleasure which, as Paula Graham suggests, is predicated on 'the fetishistic tease of presence/absence of phallic control: power and the threat of its loss ... the relation of gay men to male authority, mediated by a relationship to representations of "the feminine"' (quoted in Maddison 2000: 90). What this moment does is precisely to point up Alberto's misunderstandings of his relation to male authority, his fearful relationship to the feminine, and his fatal entrapment by (an equally misunderstood) phallic control. Elena, by contrast, sees that control and its effects at once. The suave performance of 'Youkali' and the disturbances of a camp undertow allow the audience to tune in to both these apprehensions. So this scene activates a possible heterosocial identification on the part of gay men with Elena, a homosocial (albeit impatient) identification with the clammed-up Alberto, but then – as she resorts to words and he resists them – a proto-feminist sympathy with Elena's stance which dispels the camp moment, sidelines Alberto, and makes her a different sort of minor heroine. As 'Moon River' did, 'Youkali' provisionally elevates the female lead and holds out promises which sentimentally turn to dust.

To what extent, though, can a female and gender-dissenting audience identify with Elena's abjection in the rest of the film? In the lighter film, Marga 'used' her expulsion by homosexuality from the domains of self-determination to interrupt its dynamics. This is much more difficult for

Elena. As with Marga in *Sobreviviré*, there is a formal alignment or mirror-imaging of hetero- and homosexual erotic encounters – the shifts between scenes of Alberto with Diego and Alberto with Elena – pivoting on the male protagonist which inserts Elena into the homosocial world. This is an effect greatly enhanced by the graphics of the opening credits which suggest the endless fluid interchangeability of the bodies and actions of the main players. But unlike the case as it is for Marga there is no other woman with whom to set up a sisterly alliance – she and Eva never meet, for example – and no possibility of being a disruptive presence in the anyway already fractured homosocial world of Diego and Alberto.

On the other hand, her attempts to cut through the lies, to make homosexual desire not a proximate and therefore unmentionable danger but a part of their renegotiation of their affective situation, to make Alberto see the continuity between his perceived difference and the person he is, are all acts of gender dissent. They lead in fact to an unexpected and moving instance of bonding. In a powerful scene in a restaurant off the Plaza del Rey (incidentally but not inappropriately not more than five hundred metres from the almost gay bar which features in *Sobreviviré*) Elena becomes the instigator of a crisis of abjection in Alberto which allows her to bond heterosocially with him in momentary solidarity with his entrapment in the figurations of masculinity, family, social, and paternal expectations. She is much more articulate here than Marga or the script-writers of *Sobreviviré* and is face to face with a much more complex problem. Alberto has organized the meal in order to announce his unilateral decision that the family would be better off living away from the capital (and he, therefore, away from his past and from Diego and from the truth). When she asks him direct how long he has been going with men he chokes on the little food he has been able to place in his mouth, staggers inarticulate to the door, and outside throws up. Elena's words have shredded Alberto's self-deceiving deployment of the discourse of family and fatherhood, and reconstructed the true agenda which he, with the literality of melodrama, simply cannot swallow. As he sobs in her arms in the square there is a multi-directional moment of heterosocial bonding. It can be supposed that most of the audience empathizes with both her and Alberto at this intense moment, their pity sharpened by the context of the revelation of heterosexuality's fragility; Elena is in effect comforting a man who entered the restaurant her pretend heterosexual husband and who has exited it an imperfectly outed gay man; her scene in the restaurant has abandoned the heterosexually normative by refusing to listen to the white sound of dysfunctional masculinity in denial; and most important of all, her embrace momentarily but memorably disrupts the silent secrecy of Alberto's version of eroticized homosociality by replacing Diego. Finally, there is sympathy for Diego as the unconvincing but nonetheless excluded and victimized gay man of the piece. This sequence is, then, a more convincing moment of what we could read as a form of queer alliance than that which the film so unconvincingly privileges at its tragic conclusion, the bonding of Diego and Elena in their grief after Alberto's death as they walk together through the crowd into the distance and an excessively easy closure.

Although *Sobreviviré*, as well as being a vehicle for Suárez and Diego and the music, might justifiably be considered a queerploitation movie, and *Segunda piel* a gayploitation movie (by non-Spanish audiences at least), if we view the strong, wronged women at their centres as rather unexpectedly focalizing arguments against normality in terms of gender and sexuality, power and desire, then each becomes a more interesting study in masculine denial and in the denial of homosociality's exclusionary tactics. Inasmuch as camp 'constantly plays with notions of inside and outside, masculine and feminine [and] does not locate truth in these polarities' (Bergman 1993: 94–5), 'denaturalises normality' (Dyer 2002: 21), and is a demystificatory process (51–62), then both films, at an angle, send off camp gleams which refreshingly sideline the apparent problems that their men are having in bonding right in order to concentrate – in the now time-honoured counter-tradition – on these men, and on homosocially inflected 'gayness', as a problem.

Notes

1. Songs: 'Sobreviviré' (Pablo Ortega; and Ortega, Estrella Morente); 'Sevillanas de la vida' (Ortega, Alba Molina); 'En la Habana' (Ortega); 'Moon River' (Henry Mancini/Jo Mercer; adapt. Ortega); 'Alegría de vivir' (Ray Heredia). The CD soundtrack was a significant commercial success.
2. Thus I am excluding for the purposes of this argument possible reactions to the representation of the gay male characters, on which I have written elsewhere (Perriam 2003: 113–23).

References

Alfeo Álvarez, Juan Carlos (2000), 'El enigma de la culpa: la homosexualidad y el cine español, 1962–2000', *Journal of Contemporary Iberian Studies*, 13(3): 136–47.

Allinson, Mark (1999), 'Pilar Miro's Last Two Films: History, Adaptation, and Genre', in Rob Rix and Roberto Rodríguez-Saona (eds), *Spanish Cinema Calling the Shots*, Leeds: Trinity and All Saints College.

Bergman, David (1993), *Camp Grounds: Style and Homosexuality*, Amherst: University of Massachusetts Press.

Britton, Andrew (1999), 'For Interpretation: Notes Against Camp', in Fabio Cleto (ed.), *Camp: Queer Aesthetics and the Performing Subject*, Edinburgh: Edinburgh University Press.

Dyer, Richard (2002), *The Culture of Queers*, London and New York: Routledge.

Fouz-Hernández, Santiago and Perriam, Chris (2000). 'Beyond Almodóvar: "homosexuality" in Spanish cinema of the 1990s', in David Alderson and Linda Anderson (eds), *Territories of Desire in Queer Culture: Refiguring contemporary boundaries*, Manchester, Manchester University Press.

Kleinhans, Chuck (1994), 'Taking Out the Trash: Camp and the Politics of Parody', in Moe Meyer (ed.), *The Politics and Poetics of Camp*, London and New York: Routledge.

Maddison, Stephen (2000), *Fags, Hags and Queer Sisters: Gender Dissent and Heterosocial Bonding in Gay Culture*, Basingstoke: Macmillan.

Meyer, Moe (ed.) (1994a), *The Politics and Poetics of Camp*, London and New York: Routledge.

——— (1994b), 'Introduction: Reclaiming the Discourse of Camp', in Moe Meyer (ed.), *The Politics and Poetics of Camp*, London and New York: Routledge.

Perriam, Chris (1999), '*A un dios desconocido*: Resurrecting a Queer Identity under Lorca's Spell', *Bulletin of Hispanic Studies (BHS)* (Glasgow), 76(1): 77–91.

——— (2003), *Stars and Masculinities in Spanish Cinema: From Banderas to Bardem*, Oxford: Oxford University Press.

Robertson, Pamela (1996), *Guilty Pleasures: Feminist Camp from Mae West to Madonna*, London: I.B. Tauris.

Smith, Paul Julian (1992), *Laws of Desire: Questions of Homosexuality in Spanish Literature and Film, 1960–1990*, Oxford: Clarendon.

11

¡Victoria? A Modern Magdalene
Rob Stone

'I don't need to study the roles, I just do them.'[1] Victoria Abril is an actress whose critical and public reputation is based on the psychological intensity and sexual disinhibition of her performances. In his benchmark analysis of Abril's career and screen identity, Peter William Evans captures 'the essence of experiment and transgression' that has characterized her life and most celebrated roles for Vicente Aranda and Pedro Almodóvar and observes that in the context of contemporary Spain she is 'a star formed partly by residual processes of objectification and partly by the new assertiveness' (2002: 129). In taking its cue from Evans's analysis, this chapter presents a contextual analysis of the function and evolution of Abril's screen persona in her role as Gloria Duque in Agustín Díaz Yanes's *Nadie hablará de nosotras cuando hayamos muerto* (Nobody Will Talk About Us When We Are Dead, 1995), examining the problematic identification of the Spanish audience with one of its most prominent film stars. Most specifically, in order to examine the semiotic and even synonymous fusion of Victoria and Gloria, this chapter responds to three criteria in relation to gender theory and notions of spectatorship: the iconography of Victoria Abril in Spanish cinema and society, the generic and narrative disruptions provoked by this iconography within the film and upon its audience, and the function of Victoria/Gloria within the cinematic and social stricture of a tradition of Catholic bias in the cultural and filmic representation of gender.

The role of Gloria was written expressly for Abril by an admiring and collaborative Díaz Yanes and, though she begins the film in the most demeaning way imaginable, grimy, drunk and tousled, on her knees performing oral sex on Mexican gangsters who otherwise ignore her, *Nadie*, says Abril, 'is a film about dignity, which is something we all need'. A police raid affords Gloria the chance to escape back to Madrid, where she will struggle to rebuild her relationships with her comatose bullfighter husband – 'Where is he?' – and his communist mother Julia

Figure 1 Victoria Abril in *Nadie hablará de nosotras cuando hayamos muerto*. Courtesy of Sogecine.

(Pilar Bardem) – 'Where you left him'. At the same time, Gloria will attempt to use the information gleaned as moll to rip off the Madrid-based money-laundering enterprises of the Mexican gangsters. A noirish thriller in tone if not conclusion, the film examines Gloria's problematic reinscription in the pluralist society of democratic Spain, one where social divisions are entrenched in notions of economic well-being and the legacy of out-dated but still prevalent notions of political allegiance or dissent. As a reintroduction to Socialist Spain, the film also reacquaints its female protagonist with both retrograde and evolving notions of gender, while elaborating a study of a female struggling against internal demons and external persecution, both literally, in terms of the Mexican gangsters, who allow for 'a parallel between the wartime executioners and the gangsters of today, with little difference between the patriarchal and machista values' (Bentley 1999: 339), and, more abstractly, in relation to the extant rigidity of these gender roles in a supposedly progressive Spain. 'It's a hard and powerful film', says Abril. 'Films often have their time and place, and this film, probably, if we ever manage to mature a little in the way we see and treat the world, if we ever manage to think of something other than money-money-money, well, just maybe this film about dignity will end up finding its audience among the masses that have all turned stupid from so much television.'

The legal equality that came with the 1931 Constitution had been reflected in the pre-Civil War film roles of Imperio Argentina, but the on-screen independent female in the early years of the dictatorship was invariably censored: the sexual dream of Elvira Quintillá's schoolteacher was cut from Luis García Berlanga's *¡Bienvenido Mister Marshall!* (Welcome Mister Marshall, 1952), as was the rebellious adolescent who jumps from the train and heads back to the city and her sugar-daddy gangster at the end of José Antonio Nieves Conde's neo-realist *Surcos* (Furrows, 1951). In her stead, audiences witnessed females proud to suffer for husband and country, played by stars whose iconography was manipulated to reflect and symbolize the socially circumscribed role of women. Their roles complied with the conflated morality and law of Church and State, while they themselves were groomed to be adored by a public that saw them in relation to Catholic icons, particularly when these stars ascribed their glossy good fortune in career, love and motherhood to the grace of God and the Virgin, the impossibly perfect female whose similarly unattainable ideal was analogous to the untouchable glamour of film stars. Females who dared to question or betray their circumscription did appear in Juan Antonio Bardem's *Calle Mayor* (Main Street, 1956), Luis Buñuel's banned *Viridiana* (1961) and *Tristana* (1970), and Carlos Saura's *Ana y los lobos* (Ana and the Wolves, 1972), but these were clearly exceptions from dissident film-makers, whose films utilized the suffering female as a metaphor for those who endured marginalization. Toward the end of the dictatorship, the subjugation of the independent female remained a constant in the majority of the social comedies of the *tercera vía* (the third way), whose gradual surrender to the smutty softcore of the post-dictatorship *destape* made explicit the parodic objectification of the female that underscored the genre. Nevertheless, the separate evolution of the social commentary and satire of the best of the *tercera vía* resulted in the *comedias madrileñas* (the Madrid comedies), in which liberated females such as Carmen Maura in Fernando Colomo's *Tigres de papel* (Paper Tigers, 1977) and Paula Molina in Fernando Trueba's *Ópera prima* (1980) flaunted the subjectivity of their libertine desire in front of bemused heterosexual males. These films (and the complementary off-screen antics of Maura and the Molina sisters) provided the contemporary female audience with a gleeful, somewhat vengeful use of satire that would find its most eloquent champion in Pedro Almodóvar, though the tradition of female suffering, once the key metaphor of dissident cinema, was also perpetuated in such films as Vicente Aranda's *Cambio de sexo* (Change of Sex, 1976) and *La muchacha de las bragas de oro* (The Girl in the Golden Panties, 1979), in which a teenaged Victoria Abril

Rob Stone

shouldered the burdensome metaphors of the *transición* (the political
transition) and the *desmemoria* (the pact of mutual amnesia made by
previous political opponents) respectively (Stone 2001: 115–120).

Abril was only sixteen and working as a television game-show hostess
on *Un, Dos, Tres* when she won the role of José María/María José in
Cambio de sexo by jumping on Aranda's desk to prove to a friend that 'I
could handle these film people' (Álvares and Frías 1991: 287). Married
at fifteen to her Chilean agent Gustavo Laube against the wishes of her
parents, Abril's headstrong expressiveness came through in classical
dance and singing before finding its vocation in acting and a working
relationship with Aranda through eleven films including *Amantes*
(Lovers, 1991), for which Abril won the best actress award at the Berlin
Film Festival.[2] In these and other films, including Mario Camus's *La
colmena* (The Hive, 1982) and José Luis Borau's *Río abajo* (One the
Line, 1984), Abril's slight stature and offbeat but beguiling prettiness
was characteristically the vehicle for a dramatic and erotic intensity
that matched up to the tragedy and perversity which often engulfed her
characters. In roles that invariably courted sexual excess, ambiguity
and scandal, Abril functioned both within and against the constraints
and privileges of her director-auteurs and rapidly acquired iconic status
for an emotional, dramatic and physical disinhibition that tallied with a
personal life that saw her divorce after five years of marriage and move
to Paris, where she raised her two children in 'a contract of love that
I have with them'. Her career flourished in both Spanish and French
cinema, but she also suffered in mediocre films from directors who failed
to recognize or exploit such a potentially volatile icon of female gender,
though she was also briefly perfect for the examinations of gender
fluidity and sexual response in three films from Pedro Almodóvar, with
both *¡Átame!* (Tie Me Up, Tie Me Down, 1989) and *Tacones lejanos*
(High Heels, 1991) high points in the career of a director whose name
was built on melodrama, a genre that thrives on strong, emotive women.[3]
Nevertheless, Spanish cinema has no discernible tradition of what might
be termed the 'female-in-charge' beyond that which Annette Kuhn terms
the 'gynocentric' bias of melodrama (Kuhn 1992: 301). The conclusive
female solidarity of Almodóvar's *Pepi, Luci, Bom y otras chicas del
montón* (Pepi, Luci, Bom and Other Girls On the Heap, 1980), *Mujeres
al borde de un ataque de nervios* (Women on the Verge of a Nervous
Breakdown, 1988), *Tacones lejanos* and *Todo sobre mi madre* (All About
My Mother, 1999) may have endured throughout the career of a director
who has had a profound influence on the representation of gender in
contemporary Spain, but while *chicas Almodóvar* such as Carmen Maura,

¡Victoria? A Modern Magdalene

Marisa Paredes and Cecilia Roth have largely conformed to an affectionate public's perception of them as suffering but triumphant females, all three having survived the excesses of the *movida* and various personal but well-publicized crises, the audience response to Victoria Abril has been complicated by the non-conformity and supposed *antipatía* of the actress. Abril has only ever posed for the cameras when in control of her image, in outrageous outfits from her favourite designers, or naked on her own terms as when smoking cigars in an androgynous black and white cover feature for the magazine *Cinemania*. The gossip press has never featured lay-outs of her Paris apartment and any photos of her children or lovers have come from the worst kind of paparazzi. 'There's no private life in Spain and I'm not willing to surrender mine', she asserts. 'That's why I don't think of myself as a *madrileña* anymore, because there they don't respect my privacy, my intimacy; they simply don't respect me. Which is why I left and why I won't return until my children are long in the teeth. I've still got many years of self-exile left to come.'

Abril's most indelible characters have similarly transcended boundaries of genres and stereotypes: Luisa in *Amantes*, a femme fatale in an *amour fou*, is the queen of on-screen female subjectivity and desire in post-dictatorship Spanish cinema; Marina in *¡Átame!* is a reformed degenerate in a thriller/horror film, redeemed by the awakening of her innate romanticism, and Rebeca in *Tacones lejanos* is in flight from a life defined by the husband-father/daughter Electra complex toward a belated but emotional reunion with the neglected mother/daughter dialectic at the heart and close of the film. Abril's presence does not guarantee that a film will transcend genres or stereotypes, but her performances are inevitably the medium for the transformation of those that do. Abril appears prepared to explore her iconography, prepared to let a few directors explore it too: 'I'm an actress-vehicle. I have to keep the vehicle in good order so that a good director can drive it at three hundred kilometres per hour or at thirty. Don't you know? I'm a Ferrari!' By her non-conformist lifestyle and her self-exile from Spain, Abril took an active part in the formation of her star persona and the influential gender discourse which it promoted. Consequently, while Abril embodies the view that 'the person is a body, a psychology, a set of skills that have to be mined and worked up into a star image' (Dyer 1987: 5), she also complicates the issue of star image in relation to spectatorship because, to a certain extent, her emancipation and self-determination affords a contrast with the comparative half-measures of many females in contemporary Spain.

The growth of feminist and gay activism in post-dictatorship Spain was one of the power bases of the Socialist Worker's Party (PSOE),

Rob Stone

which legitimized, tolerated and subsumed elements of the surrounding culture into its initially liberal and progressive stance on questions of national, regional and individual identity. Yet, just as the PSOE would, in time, reveal its ignorance of the distinctions between 'representing' and 'being' in talking socialism but living capitalism, so their populist façade was opportunistically imitated by many who dallied with film, fashion, art and music while jettisoning any explicit political intent in favour of remuneration and fame. The once rough-edged images of progressive individuals, such as prime minister Felipe González in rolled-up shirt sleeves, gradually erred toward vote-catching/money-making constructs that sought the control and polish of their images. Later images of González denying his involvement in the anti-ETA GAL or holidaying on Franco's yacht appeared to signal the curtailing of his potential for change and, indeed, that of contemporary Spain, where the commitment to progress waned dramatically in the early 1990s in the face of both massive corruption at the highest levels of governmental and financial institutions, and escalating problems of immigration and terrorism. Similarly, though notions of gender in the early socialist years had been reconstructed in accordance with legal reforms and the improvisation, experimentation and individuality that was evident in music, fashion, art and film, this deconstruction was seen as destructive by many Spaniards in the late 1990s, when family values were once more championed (especially by the conservative Partido Popular) in the face of a media focus on corruption, terrorism and delinquency. Nevertheless, Spain may have stopped, but Abril just kept on going. Her performance in *Nadie hablará de nosotras cuando hayamos muerto* offered a purposeful rebuttal of the returning right-of-centre politics and morality that resurrected memories and even strategies of phallocentrism, a precept of Francoism that 'depends on the castrated woman to give order and meaning to its world' (Mulvey 1992: 746).

In *Nadie*, Gloria's three-year exile shows her avoiding the circumscribed roles of mother, wife and nursemaid, while Abril's enigmatic performance similarly avoids the near-parodic representation of femininity that is characteristic of both the femme fatale and the prostitute. Victoria/Gloria refuses to recognize femininity as a construct, one that may be exploited by both men and women, while the performance/character also negates the identification of the spectator, partly because of the film's denial of erotic pleasure in a contemplation of its spectacle. Although Victoria/Gloria is involved in several sexual acts, she is never unclothed and never the focus of visual gratification. The gangsters in the first scene ignore her, while her economic/sexual transaction with

¡*Victoria?* A Modern Magdalene

two chauvinist would-be employers in Madrid is driven by her savvy: it is Gloria who puts into Marxist terms the exchange of money for her performance of oral sex on one of the men, while also putting a price on the spectatorship of the second – 'It's the same. It also costs five thousand' – an expression of control that allows her to transcend the demeaning nature of the act by both recourse to a once-routine act and by forcing the second male to assume the responsibility of his sexually confused voyeurism. The film renounces scopofilia because Abril is not an objectified Other, but an unpredictable, instinctive, even manipulative individual, who deflects the spectator's projection of masculine desire or feminine identification because she is beyond the control of her audience, both intrinsically (the paying voyeur in the office) and extrinsically (the paying voyeurs in the cinema). She resembles the integrated and co-ordinated baby in Lacan's mirror stage: her completeness confuses and belittles the spectator, who cannot measure up to her self-control, but who can disavow this Lacanian schism by dismissing her libertarianism as irrelevant degeneracy.[4] Although such a reactionary criticism suggests the legacy of Francoism, crucially it also points to the limitations of female autonomy in contemporary Spain and the problems for evaluating how people make sense of the star. To this extent, it may suit the Spanish spectatorship that Abril has lived in France for the past twenty years, has twice married and divorced foreigners and has done her best work for directors (Aranda and Almodóvar) commonly associated with the seedier side of sexuality, because all of the above dilutes Abril's relevance to the contemporary Spanish female audience. As Dyer states, 'audiences cannot make media images mean anything they want to, but they can select from the complexity of the image the meanings, feelings, the variations, inflections and contradictions that work for them' (1987: 5). In other words, one reason why Abril's audience enjoys her performance, even vicariously, is because they celebrate its exaggeration, her ability to go too far, believing that the unreality of her excessive disinhibition relieves them of the burden of identifying with her character. This ploy coincides with the attitude of Abril herself: 'When I'm in character I don't feel any inhibitions or embarrassment, but when it's about me, I mean me as in myself, a role is just a shield behind which Victoria is shitting herself.' Nevertheless, the subjectivity of desire made explicit in Abril's characteristically realistic performances of on-screen orgasms (part asthmatic attack, part fit of the giggles) complicates Linda Williams's assertion that the female orgasm is traditionally invisible on-screen (1989), because Abril's vindication of her characters' joyful participation and climax effectively prioritizes the subjectivity and desire of *her*

Rob Stone

females. *Nadie*, moreover, is the exception that proves the rule, for though the film lacks a scene in which Gloria enjoys sexual gratification, this does not render her sexless but the possessor of a female sexuality that does not depend upon male desire for its validation. Victoria/Gloria does not simply reclaim female sexuality on her own terms, but subverts the tradition of its invisibility by withholding the spectacle of erotic display from the male audience. This foregrounding of female desire and dismissal of the male equivalent is still alien to most mainstream Hollywood cinema, something which Abril rejected after playing Joe Pesci's girlfriend in Barry Levinson's *Jimmy Hollywood* (1994): 'For Christ's sake! I get indigestion just thinking about it. Big pictures bore me to death. We made *Nadie* in just six short weeks.'

The six-week guerrilla-style of film-making favoured by Díaz Yanes and Abril suited their problems of centring Gloria at the generic level because the female hero is, by her very existence, transgressive. Indeed, one reason why Abril might not provide an appropriate icon or image of the evolution of gender roles in contemporary Spain is that her star discourse is similarly transgressive; she is not symbolic but individualist, even though this individualism may ultimately leave her and her most memorable characters (Luisa, Rebeca, Gloria) alienated, marginalized and lonely. Nevertheless, Abril's enduring status as sex-symbol simultaneously complies with Paul Julian Smith's statement that 'the erotic contemplation of women [is] a process which must be defended against the supposed puritanism of feminism and political correctness' (2000: 17). The designation of inappropriate images of female-ness is derived from a feminized critical tradition, but it is one which coincides with 'a more conventional sense of feminine decorum, a sense of knowing one's place within a gendered hierarchy' (Tasker 2000: 136). Conversely, Abril's rebuttal of the gendered hierarchy of traditional patriarchal culture, in terms of both her personal life and her choice of roles, renders her a self-aware outsider in relation to its legacy in contemporary Spain and to conventional film roles for women: 'As I don't belong to any one country I've chosen a trade where I don't know where I'll be living from one year to the next', she states, while her forceful hold on her career direction is a fruitful indicator of her emancipation.[5] Such individualism suggests why *Nadie*, as Martín-Márquez argues of *Kika*, 'abandons its search for a more utopian stance on gender' (1999: 40), because it firmly believes that there isn't one. Gloria does not imitate the sadistic male or the masochistic female, for such polarization of genre types is as reductive and constricting as the strictly gendered parameters of identity; but neither is she a prophet of equality or emancipation. She may cast off the whore's pretence of sensuality and wield a jack-hammer to break through floors and ceilings (and Abril dug 90 per cent of the vault-hole in *Nadie* herself) but she does not court androgyny, nor even tomboyishness, and it is therefore not possible to read Gloria, as Tasker does the action heroines of 1980s and 1990s Hollywood, as 'a girl who has not accepted the responsibilities of adult womanhood' (2000: 15). On the other hand, her diminutive size, childish handwriting, eager-to-please smile and tense daughter/mother relationship with Julia do reveal a regression from adulthood that is finally overcome by her belated graduation from high school. Perhaps Gloria's femininity only makes sense, only adds up, when the answer is Abril herself?

Psychoanalysis 'can give an account of how women experience the path to femininity [but] it also insists, through the concept of the unconscious, that femininity is neither simply achieved nor is it ever complete' (Rose 1988: 7). In visual culture, the sexual difference of the female is equated with anatomical difference, but by the same token and criteria, this difference is only perceived: like the 1990s brand of Spanish socialism it is a 'seeming' value instead of an actual one. Ideally, Abril's dismissal of this 'seeming' value and her substitution of real others such as self-reliance, education and adaptability should authenticate her representations of the female in contemporary Spain, but this culturally specific debate over reactions and readings of Abril's place in Spanish society and cinema is problematized because 'issues of modernity are all too frequently tied up with problematic representations of women and sexuality' (Martin-Márquez 1999: 5) and analyses of Abril cannot discount the activity of the star herself in the process of audience identification and the reception of her screen persona. *Nadie* presents a redemptive arc from whore to educated woman that provides for a Marxist and metaphorical reading of Gloria as symbol of the post-dictatorship evolution of the Spanish female, but her progress from victim to 'female-in-charge' only complies with Mary Ann Doane's observation that 'sexual mobility would seem to be a distinguishing feature of femininity in its cultural construction' (1992: 765) when Gloria's real values are ignored in favour of her ironically rendered 'seeming' value of being physically equal to the traditional tasks of men, such as when Gloria deflates a whole gaggle of male conventions by shifting beer crates to secure work driving a brewery delivery truck. The effort is a masquerade of equality, a stop-gap pretence of tomboyishness for the male spectatorship of her reluctant employer, for neither Gloria nor Abril recognizes or responds to men as the hegemony which renders them bound to compete with men on men's terms, thereby refuting Doane's statement that 'it is understandable that women would want to be men, for everyone wants to be elsewhere than in the feminine position' (1992: 765), for their triumphs do not involve the flaunting of femininity or the assumption of maleness that Doane requires as evidence of the female masquerade, but the private knowledge and conviction of their individual worth. As Evans states, 'the film affirms the Abril persona's inner strength, allowing it to display its many attributes beyond the realm of sexual pleasure' (2002: 136). True feminism is 'an advocacy of women's diverse interests, grounded in the exposure of patriarchal oppression' (Martin-Márquez 1999: 5), and it is precisely this diversity and its contrast with the stagnant singularity of traditional female roles that allows for the lonely triumph of an actress/ character whose individualism takes her beyond audience identification.

Already bound up with the feminist questions of spectatorship alluded to previously, audience identification with Abril in general and Gloria in particular is further complicated by Freud's binary theory of male/female sexual difference, which extends to the gender of filmic genres and their corresponding audience: the supposedly male thriller and the so-called 'women's picture' or female melodrama. However, the transgressive nature of Abril's persona and star discourse also extends to her blurring of the distinctions between them. In this she is clearly fortunate to have collaborated with Almodóvar and Díaz Yanes, two of the post-dictatorship generation of Spanish film-makers who borrow generic codes from US cinema, thereby rejecting those of Francoist cinema, though Díaz Yanes does differ from the classically-minded Almodóvar in that he works in genres that have already been reinterpreted by contemporary auteurs such as Martin Scorsese, whose *Raging Bull* (1980) provided Díaz Yanes and Abril with their template for the redemptive tale of Gloria.

Díaz Yanes's background is in bullfighting, his father was a *banderillero*, and his academic progress was interrupted by his militancy in the Spanish communist party (PCE) and his imprisonment during the trial in Burgos in 1970 of sixteen leading members of ETA. As screenwriter of the 'female-in-charge' thrillers that Abril made for other directors – *Demasiado corazón* (Too Much Heart, 1992), *A solas contigo* (Alone With You, 1990) and *Baton rouge* (1988)) – Díaz Yanes contributed to the partial reinscription of the thriller as a female genre in contemporary Spain that has continued with Alejandro Amenábar's *Tesis* (Thesis, 1995), and Patricia Ferreira's *Sé quien eres* (I Know Who You Are, 2000) and *El alquimista impaciente* (The Impatient Alchemist, 2002). Although genre is mostly a self-conscious construct, any appraisal that seeks to measure its impact upon the imagined, abstract audience of Marxist-feminist theory is problematic because it supposes the universal spectator and ignores the probability that an audience is located in a different context from the film and that different audiences reflect different contexts. The Spanish audience, for example, with all its recent history, cannot be the universal spectator at the utopian centre of Marxist-feminist thought and, therefore, neither can it be a strictly gendered subject, though feminist and Marxist theorists (and the two combined) have mostly ignored this problem, with the result that text and context are split. Claire Johnston criticizes this film practice for failing to recognize a film as 'a production of and by subjects already in social practices which always involve heterogenous and often contradictory positions in ideologies' (1992: 298). In other words, a film may function differently in contexts where varying levels of knowledge and experience are involved and, whereas the 'female-in-charge' films of Hollywood since the late 1970s have been subsumed into a more general acceptance of the post-feminist legacy of political correctness, these differences have disrupted the stability and supposed progressive nature of gender roles in contemporary Spain. In *Nadie*, for instance, when Gloria wields the shotgun (or even the jack-hammer), she does not recognize it as a symbol of the phallic order, thereby unavoidably upholding the symbolism of the phallocentric society, but transcends its stagnant symbolism by rendering it a mere implement of female emancipation on a par with the pen that she wields at the film's climax and epilogue, using it to stab her corkscrew-wielding hit-man in the jugular and, subsequently and without irony, to complete her high school exam. Moreover, her comatose bullfighter husband, who is rendered with none of the erotic contemplation of Lydia (Rosario Flores) in Almodóvar's *Hable con ella* (Talk To Her, 2002), may even constitute a parody of the passive male spectator, in which the tables have been turned to such a degree that the objectification of the male signifies not female desire but disinterest. As Studlar argues, 'it is an oversimplification to collapse the entire signification of woman to phallic meaning' (1992: 780) and Victoria/Gloria avoids the interpretation that mixes psychoanalysis with Marxism by refusing to settle for the binary readings of sexuality and the easy symbolism of her use of phallic weaponry as the compensation of her lack, that which Mulvey terms 'woman's entry into the symbolic achieved by possession of the penis' (1992: 747). Instead of wasting time in reclaiming a now-redundant phallus, Victoria/Gloria posits a second lack: a gap between femaleness and the concept of femininity as it appears in popular, secular and traditional Spanish cultures.

Against a policy of circumscription which promotes conformity and adherence to the values of hegemony, Abril has often performed transgressive characters whose survival has convinced them of the value of retaliatory or dissenting acts. As her Luisa says in *Amantes*: 'I killed my husband and I'm still here'. Similarly, the self-justified criminality of Rebeca (double-murderer) in *Tacones lejanos* and Gloria (prostitute-thief) in *Nadie* present Abril as a figure within which female power is unified with self-control over instinct and a reasoning-out of criminal activities for personal well-being. This series of acts both *within* films, *between* them and *beyond* them in the private life of Abril, creates a narrative of female resistance that is legitimized by genres (melodrama and thriller) while simultaneously exposing the shortcomings of their conventional representation, especially in relation to the place of the female in popular culture and, indeed, the politics which promote it. In simplistic generic terms, *Nadie* resembles a thriller, one which may be opportunistically embedded in the sub-genre of female warriors that appeared in Hollywood cinema at the end of the 1970s and delighted and confused critics by mixing the cerebral with the visceral, which included Sigourney Weaver in the *Alien* films, Linda Hamilton in the *Terminator* films, *Thelma and Louise* (Ridley Scott, 1991) and Linda Fiorentino's revisionist femme fatale in *The Last Seduction* (John Dahl, 1993). Subsequently, the presence of the female as an element of spectacle in commercial narrative film began to counter the claim that 'her visual presence tends to work against the development of a story line, to freeze the flow of action in moments of erotic contemplation' (Mulvey 1992: 750). These women were not sexual objects, but subjects that led with their subjectivity and desire, rendering males either victims or sexual prey, and inevitably liberating the female spectator from the trap identified by Mulvey, that of identification with the passive female, because this was replaced by kinship with an active heroine. Wielding a gun did not correspond solely to Freudian ideas of a female's lack of phallus and its compensation, primarily because times had changed and these women were no longer outside codes of femininity. The female-in-charge did not become symbolically male, though she was equally appropriated and decried by the militancy of the feminist movement, which debated these heroines' relationship to a male audience rather than the female one and, by fixating on the political representation, failed to legitimize the pleasure afforded a female audience. Yet, if 'man is reluctant to gaze at his exhibitionist like' (Mulvey 1992: 751), then many women held no such compunction about championing the cinematic spectacle of the female-in-charge. 'A certain masculinization of spectatorship' (Doane 1992: 765) was avoided by the explicit recognition of the causes of these females-in-charge as traditional female concerns, such as the blossoming maternal instinct of Ripley in *Aliens* (James Cameron, 1986) and Sarah

¡Victoria? A Modern Magdalene

Connor in *Terminator 2: Judgement Day* (James Cameron, 1991) and the self-defence and solidarity of *Thelma and Louise* against a rapist and the rigid, patriarchal forces of the law-enforcement system which pursued them. Likewise Victoria/Gloria, who functions beyond any political or social circumscription of her potential, beyond the metaphorical or symbolic function of the female.

Although a Marxist-feminist reading of Gloria's odyssey would undoubtedly track her narrative path from whore to anonymous member of the proletariat as the resolution of an imbalance that sees the whore as analogous to the wife in the economic exchange of marriage (wherein the redemption of the prostitute may also be taken for the economic redemption of the worker), such a reductive dismissal of the prostitute role as wholly victim becomes problematic and facile when subject to the constraints and legacy of forty years of Francoism and several centuries of Catholicism. As Rosa Montero states, 'when women are the exception at work, as in the early stages of integration, it is hard to do more than adapt to traditional male values' (1995: 381), but Gloria's return to her high school exam signals the importance of education in attaining autonomy, one that may be read as indicative of the educational basis of female independence in contemporary Spain and thereby equates with the affirmation that Spanish women 'in general are represented as the motor of contemporary social change' (Brooksbank Jones 1995: 386).

In taking Gloria beyond the dangers of parodying femininity through its masculinization for the sake of spectacle, Abril also challenged the tradition of religious symbolism and iconography to which the Spanish female had been subscribed both on-screen and in society. Marsha Kinder claims that *Nadie* expresses a 'born-again neo-Catholicism [in which] violence is seen as religious sacrifice that reaffirms traditional Spanish institutions, [and its] intense reengagement with Catholicism (however parodic) evokes the kind of mentality that made both González's defeat and Aznar's coalition possible' (1997: 18). Gloria, says Kinder, 'comes to symbolize ... a revitalised Spain' (1997: 19). However, I would argue that when examined in the context of traditional Catholic iconography and its circumscript models of female behaviour, the values associated with the ultimately lonely but triumphant Gloria remain transgressive; for she is independent, resolved through education to be free-thinking, and contemptuous of the social conventions that treat masculine traits as superior and the family unit as sacrosanct. Perhaps, if there were more range in the Christian dimensions of femininity between the extremes of the virgin and the whore, one might attain some sense of Gloria's place in contemporary Spain, but how exactly might one situate Victoria/Gloria

Rob Stone

as a woman between the oppressive weight of extant Catholic hegemony and the gradual dismissal of its dogma in contemporary Spain? Abril has described Gloria as 'a modern Magdalene', probably as a consequence of Díaz Yanes' admission that 'for the character of Gloria I went back to the metaphor of Mary Magdalene, looking at various paintings, to explain to Victoria exactly how I had conceived of this woman, because the physical appearance is easy, but what's inside is much more difficult to express' (Heredero 1997: 354). Gloria clearly responds to the popular but erroneously conceived figure of Magdalene as 'a repentant prostitute, ... the very incarnation of the age-old equation between feminine beauty, sexuality and sin' (Haskins 1993: xii–xiii). Common knowledge maintains that Magdalene was the woman who cleaned herself up to became Christ's companion and witness to his crucifixion and resurrection. However, in *Nadie*, the appropriateness of this analogy is ultimately dismissed by the failure of Gloria's husband and supposed master to resurrect himself. It is also pertinent that the sexless icons of Catholicism have provided a recurring contrast with characters played by Abril, such as the portraits of the Virgin at the beginning of *¡Atame!* and that which the virginal Trini (Maribel Verdú) lugs about in *Amantes*. Religiosity *is* prevalent in *Nadie*, most explicitly in relation to the ritual and iconography of bullfighting, whereby the central but immobile figure of Gloria's comatose bullfighter-husband provides the Christ figure to Gloria's Magdalene; yet, rather than faithful devotion, a traumatized Gloria leaves her comatose husband in the care of his mother and seeks penance as a prostitute in Mexico – 'I've done terrible things' – perhaps by these means of sacrifice promoting his resuscitation (much like Emily Watson's character in Lars Von Trier's 1996 film *Breaking the Waves*). But this Christ figure does not awaken; instead his communist mother kills him. In this inverted gospel, the communist Julia (based on communist Díaz Yanes' own mother) recognizes Gloria's kindred suffering and is inspired to solidarity and sacrifice, thereby providing the flipside to Martín-Márquez's statement that 'a Catholic environment ... is shown, paradoxically, to facilitate women's erotic attachments' (1999: 247) by foregrounding a relationship between females that is based on affinity, equality and a distancing from relationships delineated by their sexuality toward an environment underscored by communism in which relationships are based upon emancipation from such circumscription. Consequently, Julia and Gloria are linked by Julia's recognition of the same fight passed to a younger generation with Julia's sacrifice and gift of money being intended to help Gloria return to her studies and make the most of the social opportunities that Julia never had.

¡Victoria? A Modern Magdalene

In choosing education as the means of emancipation and self-determination, Gloria has far more in common with the little-known figure of the true Mary Magdalene, who is actually mentioned very few times in the Bible. She is not the prostitute that Christ rescues from a stoning. The only things written about her are that Christ cast seven demons from her, that she was at the crucifixion and witnessed Christ's burial, and that she was later with the group of women who went to Christ's tomb after he was buried, being the first of them to see Christ risen. The reputation of 'repentant prostitute' most likely originates with the ancient discomfort with the female having any sway in spiritual matters, which prompted the early Christian Church to phase out the importance of Magdalene by reducing her to the status of whore. Nevertheless, revisionist historians often cast Magdalene as the first apostle and ascribe authorship of a fifth gospel to this woman who was written out of history by male scholars, much like the invisible history of the woman in Spain. Correlatively, although in *Nadie*'s first scene Gloria protests her negligibility to the police by accepting the label – 'Sólo soy una puta' (I'm only a whore) – and is thereafter referred to as 'la puta' throughout the film, at her climactic stabbing of her hitman she proclaims her rejection of such victimhood thus: 'De puta, nada' (There's nothing of the whore in me). In truth, Magdalene is 'the woman by the cross [who] represented the more positive aspects of woman in Christianity: her ministering role, strength, courage and faith are in sharp contradistinction to traditional 'feminine' meekness and passivity, traits which had long served only to subordinate women' (Haskins 1993: 359).

Gloria's final redemption through education allows her to express her own history and philosophy or 'gospel' by employing her motto of 'the poor are princes who have to retake their kingdoms' in her answer to the final question on her high school *bachiller* exam. This potential for reclaimed dignity is earlier signalled in her formal dressing of herself in a bullfighter's cape for the tuition of a neighbour's son and in her subsequent putting of her head under a running tap that offers both sobriety and baptismal purification. Although Gloria's donning of the cape may be read as her adoption of the absent husband's role, her precise and forceful gestures attest to her own independent mastery of the role, as well as her insider knowledge of the ceremony and ritual of the male-dominated culture of bullfighting, something that is underlined by the shot of Gloria walking to her husband's funeral flanked by but equal to such famous bullfighters as Curro Vázquez.

The metaphor of Magdalene certainly suits Abril, whose characters have suffered more than those of any other actress in Spanish cinema:

beaten up in *Cambio de sexo*, abused in Aranda's *Si te dicen que caí* (If They Tell You That I Fell, 1989), raped and slain in *Libertarias* (Freedom Fighters, 1996), a recovering junkie in *¡Átame!*, imprisoned in *Tacones lejanos*, beaten, abused and knee-capped by corkscrew in *Nadie*, etc. Moreover, like Magdalene, Abril's individualism has frequently prompted a backlash that has purposefully tainted her with the degeneracy of the whore, for, as Abril herself states, 'actors in Spain are treated like whores'. Ultimately, however, this reductive and false labelling of Victoria/Gloria/Magdalene as whore also complicates her relevance to the contemporary Spanish female, particularly when definitions of the whore criss-cross each other, dragging behind them precepts of Marxist and fascist dogma: hardline feminists see dutiful wives as whores, while Church-educated *machistas* see unmarried, sexually active women as whores. Yet, this unholy trinity of Victoria/ Gloria/Magdalene is beyond them all, combining forces in a battle to reverse the view that individuality of any kind should be countered with alienation. There was a time when dissident Spanish cinema based itself on the individual auteur, whose autonomy was a response to the state control of cultural expression. And, even now, as auteur of her own persona and star discourse, Abril embodies the ability to 'articulate both the promise and the difficulty that the notion of individuality presents for all of us who live by it' (Dyer 1987: 8). In sitting her high school exam, Gloria corrects her misspelling of the verb *echar* (to throw away) by remembering to 'echar la 'h' por la ventana' (to throw the 'h' away). The misspelt *hechar* suggests the participle *hecho* of the verb *hacer* (to do or to make), meaning something that is already done or made, whereas by correcting it to *echar*, Gloria throws all that away. Christ does not resurrect and this modern Magdalene must get on and triumph on her own terms, much like Abril: 'It's been a struggle, but right now I'm feeling good about things. The essential things in life are going well.'

Notes

1. All quotes from Victoria Abril, unless otherwise stated, are from an interview with the author.
2. The relationship between Abril and Aranda has recently foundered acrimoniously. Abril's other films for Aranda include *Tiempo de silencio* (Time of Silence, 1986), *El Lute, camina o revienta* (El Lute:

Forge on or Die, 1987), *Los jinetes del alba* (Riders of the Dawn, 1990) and *Intruso* (Intruder, 1993).

3. Abril's third film for Almodóvar is *Kika* (1993) though there are four if you count her cameo in the first nightclub scene in *Ley del deseo* (Law of Desire, 1987). She was also due to play Veronica Forqué's role in Almodóvar's *¿Qué he hecho yo para merecer esto!* (What Have I Done to Deserve This!, 1984) but felt the role of the prostitute was too close to the role of a prostitute that she had just played in Borau's *Río abajo* (On the Line, 1984).

4. This response to Abril's overtly sexual but commandingly subjective star persona becomes particularly acute when she explores bisexuality on-screen in *Cambio de sexo* (1976), *La muchacha de las bragas de oro* (1979), *French Twist* (1995) and *Reykjavik 101* (2001) among others. A critical and public dismissal of such performances as sensationalism may defuse her threat to phallocentricism, but Abril replies to these accusations with characteristic scorn: 'I think we all have a homosexual side to us, awake or not, God put it there. In the majority of cases it's asleep and it will never wake up, but sometimes it does, because it's enough that life, which is the art of meeting people, makes these things happen by chance. I'm sure that love is stronger than sex. You might start out believing you have a certain sexuality, but then along comes someone who says that's wrong, who says they're going to show you things from another perspective, and besides, you're going to like it. In the right place, at the right moment with the right person, everyone can be queer.'

5. Abril has turned down roles for Almodóvar and Aranda and has lately declared herself available to any new director with an interesting script, such as Balthasar Kormakur, first-time director of *Reykjavik 101* (2001).

References

Álvares, Rosa and Frías, B. (1991), *Vicente Aranda, Victoria Abril: El cine como pasión*, Valladolid: 36 Semana internacional de cine.

Bentley, Bernard P.E. (1999), 'The Eroteticism of "Nadie hablará de nosotras cuando hayamos muerto"', in P.W. Evans (ed.), *Spanish Cinema: The Auteurist Tradition*, Oxford: Oxford University Press.

Brooksbank Jones, Anny (1995), 'Work, Women and the Family: A Critical Perspective', in H. Graham and J. Labanyi (eds), *Spanish Cultural Studies: An Introduction*, Oxford: Oxford University Press.

Rob Stone

Doane, Mary Ann (1992), 'Film and the Masquerade: Theorising the Female Spectator', in G. Mast, M. Cohen and L. Braudy (eds), *Film Theory and Criticism*, 4th edn, Oxford: Oxford University Press.

Dyer, Richard (1987), *Heavenly Bodies: Film Stars and Society*, London: Cinema BFI series.

Evans, Peter William (2002), 'Victoria Abril: The Sex Which is Not One', in J. Labanyi (ed.), *Constructing Identity in Contemporary Spain*, Oxford: Oxford University Press.

Haskins, Susan (1993), *Mary Magdalene: Myth and Metaphor*, New York: Riverhead.

Heredero, Carlos F. (1997), 'Agustín Díaz Yanes: La ética del trabajo', in *Espejo de miradas*, Madrid: Festival de cine de Alcala de Henares.

Johnston, Claire (1992), 'The Subject of Feminist Film Theory/Practice', in J. Caughie and A. Kuhn (eds), *The Sexual Subject: A Screen Reader in Sexuality*, London: Routledge.

Kinder, Marsha (1997), *Refiguring Spain: Cinema/Media/Representation*, Durham NC: Duke University Press.

Kuhn, Annette (1992), 'Women's Genres', in J. Caughie and A. Kuhn (eds), *The Sexual Subject: A Screen Reader in Sexuality*, London: Routledge.

Martín-Márquez, Susan (1999), *Feminist Discourse in Spanish Cinema: Sight Unseen*, Oxford: Oxford University Press.

Montero, Rosa (1995), 'The Silent Revolution: The Social and Cultural Advances of Women in Democratic Spain', in H. Graham and J. Labanyi (eds), *Spanish Cultural Studies: An Introduction*, Oxford: Oxford University Press.

Mulvey, Laura (1992), 'Visual Pleasure and Narrative Cinema', in G. Mast, M. Cohen and L. Braudy (eds), *Film Theory and Criticism*, 4th edn, Oxford: Oxford University Press.

Rose, Jacqueline (1988), *Sexuality in the Field of Vision*, London: Verso.

Smith, Paul Julian (2000), *The Moderns: Time, Space and Subjectivity in Contemporary Spanish Culture*, Oxford: Oxford University Press.

Stone, Rob (2001), *Spanish Cinema*, Harlow: Longman.

Tasker, Yvonne (2000), *Spectacular Bodies: Gender, Genre and the Action Cinema*, London: Routledge.

Williams, Linda (1989), *Hard Core: Power, Pleasure, and the 'Frenzy of the Visible'*, Berkeley: University of California Press.

–12–

Theatricality, Melodrama, and Stardom in *El último cuplé*

Kathleen M. Vernon

The melodramatic utterance breaks through everything that constitutes the 'reality-principle', all its censorships, accommodations, tonings-down. Desire cries aloud its language in identification with full states of being.

Peter Brooks, *The Melodramatic Imagination*

Postwar Spanish cinema's first authentic 'blockbuster,' *El último cuplé* had its première at Madrid's Cine Rialto on 6 May 1957, although at that moment there was little evidence of the film's future trajectory, in which it would roll up box-office records across the Peninsula, in Latin America, and even the Soviet Union, making a movie star of Hollywood proportions out of lead actress Sara Montiel and generating a series of would-be sequels starring Montiel and others. Montiel herself was absent from the première, having returned to Los Angeles with her husband, film director Anthony Mann. The film's director and producer Juan de Orduña had struggled to find financial backing for the project and when the search for a distributor proved nearly impossible he ended up selling the rights to CIFESA studios for 'a plate of lentils' (Castro 1974: 298).

Contemporary press reports and reviews acknowledged and largely celebrated *El último cuplé*'s unprecedented success. The film journal *Triunfo* reported: 'Everybody is talking about *El último cuplé*' (*Triunfo*, 22 May 1957*)*; reviews from Tenerife and Cordóba spoke of the film as 'an authentic cinematic event' (16 November 1957) and a 'cinematic phenomenon' (5 November 1957). Provincial papers pointed to the build-up of expectation for the film's arrival in their region: 'We don't believe there has ever been a Spanish or foreign film whose arrival in Oviedo was awaited with so much curiosity' (*Región*, 1 October 1957); 'The "bomb" of the current cinema season has finally exploded' (*Información*, Alicante, 1 October 1957). A number of the reviews cast the film as a national triumph for Spanish cinema: 'Una obra españolísima... A highly Spanish work from start to finish' (*Patria*, Granada, 12 October 1957); '*El último cuplé* is a great Spanish film capable of holding its own against the best foreign cinema' (*Diario de Cádiz,* 16 October 1957); or as *Triunfo* has it, 'winning a major battle for Spanish cinema this season'.

In the midst of such expressions of nationalistic pride certain voices were nevertheless heard to question the reasons behind the success of a film that they recognized as hardly innovative or artistically distinguished. Thus, while the dean of Franco-era cinema criticism, Fernando Méndez-Leite, would trumpet the film as 'the most significant triumph of [Spanish] national cinema in its already long history' (1965: 270), director Orduña himself was singularly dismissive in his judgement: '*El último cuplé*, apart from some scenes handled with sensitivity, is technically about as ordinary and common as is possible. It was made quickly and on the run, without the slightest aspiration to anything more' (Castro 1974: 298).

What was it then that enabled a low-budget domestic film to triumph over competing 'quality' products from Spain and abroad? What were the sources of the film's nationalistic appeal? And why, despite its nearly mythic status, has *El último cuplé* remained, in Román Gubern's words, 'one of the most singular and worst studied phenomena in the history of Spanish cinema' (1984: 187)?[1] This chapter will propose a series of answers to those questions, focusing on the film's mobilization of a highly effective form of melodrama, rooted in the revival of a popular pre-civil war song and performance genre, the *cuplé*, and with it, the elaboration of a complex model of female stardom and behaviour.

Escapism and Theatricality

As many of the reviews and Orduña himself recognized, *El último cuplé* is on many levels a baldly formulaic film, with little pretence to originality or depth, whether of plot or of character. The familiar fiction of a female performer's rise to fame and the conflicts thus entailed between private and public success is a standard storyline for countless musicals from Hollywood to Bollywood and places in between.[2] In *El último cuplé*, however, the primacy and priority of the musical repertory clearly subordinate narrative to song. As a result, narrative structure, action, and character function as pure pretext, shaped by the indispensable appearance of well-known songs recognized by Spanish audiences as central to the cuplé genre. The film opens with a self-reflexive 'prologue' that calls attention to this inversion of normal dramatic motivation and points to the narrative void at the origin of the film. The initial image and background for the opening credits shows a theatre stage covered by a heavy red curtain. When the credits end, the curtain rises, and still another red curtain parts from the centre. Contrary to expectations the rising curtains fail to provide access to the story. Instead a spotlight illuminates the centre of the empty stage, while an off-screen voice announces a dedication: 'In memory of those women who once moved us with the brief magic of the *cuplé*, this homage: a mosaic of famous songs gathered within an invented story that could have been true'. With that, the curtain descends once again.

This hesitation between flesh-and-blood women and their fictional evocation, between invention and history, nostalgic recollection and vicarious contemporary romance, shapes the unfolding narrative and no doubt offers one clue to the film's exceptional appeal. The closed-off stage of the false opening is followed by a street scene, stock shots of contemporary Barcelona (identified by a superimposed title as set in 195–) that stand out all the more in a film composed almost exclusively of studio-based shooting. A theatre façade in the city centre gives way to the interior of a third-rate theatre where María Luján (Sara Montiel) is performing amid a motley assortment of can-can dancers and singing acts, as we are belatedly granted access to the story behind the curtain. Unbeknownst to the down-on-her-luck singer, who needs a belt of whiskey before emerging on stage, a pair of old friends have come to watch the performance. The subsequent reminiscences in her dressing room trigger a long flashback evoking María's eventful career: her seemingly unstoppable rise from the *zarzuela* (Spanish comic opera) chorus line to individual stardom, international travel and growing personal and financial independence; the loves lost and found; and her later decline into drink, ill-health and penury. Fashioned by and around the performance of well-known cuplés, the narrative takes Luján from the popular quarters of Madrid to Paris and New York, her artistic choices and personae shaped by the different audiences' expectations, for the cheeky *chulapona* (popular female Madrileñan street type) or the 'authentic' embodiment of more exotic, regional forms of Spanishness – Andalusian and Valencian, respectively. Her romantic life too, with its varied cast of male admirers, seems matched to the musical repertory, from her first love, the clockmaker's apprentice Cándido, to the worldly impresario Juan Contreras, and the young bullfighter, Pepe Domingo.

More so, and more overtly, perhaps, than the majority of popular culture texts, *El último cuplé* reveals itself as highly overdetermined, crossed by multiple causalities and motivations external to the 'integrity' of the story. In his study of the film, Gubern signals its archetypical form and function, marked by the presence of plot devices and topoi drawn from fairy tales and other popular mythologies more specific to the period. Gubern also reviews the film's financially precarious production history prior to its box-office take-off as evidence of the fact that the film was not originally perceived as a commercial venture, contrary to its subsequent reputation in the press. His larger point is that commercial success is never a given and that popular taste is unpredictable and often resistant to market manipulation (1984: 187). We might go still further to argue that the production and reception history of *El último cuplé* offers a critique of the view of commercial cinema as a commodified delivery system for imposing dominant ideologies on a defenceless public, revealing significant indeterminacies and even contradictions in the process and product.

El último cuplé in this regard has much in common with the popular, 'escapist' cinema of the Italian fascist period studied by Marcia Landy. Landy questions the commonplace understanding of the function of cinema entertainment as transporting viewers outside and beyond their own social reality. In her analysis the very anti-realism of such forms as melodrama and the film musical is seen as key to providing for a different kind of spectator position vis-à-vis both the film viewed and its context. Deviations from the norms of classic cinematic realism, whether through melodramatic excess or a deficit in conventional dramatic motivation, direct the viewer's attention toward a recognition of the 'theatricality of feature films, their metacinematic character, the ways in which the films perforce share with their audiences a knowledge of their commodity status, a slippery relation to conformity and opposition, and a simultaneous sense of involvement and detachment' (Landy 1998: 29). Landy deploys the notion of theatricality to complicate the binary categories that have structured previous approaches to commercial film genres. Excess is held to promote a defamiliarizing distance from the film as artifice and an awareness of the spectator's own role as consumer of a commercial product, and yet such knowledge does not constitute a necessary barrier to affective engagement. Textual excess may detract from the centrality of narrative, directing the spectator's focus to other elements of the film, the star performance, certain images, the role of gesture. The film musical offers a particular example of such reflexive forms of anti-realism and their effects with its frequent plot device of the show within the film 'that serves to present art as life and to celebrate performance over naturalism' (Ibid.: 51).

In *El último cuplé*, as we have seen, theatricality is palpable from the opening image. Over the course of the film, the apparent opposition expressed in the opening juxtaposition of stage and street will give way to an increasing fusion between on- and off-stage realities, emotions, and behaviour. Moving beyond a melodramatic 'imitation of life', the film will proclaim the identity of art and life, as embodied in the female *cuplé* singer's performance.

Documenting the Cuplé

Landy's discussion of the commercial film highlights a fundamental characteristic of the popular-culture text, namely its capacity for accommodating divergent sources and discursive models. Acknowledging the primary theatricality of *El último cuplé* should not blind us to the film's compound character, to the coexistence of contrasting yet converging narrative logics: melodrama, sentiment and nostalgia on the one hand, in conjunction with a certain documentary 'realism' (in very attenuated form of course) on the other, the latter centring on the evocation of Spain's early twentieth-century 'Belle Epoque', and charted through the evolution of the cuplé as social entertainment and a performance genre.

In this respect the choice of musical repertory is once again a determining factor. *El último cuplé* shares many generic features with the dominant musical cinema genre of the 1930s and 1940s in Spain, the Andalusian folkloric musical or *españolada*. These include the focus on the singing female lead and the interclass love plot.[3] Yet significant differences follow from the content and cultural context of the two musical repertories. As numerous commentators have noted, the world evoked by the Andalusian *copla* and its cinematic setting is largely that of an idealized, rural, pre-industrial Spain largely disconnected from any specific historical referent. And while the *españolada* also generated a female star system, the actresses and singers identified with the form – the so-called *folklóricas* (female folkloric performers), from Imperio Argentina and Estrellita Castro to Juanita Reina and Carmen Sevilla – were not noted for their sensuality, covert or otherwise.[4] Despite their sassy demeanour and ready lip, the women protagonists of the Andalusian musical remained well within the bounds of Spanish sexual propriety.

In contrast, the world of the *cuplé* evoked in Orduña's film is rooted in an explicitly 'modern', urban setting while the role of the *cupletista*, in the person of actress Sara Montiel, stands in erotic opposition to the chaste *folklórica*.[5] Although cultural historian Serge Salaün defines the *cuplé* as a fundamentally escapist genre on the basis of its lyrics,[6] the film's dual focus on the songs and the cultural context in which they were performed provides for an identification with a specific historical moment, beginning around 1900 and centring on the *cuplé*'s 'golden age' stretching from 1910 to 1925 and tied to a particular urban culture, in this case that of Madrid, and its performance venues.

As Salaün's studies of the cuplé demonstrate, the history of the emergence of the stand-alone song as a performance genre, over the course of the nineteenth and early twentieth centuries from earlier settings within the *zarzuela* or *género chico* (one-act comic opera), reflects and even anticipates the history of modernization in Spain. Urbanization and the growth of the middle class brought about the development of new forms of public entertainment and entertainment venues beyond theatre and opera – music halls, *cafés cantantes*, *salas de variétés*, cabarets – that in turn favoured the development of new forms of sociability. The emergence of a variety of public spaces given over to entertainment and leisure activities bespeaks the creation of alternatives to previous forms of professional or private life. In Salaün's words: 'This urban culture, in counterpoint to traditional rural culture, marks the emergence of modernity with a more 'civic' or lay character' (1996: 22). The liberation of the song form from the more elaborate productions, higher overheads and infrastructure required by the formal musical theatre of the *zarzuela* meant a new range of economic options and accessibility. The creation of programmes of songs and *variétés* offered at multiple daily sessions and popular prices could attract audiences from a broad range of classes, although still predominantly male in composition. The songs themselves reflected this democratizing urge as well as an anti-aristocratic and anti-monarchic spirit. Performers, audiences and composers championed this native song as an alternative to foreign opera or bel canto (Salaün 1990: 17). Thus the *españolismo* that Franco-era critics celebrated in the film was already in evidence, albeit in the form of a decidedly populist nationalism.

Despite this apparent chauvinism, paradoxically the *cuplé* was also the recipient and vehicle of numerous international influences. While its name derived from the French *couplet*, the music absorbed and reflected sources in Portuguese fado, North American fox trot, cakewalk, and jazz, and Latin American rhythms as well as domestic traditions, primarily Andalusian and Madrileñan. With its cosmopolitan vocation, the *cuplé* provided a source of cultural and social energy to a modernizing nation: 'The *cuplé* indisputably has a role as transmitter on a national scale and, moreover, a national responsibility, as much for its permeability as for its attachment to national traditions' (Salaün 1990: 124).

In telling the story of singer María Luján's rise from the chorus of the *zarzuela* to international success as a *cupletista*, the film brings historical substance to the outline of the conventional backstage musical in order to chronicle the evolution of the *cuplé* genre as studied by Salaün and others.[7] Luján's breakthrough coincides with the period of transition around 1910 from the provocative and disreputable eroticism of the so-called *género ínfimo* (negligible genre; the term plays on the notion of this form being slighter or less valued than the *género chico*) or *sicalipsis* (an untranslatable neologism meaning bawdy or obscene) to the more dignified *cuplé sentimental*, which sought to expand the audience for the genre to a mixed public of men and women. In the film María accompanies the impresario Juan Contreras to a performance of the song, *Tápame* (Cover Me Up), a number typical of the suggestive style of the overtly erotic *cuplé*, during which the singer invites a rowdy bunch of male spectators to cover up her rain-soaked and chilled body. Embracing the opportunity for advancement but rejecting both such cheap erotic effects and down-market audiences, María declares, 'I would do it another way'.

Both the film and the standard histories stress the central role of individual stars in bringing about the transformation in the genre, what Javier Barreiro characterizes as the 'dignification' of the cuplé (Barreiro 1996: 45). Historians credit La Goya (Aurora Mañanós Jaufret) and later Raquel Meller with developing the full dramatic possibilities of the individual song, with each designed and performed as a mini theatre piece accompanied by its own costumes, lighting, and décor.[8] With increased respectability and artistic recognition for the cupletista, now celebrated as much for her acting skills as for her singing, came an increase in financial standing, or perhaps, as Barreiro suggests, the latter drove the former. This was also the period in which – a development also reflected in María Luján's story – the cuplé became increasingly globalized by means of tours to the rest of Europe and North and South America, where Salaün reports, the real money was to be made.

Notwithstanding the *cuplé*'s role as an agent and index of modernization in Spain, Salaün considers its ideological effects to be largely negative and retrograde, especially with regard to the position of women in society. In his view the song-spectacle naturalizes and legitimizes the consumption of women as aesthetic and/or sexual objects and commodities. He argues that by situating the stage woman beyond and outside social norms and the family, and thus as inferior to the 'normal woman', the *cuplé* and other popular performance genres serve to reinforce the double standard that has men seeking sexual satisfaction outside the home (1996: 31).[9]

Paradoxically, success on the stage was sought by the majority of female performers, Salaün claims, as a means to reenter respectable society while achieving social and economic advancement via marriage:

> There is absolutely no doubt that the desire for respectability is what motivates the immense majority of women involved in the profession: the stage is a risky step up, but it is an efficient one to 'place oneself' and return to the flock of high-minded, 'decent' society and never a tribunal to struggle for the evolution of the female condition. (1996: 38–9)

Stardom, Melodrama and the Cuplé

As much as the film offers a confirmation of much recent scholarship on the *cuplé*, in other respects it issues a challenge to the view of the genre as entirely complicit with conservative values and the subordinate role of women. As we have noted, the history of the *cuplé* genre reveals the existence of a kind of symbiosis between well-known songs from the repertory and the stars who first made them popular. A review of the film in the Salamanca paper, *El Adelanto*, highlights this phenomenon: 'The *cuplé* was completely identified with the performer and in this way the artists were made famous by the *cuplés* they sang, and the *cuplés* by the artists who sang them' (25 May 1957). Hence Raquel Meller's pique toward Sara Montiel who she felt was usurping both her song(s), *El relicario* (*The Reliquary*) in particular, and her life story (*El Alcázar*, 25 September 1957).

This type of identification between performer and song, between 'real', historical person and role is explored in Christine Gledhill's study of the interface between melodrama and stars. Following Richard de Cordova and others, Gledhill sees stardom as arising 'when the off stage or off screen life of the actor becomes as important as the performed role in the production of a semi-autonomous persona or image ... This slippage between the player's performance of a role and the player's personal life suggests an intensification of the process of personalization in which the relation between the emblematic, moral schemae of melodrama and social reality is recast' (1991: 212).

El último cuplé condenses and dramatizes this process of personalization and fusion between off-screen life and stage persona and between 'genuine', intimate emotion and its musical expression. The film explicitly situates this process in institutional terms, with respect to the evolution of the genre and performance styles. Not for María Luján the conventional stage names, 'La Bella' this or that, of her predecessors in the *género ínfimo'*. That practice, notes impresario Contreras, 'belongs to an era that must be left behind'. Instead she will perform as herself, María Luján.

Another aspect of this condensation can be seen in the function of the songs in the film. As many commentators have noted, particularly with respect to the *canción escenificada* (staged song) style of the golden age, the *cuplé* itself is a highly compressed form of melodrama. 'The song has a plot, rising action, and denouement. It has drama or comedy, performers, music and text, scenery, lighting, appropriate costumes and even choreography' (Salaün 1996: 24). The *cuplé* marshals the basic weapons of melodrama; in its dramatic arc, form of address, reliance on gesture, costume, and corporealization, the cuplé performs an exteriorization of emotion inexpressible through other means.

The convergence between song and story in the film has not gone entirely unremarked upon. Terenci Moix has noted how the cuplés sung by Luján express a commentary on the action and serve to reinforce emotions (1993: 242). This process reaches its apex in the film as María's career arrives at its high point and she falls passionately in love with the would-be bullfighter José 'Pepe' Domingo. There initially appears to be an almost textbook Freudian economy at work in the relation between love and career, emotion and song in María's rise and fall. In setting aside her first love, the working class Cándido, she implicitly accepts the impresario's judgement that for the true artist the only love that counts is love of her art.[10] This lesson holds in the developing relationship between Contreras and his protégée as gratitude and respect on her part provide the dominant note. In her subsequent romance with the younger man it is as if all the passion that was sublimated into her art comes rushing forth. And yet, rather than a loss of emotional energy available for performance, we find an intensification of the relation between life and art as the songs increasingly predict and echo the ups and downs of their relationship, and lines of dialogue circulate between 'real life' and their incorporation into songs.

Thus when Luján finds herself caught up in a love triangle with Pepe and his hometown girlfriend Trini, she is told that Pepe has been boasting of his conquest of the famous singer, that 'él va pregonando que [ella] está medio loca por él' ('he is going around proclaiming that she is half-crazy for him'). The next scene cuts away to her performance of the *cuplé Y tú no eres eso* (And You Are Not That) whose verse repeats those exact words, as Pepe watches and listens from his seat in the theatre. Their subsequent reconciliation scene, filmed in the privacy of her carriage, ensures we have noticed the echo effect. Chastened, Pepe swears to 'love her until death', to which she replies, 'There is music to go with that'. His response indicates that he used those words so she might sing it back to him, which she does, intoning the opening stanza of *Nena* (Darling): 'Juró amarme un hombre sin miedo a la muerte' (A man swore to love me without fear of death). The shift between stage/d confrontation and intimate reunion only emphasizes the accelerating collapse of boundaries between public and private, art and life.

One reading of these scenes might suggest that the characters are playing out a pre-existing script, like Madame Bovary or Ana Osores under the influence of a diet of romantic novels. Certainly it could be argued that for more modern subjects, mass culture forms such as songs have replaced romantic literature as 'dangerous' models of behaviour or feeling. Moix seems to be responding to this extreme level of determinism with its fusion of song and story when he remarks 'More than something new in the history of the musical, it was a new condition of melodrama as genre' (1993: 243).

Throughout the course of the films two songs in particular take on a protagonizing role. Both *Nena*, first heard in an instrumental version over the opening credits, and the Meller standard *El relicario* evoke a cult of love and death, fate and fatalism. They become a form of musical prophecy, announcing the bullfighter's demise. In fact, the film makes quick work of Pepe's actual death, with the emotional response on María's part displaced to before and after his actual fatal injury in the bull ring. With the singer at home preparing to attend his debut in Madrid, the strains of *Nena* on the sound track announce a death foretold as María imagines and visibly suffers over a goring depicted in vivid detail. His real-time death, with María present in the stands, is anticlimactic as the camera cuts abruptly from the scene to a close up of María's face swathed in a Madonna-like white mantilla and then without transition to another close-up of the performer in a black mantilla. The plotting and editing have taken us where we need to go, to Luján/Montiel's performance of the classic song narrative of the tragic love between a singer and a bullfighter, *El relicario*.[11]

In her performance following the bullfighter's death, the artist doesn't simply seek inspiration for public expression in private emotion à la Method-acting but actively experiences mourning for her lost love on stage in the form of song. The proof of this melodramatic fusion of off-stage/screen sentiment with public performance is offered in her literalizing somatization of emotional suffering as a physical symptom that banishes her from the stage under pain of death. Luján is driven into involuntary retirement at the height of her career by her heart, which according to her doctor, cannot resist the excess of emotion expressed in her song. This same capacity is reactualized, just like the *cuplé* being given new potency in its film revival, upon her 'successful' comeback in Madrid some 20 years later. Hence her prophetic advice to present-day *cupletistas*: 'to be born and die in each *cuplé*'. Indeed, Luján proves as good as her word. Rescued by Contreras and brought to Madrid for a gala reintroduction to her hometown public, she collapses and dies immediately following a final rendition of *Nena*, a melodramatic finale both predetermined and arbitrary, predictable and yet moving.

To further understand the appeal and meaning of *El último cuplé* for Spanish audiences in 1957 it is useful to consider the broader social and cultural functions of melodrama and the star persona. Thomas Elsaesser has suggested that the melodramatic imagination becomes particularly active during periods of intense ideological crisis (1987: 47). In the second half of the 1950s Spain found itself in transition between two opposed economic models and value systems as the inward-directed model of economic – as well as cultural and political – self-sufficiency gave way to the open embrace of an international market economy and consumerism. December 1956 had seen a major reshuffle of the Franco cabinet with the entry of a number of technocrats linked to Opus Dei. The presence of actress Sara Montiel was also a reflection of this new mentality. Montiel had abandoned the Spanish film industry in 1950 for greater acting opportunities in Mexico and Hollywood. The performer who returned to Spain had honed her acting skills along with her technical knowledge of the medium and harnessed a consequently greater control over her own screen image. In *El último cuplé* the actress projects an anachronistic 1950s sensibility and sensuality as well as a highly developed concept of star power schooled in North America's two most potent film industries, qualities which she grafts onto the historical persona of the *cupletista*.

In a similar vein, Richard Dyer links the development of intense star-audience relations, projected through the star's 'charisma' to performers' embodiment of ideological contradiction, suggesting that the rise of particular stars can be traced to their condensation of values felt to be under threat or in flux at a particular moment in time (1991: 57–9). It is clear that in various ways Montiel's role in the film fulfils this function. Gubern stresses the place of transgression and taboo in configuring the film's relation to the popular mythologies of the time. Thus María Luján 'earns' her tragic destiny and death for having dared to contravene dominant values regarding women's traditional roles in a romantic relationship. Gubern identifies five broken taboos entailed by her romance with the bullfighter: her expression of overt carnal, sexual desire; the cross-class and cross-age dimensions; her role as protector; and the fact she breaks up the 'natural' couple, Pepe and Trini (that is, both stem from the same socio-economic milieu and age group) (1984: 193). Of course, cross-class romances were a staple of romantic fiction and film, including folkloric musicals, in which they share the traditional comedic function of promoting reconciliation of contesting social elements. Nevertheless, this is film that is more engaged by a set of unresolved conflicts, centring around issues of gender. The film would appear to flaunt a series of role reversals, by having Luján duplicate in her relationship with the younger bullfighter the role of financial supporter and career promoter that Contreras once played for her. The notion that an older 'protector' may enact a double role in initiating a protégé into the ways of the world in both professional and sexual realms is portrayed as acceptable but only when the older and wiser mentor is male. The parallelism that has Luján successively on both the receiving and the giving ends of such activity would seem to criticize or at least call attention to the 'gender dimorphism' that Salaün (1996: 26) finds so pervasive and unmovable in the world of spectacle.

Gubern contrasts this overt violation of male-female social norms and power relations with the film's relative discretion as regards the protagonist's 'moral' status. A reflection of the ambiguity, in Gubern's words, 'typical of melodrama', Luján's rise to fame is offered as an 'honorable, exemplary model for female spectators' (Gubern 1984: 194). While he details the varied contexts and motivations for the five kisses bestowed by the heroine on her various love interests, he also observes that there is no textual evidence that she actually slept with any of the men she loved. Likewise the film makes much of her rejection of the established practice for *artistas* to accept gifts and money from wealthy 'admirers'. Early in the film María and her companions express their disdain for the aging *cupletista* La Palacios and the succession of corrupt minor government officials courting her in the wings with gifts and the promise of influence. Luján subsequently makes clear her refusal to accept any sort of quid pro quo in return for Don Juan Contrera's support of her career. And when the triumphant singer sends back a ring in Paris from a Russian count (played by well-known Spanish leading man Alfredo Mayo), her substitute stage-mother Doña Paca can only lament her niece's excessive 'decency'. Yet apparently other viewers were to interpret the protagonist's behaviour in the film in significantly different ways. Critic Francisco Llinás, in opposition to Gubern, celebrates Luján/Montiel's presumably overt sexual behaviour: 'Unusual for the time, María Luján evidently slept with her lovers, she chose her men and did not hesitate to make use of her charms to advance her career' (*Liberación*, Madrid, 16 November 1984).

To that extent Montiel was perhaps the quintessential female icon of her time, personifying the ambivalences of a society caught between moralizing and modernizing impulses, and reflecting back to spectators the face of Spain as shaped by their own beliefs and desires. As such, the character of Luján not so much provides the opportunity for the reconciliation of opposites as instead embodying a state of active contradiction summarized in Terenci Moix's oxymoronic characterization of Montiel as 'la ingenua libertina' (the innocent libertine) (1993: 242). Luján's fate in the film underlines this dual message. Death takes the performer at the moment of her greatest triumph. Yet a certain undecidability persists: payment for her sins of moral and social/gender transgression, or death as consecration on the altar of melodrama's 'full states of being', in the words of Peter Brooks?

Epilogue: Gender, Politics and the Cuplé

The history of the cuplé and the forms of sociability and performances of gender identities that developed around it reveal a further dimension not directly referenced in the film but key to understanding the changing ethos reflected by it. While, as we have seen, Salaün is highly critical of the way in which the medium models and reinforces traditional male and female roles, he also remarks on the extent to which the world of the stage offered 'a space of liberty and creativity for homosexuals', both for well-known performers of the era such as Miguel de Molina, Edmond de Bries and Tomás de Antequerra (the latter two of whom performed dressed as women), as well as authors, composers, and scene designers such as lyricist, writer and participant-chronicler of *arte frívolo* (the frivolous arts) Alvaro Retana (Salaün 1996: 40). A later film, Pedro Olea's *Un hombre llamado Flor de Otoño/A Man Called Autumn Flower* (1978), extends this theme of personal sexual liberation achieved through the *cuplé* to the political sphere. *Flor de Otoño* narrates the true story of a member of the Barcelonan upper class who leads a triple life as a labor lawyer and dutiful mother's son by day and transvestite *cupletista* and anarchist militant by night. The film insists on the association between the world of the *cuplé* with its radical gender politics and the cause of political revolution, as the protagonist enlists his nocturnal companions in a plan to assassinate dictator Primo de Rivera. Although the plot fails and the men are executed at the film's conclusion, the story celebrates the full range of their transgressive acts and their role as pioneers and martyrs – not unlike María Luján – in an ongoing struggle to love, sing and live in freedom.

Notes

1. The film's reputation is alluded to in the title of Francisco Llinás's article (1984) in the short-lived Madrid daily *Liberación*, 'El último cuplé: un mito para españoles'. Nevertheless, Gubern's article (1984) remains one of the few attempts at extended analysis of the film.
2. The key studies for understanding the American form of the genre are those of Altman (1990) and Feuer (1993).
3. For a more nuanced understanding of the *españolada* or folkloric musical, see Woods (2000), Labanyi (1997), and Vernon (1999).
4. Daniel Pineda Novo defines the *folklórica* and the films in which they appeared in these terms: 'They were romantic, lovable, schmaltzy films ... which project a false image of a sometimes gentle, sometimes fierce woman – usually gypsy – although affectionate and pure and even puritanical, "everybody's sweetheart". And in the background, the strumming of guitars, stamping heels and the clatter of castanets' (1991: 8).
5. Although a number of *El último cuplé*'s critics cast the cuplé film as a worthy successor to the earlier folkloric musical, this sequencing reverses the historical relation between the two song genres, with the *copla* or *canción española* emerging as the cuplé was losing its dominant role on stage. There is in fact a good deal of overlap, in terms of both performers and repertory, between the cuplé and the copla, despite the presumed contrasts in content and performance style: cosmopolitan and suggestive if not erotic for the cuplé vs local and sexually unthreatening for the copla.
6. This in contrast to Barreiro, who claims that 'the *cuplé* is completely imbricated in everyday life and ... in it we can find continuous references to events great and small of the time: the Russian Revolution, syndicalism, the Moroccan War, inventions, fashion, female emancipation, sport' (1996: 43).
7. In addition to Salaün and Barreiro, see the more anecdotal studies by Zúñiga (1954), Villarín (1990), Díaz de Quijano (1960), and Retana (1964).

8. Born in Bilbao, 5 December 1891, Jaufret made her debut in June 1911. She quickly became a star. 'The reform of the *cuplé* is attributed to her, which consisted of eliminating all remaining traces of the *género ínfimo*. She imposed the model of performing each song wearing a costume appropriate to it. She retired from the stage in 1927 following her marriage to writer Tomás Borrás and would only return for a series of benefit performances during the Civil War' (González Peña et al. 1996: 198). Meller was born in Zaragoza on 9 March 1888. According to González Peña et al., less an innovator than a masterful interpreter – 'she perfected the genre initiated by La Goya' – Meller went on to international acclaim in Paris and New York (1996: 198). In Los Angeles she befriended Charlie Chaplin who would use the music from one of her standards, *La violetera* (The Violet Seller), in his film *City Lights*. Meller herself had a successful film career, primarily in France. She was known for her diva-esque temperament as well as for her interpretations of more dramatic *cuplés*, such as *El relicario* (The Reliquary).

9. One indication of that on-stage/off-stage distinction and double standard of permissible and non-permissible behaviours occurs in the film's first scene set in the 1950s. In her dressing room preparing to go on stage, María Luján's décolletage is partially covered by a veil which disappears when she is on stage and reappears after her performance when she is once again in her dressing room. The on-again off-again veil would seem to distinguish between a kind of off-stage and on-stage existence in which different rules of behaviour apply. When María is speaking to the little girl who brings her laundry, or is perceived by the film's spectators as a 'normal woman', she must observe certain norms and limits of dress, but when she is on stage she exists in an outside realm, beyond social norms.

10. The suggestive overtones of the name Cándido and the notion of love sacrificed for art and career hit all the familiar, archetypical notes. Nevertheless, the Cándido storyline also evokes the historical referent of Spain's African colonial wars when the young boyfriend pays off his debts by taking the place of a more wealthy draftee and shipping off to Africa.

11. In this plot device the film exploits the familiar romantic topos of the bullfighter and female singer/dancer, an early instance of celebrity coupledom played out before the press and public by Spanish performers from Pastora Imperio to Rocío Jurado and Isabel Pantoja.

Kathleen M. Vernon

References

Altman, R. (1990), *The American Film Musical*, Bloomington: Indiana University.

Barreiro, J. (1996), 'Las artistas de *variétés* y su mundo', in María Luz González Peña, Javier Suárez Pajares and Julio Arce Bueno (eds), *Mujeres de la escena, 1900–1940,* Madrid: Sociedad General de Autores y Editores.

Brooks, P. (1976), *The Melodramatic Imagination*, New Haven: Yale University Press.

Castro, A. (1974), *El cine español en el banquillo*, Valencia: Fernando Torres.

De Cordova, R. (1990), *Picture Personalities: The Emergence of the Star System in America*, Urbana: University of Illinois Press.

Díaz de Quijano, M. (1960), *Tonadilleras y cupletistas. Historia del cuplé*, Madrid: Cultura Clásica y Moderna.

Dyer, R. (1991), 'Stars and Society: Charisma', in Christine Gledhill (ed.), *Stardom: Industry of Desire,* London: Routledge.

'*El último cuplé* y la "nueva" Sara Montiel', (1957), *Triunfo*, Madrid, 22 May.

Elsaesser, T. (1987), 'Tales of Sound and Fury: Observations on the Family Melodrama', in Christine Gledhill (ed.), *Home is Where the Heart Is*, London: BFI.

Feuer, J. (1993), *The Hollywood Musical*, 2nd Edn, Bloomington: Indiana University Press.

Gledhill, C. (1991), 'Signs of Melodrama', in Christine Gledhill (ed.), *Stardom: Industry of Desire*, London: Routledge.

González-Peña, M.L., Suárez Pajares, J. and Arce Bueno, J. (eds) (1996), *Mujeres de la escena, 1900–1940*, Madrid: Sociedad General de Autores y Editores.

Gubern, R. (1984), '*El último cuplé*', *Cahiers de la Cinématèque*, 38/39: 187–94.

Labanyi, J. (1997), 'Race, Gender and Disavowal in Spanish Cinema of the Early Francoist Period: The Missionary Film and the Folkloric Musical', *Screen*, 38(3): 215–31.

Landy, M. (1998), *The Folklore of Consensus: Theatricality in Italian Cinema, 1930–1943*, Albany: State University of New York Press.

Latino, J. (1957), 'Fenómeno cinematográfico', *Córdoba*, Córdoba, 5 November.

Less, A. (1957), 'En el Campoamor, *El último cuplé*', *Región*, Oviedo, 1 October.

'Los estrenos' (1957), *Información*, Alicante, 1 October.

'Los estrenos' (1957), *Patria*, Granada, 12 October.

Llinás, F. (1984), '*El último cuplé*: Un mito para españoles', *Liberación*, Madrid, 16 November.

Méndez-Leite, F. (1965), *Historia del cine español*, Madrid: Ediciones Rialp.

Moix, T. (1993), *Suspiros de España: La copla y el cine en el recuerdo*, Barcelona: Plaza y Janés.

Pedraz, S. (1957), '*El último cuplé*', *El Adelanto de Salamanca*, Salamanca, 25 May.

Pineda Novo, Daniel (1991), *Las folklóricas y el cine*, Huelva: Festival de Cine Iberoamericano.

Retana, A. (1964), *Historia del arte frívolo*, Madrid: Tesoro.

Salaün, S. (1990), *El cuplé*. Madrid: Espasa-Calpe, 1990.

—— (1996), 'La mujer en las tablas', in María Luz González-Peña et al. (eds), *Mujeres de la escena, 1900-1940*, Madrid: Sociedad General de Autores Editores.

'Scaramouch' (1957), '*El último cuplé* constituye un auténtico acontecimiento del cine español', *Heraldo*, Santa Cruz de Tenerife, 16 November.

'Teatro Anadalucía – *El último cuplé*,' *Diario de Cadiz*, Cádiz, 26 October.

Vernon, K. (1999), 'Culture and Cinema to 1975', in David T. Gies (ed.), *Cambridge Companion to Modern Spanish Culture*, Cambridge: Cambridge University Press.

Villarín, J. (1990), *El Madrid del cuplé*, Madrid: Comunidad de Madrid.

Woods, E. (2000), *From Rags to Riches: Ideological Contradiction and Female Stardom in the Andalusian Musical Comedy Film*, PhD Dissertation, State University of New York, Stony Brook.

Zúñiga, A. (1954), *Una historia del cuplé*, Barcelona: Barna.

-13-

Radio Free *Folklóricas*: Cultural, Gender and Spatial Hierarchies in *Torbellino* (1941)

Eva Woods

Recent scholarship on Spanish popular films before 1950 tends to agree with Stallybrass and White, who demonstrate that high/low opposition is fundamental to ordering and sense-making in European cultures (1986: 3). Focusing on the disruption of official dichotomies and the fabrication of consent (Labanyi 2001: 85 and 2002: 209; Marsh 1999; Vernon 1999; Woods 2000), such studies explain fascism's inability to impose official culture by its failure to control the making or reception of meaning. My argument in this chapter is that within the restricted confines of Francoist culture, Andalusian musical-comedy films were nevertheless able to privilege an ambitious, independent, female protagonist who thrived in the ambiguous world of entertainment spectacle. *Torbellino* (Marquina, 1941) is typical of this film genre, dramatizing what Stuart Hall identifies as the tendency of popular culture to negotiate between high and low constructions, and between adaptive and dissident elements (Hall and Whannel 1965: x). In this film, feminized and massified flamenco culture (personified by the Sevillian singer, Carmen) triumphs over high art, and the North (symbolized by the male Basque owner of the radio station and classical music aficionado) surrenders to flamenco via the highly contested mass medium of the radio.

Under Francoism, oppositional popular discourses often competed with traditional material which was supported by Francoist cultural policy because it was based on 'authenticated' values and customs that reflected 'hierarchical and reactionary social order and a unitary state...' (Boyd 1997: 235). In Andalusian musical comedies, for example, rise-to-stardom narratives pose as oppositional rhetoric (Woods 2000): stardom is consistently cast as a powerful vehicle of change (a *torbellino*) which disrupts static structures of class and identity. Indeed, *Torbellino* debunks what Graham calls 'national patriotic "high" cultural material' (1995:

238) through its peculiar construction of female *folklórica* stardom. But the filmic representation of radio in Torbellino does not celebrate the *folklórica* as an expression of the peasantry and the working classes. The *folklórica* instead comes to represent the hybrid commercial flamenco music known as *canción española*. The gradual dominance of this 'inferior' artistic style from a devalued geographical region represents a complex hegemonic process. The film's capitalist discourses, disguised as popular ones, enact consent between competing class interests ultimately making *Torbellino*'s 'home-grown' version of capitalist culture an acceptable one. If cultural domination in Spain depended upon who controlled the transmission and diffusion of song (Salaün, 1990: 155), then *Torbellino* recounts the struggle between the interests of different classes, who sought to define national taste by imposing their own regional music styles through radio and film.

Nation Narration

Debates on high and low art, notions of taste, the popular, and the role of these in a national cinema, comprise the ideological context in which Andalusian musical-comedy films were produced and received. Between the 1920s and the 1940s, cinema magazines such as *Cinegramas*, *Nuestro Cinema*, and later, *Primer Plano* published countless articles on what should constitute a Spanish national cinema. Two camps emerged: one was formed by directors such as Florián Rey, who argued that the *españolada* (or films devoted to portraying Spanishness) could faithfully represent an authentic Spanish diversity. The other group, made up of both pro-dictatorship and liberal intellectual elites, saw the *españolada* as the downfall of the industry, arguing that it promoted a stereotyped and false view of Spain's reality by privileging the topoi of Andalusian settings and folklore to the detriment of those of other regions. In a radio broadcast interview from 1946, *Torbellino*'s writer and director, Luis Marquina, states:

> Because the *españolada* is nothing more than a deformation, an excess of what is Spanish that we, naturally, are the first to reject; ... these films deprive us of all the artistic wealth, the diversity of environments, the profusion of topics and even the variation of sentimental motives that the different Spanish regions make available to us. (Pérez Perucha, 1983: 144)[1]

What constituted 'the unknown authentic Spain' was therefore a hotly contested affair. Marquina, like the Álvarez y Quintero brothers, felt that Andalusian motifs, if used correctly, could still raise the cultural level of the general public through the medium of radio and film. Both Marquina and the Álvarez and Quintero brothers were involved in *radioteatro* (radio plays), and scores of films from the 1930s to the 1950s were adapted from plays by the Álvarez and Quintero brothers. (*Torbellino* has been described as 'an almost Quinterian popular show'.)[2] Antonio Quintero, Rafael de León, and Manuel Quiroga, the playwrights and composers *par excellence* of folklore musical theatre, were in large part responsible for what Álvaro Retana calls 'the dictatorship of the Andalusian setting' and many of the plays authored by the trio occupy a liminal space between high and low culture. De León's songs, for instance, have been compared to Federico García Lorca's poetry, yet the authorial trio and their contemporaries maintained that it was necessary to raise the intellectual level while at the same time pleasing the public: on the one hand 'reformist and conscious', and on the other, catering to popular tastes (Romero Ferrer 1996: 50). But critics of the *españolada* refused to accept that the stability and meagre success of the Spanish film industry was largely due to this embarrassing *cine de pandereta* (literally, cinema of the tambourine, but referring to folkloric musical styles catering to a supposed lower-class taste). According to a fascist critic, this cinema glorified 'that Spain of "generous bandits" constantly fighting with the law and all that symbolizes authority and discipline', and formulaically featured a famous bullfighter in love with 'a dark and robust woman'.[3] Replete with elements inconsistent with an official or intellectual mythology of Spanishness ('portraying the criminal lives of these people, who living on the verge of misery, entertain the placid bourgeoisie and foment resistance among those whose lives constitute a constant struggle against adversity'), these films nevertheless continued to be produced, and even increased during the 1940s.

Aided by the Church, the Franco regime was well aware that nation narration – or even the creation of personal and regional identity – depended in part on controlling how the media produced and disseminated knowledge for mass consumption. Cinematic sound supported the regime's emphasis on a specific kind of national identity: films could be dubbed, subtitled in Castilian, and regional music could be used to reinforce a sense of belonging. Yet clearly, the regime had not succeeded in controlling cultural discourse, for despite ubiquitous censorship, the cinema and radio remained to a large degree privately owned or collective enterprises. Therefore, cinema under Franco was not and could not be merely the product of a homogenous political machine. As Besas affirms, Franco's cinema policy 'was not to interfere in the workings of the industry, but merely to ensure the established order. The cinema was farmed out among the victors in the war. The Church took charge of its morality; the state unions got its administration, racketeers and the rich the chance to make a buck' (Besas 1985: 37). Discourse on national cinema and, inevitably, the films themselves were shaped by a complex amalgamation of capitalist entrepreneurs (managers, stars, theatre companies, the *cuplé* industry, lower-level employees), investors and intellectuals, some pro-regime, others not. These varied interests competed to establish their own (profitable) versions of nation and identity while simultaneously trying to appease state censors. It should come as no surprise, consequently, that *Torbellino* tells an ambiguous, many-sided story. It includes the struggle for a feminized popular culture against a masculine high culture, but also shows how that very conflict became a key theme, typifying the radio-dominated mass entertainment industry, and largely enabling its success.

High and Low: Cultural, Gender, and Spatial Hierarchies

The beginning scenes of *Torbellino* immediately draw the spectator into the debate between high and low art. The camera opens to the set of a radio station's recording studio where an opera singer's shrill voice clearly marks her as parodic. Her singing becomes the subject of an argument over the merits of popular vs classical music that develops between the managers of two radio stations: 'Alegría de la vida' ('The Joy of Life') and 'Radio Ibérico' (also the name of one of the first radio stations in Spain). Radio Ibérico's manager is Don Segundo Izquierdo, whose name mocks liberal left-wing intellectuals as guardians of high culture. He symbolizes high art's desire to separate itself from mass culture:

> *Manager*: But do you really think you can advertise 'The Joy of Life', which is the title of our house with this tragic program that invites death by asphyxiation?
>
> *Don Segundo*: What you mockingly call tragedy is art, pure art; the true tragedy is in mixing, in an absurd alliance, what is artistic with the greed for money.

Don Segundo has only contempt for art that displays hybridization, as opposed to a 'pure' form, or reveals a desire for profit (two qualities inherent in Andalusian musical-comedy films). Unlike his Sevillian business partner, Don Segundo lives the life of pure art and taunts the manager for his lower-class taste for cheap flamenco tavern entertainment and its drinking culture, both of which he associates with an essentialist Andalusian identity. But the manager of Alegría de la Vida argues that by marketing only classical music, Don Segundo has become too distanced and insensitive to the 'needs' of the public. His partner tries to convince him to mix in some popular culture – 'but mix man, mix ... come off that high horse' – and suggests that *la rutina* (routine), the kind of music that the people are used to encountering in their daily lives, should be the focus of Radio Ibérico's programming. 'Mixing' implies passion and identification rather than coldly objective or distant observation. But ironically, casting popular song in these terms also tends to disguise its status as a cleverly marketed commodity.

Interestingly, the characterization of the radio in *Torbellino* is remarkably similar to historical anecdotes about 'Unión Radio', one of the first Spanish radio stations (constituted in 1924, inaugurated in 1925, and after 1939 called La Ser, Sociedad Española de Radiofusión), which remained profitable, pleasurable, and strongly distanced from its role as Primo de Rivera's or Franco's cultural loudspeaker. Seen as the paragon of modernity, Unión Radio's director Ricardo Urgoiti was an engineer, a monopolist business man, and the visible head of several large corporations. Simultaneously, he was criticized as 'liberal, Masonic, and red' (Diaz 1997: 131). Between 1926 and 1929 he was known as the man who monopolized the airwaves (Ibid.: 131). As Armand Balsebre states, Urgoiti's modernity came from his capacity for understanding that the radio needed to attract listeners and clients who could finance publicity (Balsebre 1992: 148). For Urgoiti, programming that sought equilibrium between elitism and lowbrow genres was important in order to break with the amateurism of the early broadcasts in Spain (Balsebre 1992: 150). *Torbellino* echoes the changes affecting Unión Radio in the 1920s by portraying the competition between radio stations (Radio Ibérica, Unión Radio and Radio Castilla fiercely fought over the Madrid market in the mid-1920s, [Balsebre 1992: 145]), and by stressing the issue of mixing high and low. Urgoiti's strategy of integrating high musical tastes (classical music and opera) with popular music (*zarzuela*, 'música española', flamenco) and music such as jazz and the foxtrot (Balsebre 1992: 152) had appealed to a broad audience, partly because radio was inherently an interclass genre (Díaz 1997: 34; Balsebre 1992: 142).[4] Radio is a powerful means of disseminating information, but the public saw it principally as a music box. From the beginning, its musical identity was mixed: classical music and opera were regularly featured alongside flamenco and *canción española*. In 1924, Radio Ibérica broadcast a live transmission of the flamenco group, Rita y Pepe Ortega, El Niño de las Marismas, followed by a baturro group (Díaz, 1997: 52, 98).

The strong undercurrent of capitalist competition in *Torbellino*'s narrative alternates with discourses on the value of art and modernist aesthetics, complicating the film's ideological structure. Like Ortega y Gasset's writings, the film evokes the intelligentsia's attempts at inventing the nation. Such efforts underlie the characterization of don Segundo, an elitist unwilling to compromise his musical taste (and therefore in danger of losing his business). Ortega y Gasset defended modernist, or pure, disinterested art, against a takeover by the anonymous, chaotic, vulgar and undifferentiated masses who imposed 'the passions' on artistic production. In contrast, bourgeois realism and romanticism, instead of concentrating on form, emphasized human relations and the power of pathos, reducing the distance between work and the emotions, and encouraging an identification with the work of art that came to be called 'psychic contagion'. Andreas Huyssen calls such a discourse the Great Divide, stressing that modernist high art increasingly distances itself from the commodification of culture associated with low art (Huyssen 1986: 17).

The commodification of art evoked an upper-class fear of the increasing social mobility brought about by modernization. Between the late nineteenth and the first third of the twentieth century, the debate about high and low culture focused on transformations in private life. The changing role of women sparked fears of anarchy (that is, the women's movement and socialism) that could only be quelled by accusing women of immorality, satirizing them, and devaluing their production as mass culture (Sieburth 1994: 7). In turn, the proliferation of feminine mass culture was stigmatized as a sign of cultural decline, a loss of the Benjaminian 'aura'. Authentic folk and high culture, on the other hand, connoted masculinity. The privileging of *deep song*, or *cante jondo*, for instance, showed how 'upper class interest in expressive styles' (Mitchell 1994: 99) gave the rich 'a more frank way of dealing with the opposite sex' and allowed them to 'slum', or spend a night of debauchery and then return to their homes (Mitchell 1994: 108).

Flamenco performance had traditionally been a closed affair, mostly catering to wealthy all-male audiences who could hire a flamenco group to entertain a private coterie for an evening. After its institutionalization through mass-public theatres, however, flamenco spectacle filled coliseums and venues formerly reserved for the *variétés*. Flamenco musicians began to play with an orchestra, hybridizing the *canción andaluza* and the *cante jondo* and drawing scathing criticism from cultural elites. *Torbellino* celebrates the commodification of flamencoized music and thereby undercuts critiques by non-Calé (non-'Gypsy') flamencologists who were intent on preserving the exploitative labour relations that oppressed flamenco performers during the late nineteenth and early twentieth centuries. Álvarez Caballero, for instance, laments how *cantaores* such as Pepe Marchena 'frivolized' and softened *opera flamenca*, adding orchestra, falsettos, personal creativity, and most importantly, the explicit seduction of a mass audience, all of which degraded the 'seriousness' of deep song into a 'a pretty song' instead of 'true song' (Álvarez Caballero 1994: 224). Such changes depleted flamenco of its 'mystical' aspects but speeded the development of the *canción española* on the radio and in musical-comedy films, where it was sung by *folklóricas* and *cupletistas* such as Concha Piquer, Estrellita Castro, and Imperio Argentina. A corresponding rise in professionalism, embodied in contracts, salaries, managers, the personalism of the performer and mass spectacles held in squares or bull rings, contributed to the perceived decline of authentic deep-song practice (Álvarez Caballero, 1994: 230–1). The attempt by intellectuals to fossilize flamenco as an ethnically pure cultural form (a form particularly apt for male *initiates*) was a response provoked by the threat of modern mass culture in the form of *españoladas* and *folklóricas*.[5]

Nietzsche had said that Wagner and the theatre – mere spectacle and illusion – epitomized mass taste and the feminization of culture. Popular theatre was emotional, affective (Nietzsche was swept away by *Carmen*); high art distanced the audience, keeping them from surrendering to the play. Women had a significant place in the theatre because their acting was imitative and unoriginal, thus not a threat to high art. The insistence on gendering mass culture as feminine recalls the 'masculinist mystique' of modernist thinkers such as Marx, Nietzsche and Freud. Freud's notion of stable boundaries between the ego and the id parallels Marx's elevation of production over consumption, the id and consumption being the feminine counterparts in each case (Huyussen 1986: 37). The privileging of production over consumption, moreover, as well as 'the effect of commodification in the music material' (Huyussen 1986: 37) and the gendered connotations that cling to consumption and commodification, are ideas that appear in the later writings of Adorno, whose essays significantly affected mid-twentieth-century Spanish criticism of *españolada* films. *Torbellino* establishes Don Segundo as an emblem of Orteguian modernist thought, only to debunk this image in favour of the transformed Don Segundo, who finally, by the grace of capitalist logic, is able to grasp the exploitable potential of 'Andalusianified' mass culture.

Spatial Hierarchies

As in all Andalusian musical comedies, the representation of high and low in *Torbellino* alternates between a class/taste register and a geographical one (the South is the feminized counterpart of the masculinized North). Reflecting on the history of power relations between North and South in Spain, Ortega y Gasset argued that during the late 1920s, Andalusia enjoyed intellectual predominance while other regions were apparently in decline. Recalling a similar time in the nineteenth century, when Andalusia was the centre for the development of the new social sciences, Krausism, and university reform, Ortega y Gasset wrote 'Theory of Andalusia', a racist and degrading explanation of Andalusian psychology, but also perhaps a parody of writings spawned by this regionally-centred intellectual fad. Characterizing Andalusia as the feminized and racialized other whose affected manner denotes a passivity similar to that displayed by the Chinese, he wrote:

> When you see the frivolous, almost effeminate gesture of the Andalusian, keep in mind that it has been functioning in almost the same way for over a thousand years [;] ... this tenuous gracefulness has been invulnerable to the terrible invasions and convulsive catastrophes of the centuries. Looking at it this way, the Sevillian's little gesture takes the shape of a tremendously mysterious sign that sends shivers up the spine. It is similar to the impression produced by the enigmatic smile of the Chinese – what a strange coincidence! – that other ancient people aligned on the opposite end of the Eurasian massif. (Ortega y Gasset 1983 [1927]: 113)

While in the north of Spain the soldier-warrior figure was admired, in Andalusia the heroes were, paradoxically, the villain and the lazy *señorito*. Andalusia's historical role was to surrender to conquerors, thus to preserve its vegetative yet paradisiacal existence. Residual discourses (nineteenth-century Romanticism) and more emergent ones (Ortega's brand of centralist nationalism) intersect in *Torbellino*'s romantic plot, which runs parallel to the actual struggle over popular music in the country's radio stations. Don Segundo swears allegiance to art, science and sport, while Carmen's proven lack of athletic ability (she loses at tennis) means that her Andalusian blood makes her suitable only for 'feminine' activities. But unlike Don Segundo's blond secretary, a woman of questionable reputation who furtively plots with Don Segundo's enemies to ruin him, Carmen remains loyal, taking in hand the station's problems and protecting Don Segundo's business.

As in Prosper Mérimée's novel, *Carmen* (1845), the foundational fiction for later stereotypes of Andalusia, *Torbellino*'s male protagonist is Basque and hopelessly captivated by Carmen, the personification of Andalusia. But *Torbellino* has no violent subtext. It ends happily (Carmen does not die and her lover remains with her), and Carmen is no dark and exotic 'Gypsy' but a merry, white-skinned woman, untroubled by the destructive nature of her original. Mérimée's Carmen was a wage-earning, working-class *cigarrera* who cherished her freedom more than bourgeois romantic love. But her more recent incarnations whitewash both revolutionary connotations and even the feeble bohemian fetishistic aspects, refashioning Carmen into a more acceptable image of the nurturing motherland or suffering victim (for example *Carmen, la de Triana* [Florián Rey, 1938]). *Torbellino*'s Carmen underscores the nature of consensual relations: the Carmen myth is profitable for cultural producers but must also be acceptable to the regime's definitions of womanhood and nation. *Torbellino*'s *folklórica* promotes business and is an acquiescent worker, while the ethnic and national tensions evident earlier in the film dissolve into a harmonious union between Northern hero and Southern heroine.

As folkloric songs, and especially the *canción andaluza* grew in demand, almost every *cupletista* star rushed to include them in their repertoires. Many *cupletistas* moulded themselves into principally Andalusian folkloric singers, furthering their careers via the radio, recordings, and eventually the folkloric cinema industry, the epitomy of feminized mass culture. These films, produced by men, concentrated on women's amorous adventures and their climb to professional success. In effect they were elegies to the vitality and cleverness of actual women who had 'made it' both romantically and financially. On film, not only are the female protagonists articulate, but their language is rich with double entendres, puns, and twists of meaning that mock the male supporting characters. The tongue-in-cheek humour deriding the Northerner or the Frenchified Spaniard is also exploited, for example in *Morena Clara* and *La Lola se va a los puertos*, where the female 'Gypsy' protagonist from Andalusia falls in love with a Northerner or a character aligned with European, rather than 'Southern Spanish' values. In *Torbellino*, Don Segundo's Basque doorman's caricatured stiffness and brusqueness contrast with Carmen's humour and Andalusian accent. Because only the audience is privy to her disguise, her conversation with the doorman, who is outside the joke, underscores her cleverness.

Indeed, Andalusian musical-comedy films often responded to elitist cultural criticism by providing a world in which Andalusian mass culture

Eva Woods

and *folklóricas* ridicule characters representing high culture.[6] *Torbellino* closes with Don Segundo's transformation into an 'Andalusian', a metaphor for the unity of the Spanish nation and the resolution of difference. Standing outside Carmen's wrought-iron window grate in Sevilla, Don Segundo is instructed by Carmen on how to seduce her, Andalusian style. Wearing a wide-brimmed, flat-topped flamenco hat, he adopts the correct posture (one hand in the coat pocket, leaning against the window with legs casually crossed) and woos her with *soleares*, a classic flamenco rhythm. This superficial transformation recalls what Jo Labanyi correctly refers to as a mutual mimicry of cultural codes by characters portraying subalterns and members of the dominant class (Labanyi 2002: 97).

Nevertheless, the majority of the film deals with Carmen's untraditional pursuit of career and the interdependent relationships between stardom, technology and mass culture. The film climaxes with the union of Don Segundo and Carmen and the success of Carmen's strategy for saving Radio Ibérico from ruin. In a nation-wide contest between radio stations for the best musical programme, she changes the music from classical to flamenco, creating the winning programme (Castro's final song) that will also provide a boost to her career. In one sense, then, the film is an homage to feminine prowess, and to women who overcome their economic conditions, thereby contesting traditional notions of womanhood. But of course it is also like many other backstage musicals that chronicle 'the neophyte entertainer in the process of becoming professional, a star in the process of being born' (Feuer 1993: 15). *Torbellino* celebrates both the production of popular music, and the process by which Carmen's 'spontaneous' and 'natural' performances lead to her triumph in the radio contest. Indeed, radio contests such as 'In search of a starlet', 'Come up on stage' or 'Mysterious artistes' gained listener support and donations, and promoted the station's other products. Contests, like radio in general, transformed the domestic sphere into a theatre, creating the illusion of a community of listeners that despite geographical distance were connected in an intimate way by voices that could penetrate the home.

Radio: Ambivalent Freedom

Radio, which rapidly developed after 1923 (Salaün 1995: 93), significantly influenced the way in which Spaniards consumed folklore and song. One of the cheapest forms of entertainment and the most accessible to the entire class spectrum (it avoided the problem of literacy), radio transmitted programmes on everything from *variétés*, contests, *radioteatro*, and the radio serials/soap operas, to song (Abella 1996: 156). During the 1940s, radio would become a 'ubiquitous medium in working- and lower middle-class homes' (Graham 1995: 238). In 1933, there were 153,662 radio transmitters (6.4 per 1,000 inhabitants); in 1936 there were more than 300,000, and in 1943 more than a million (Díaz 1997: 134). People listened to the radio from taverns, casinos, unions, neighbourhood patios, and private homes.

Luis Marqina's introduction to the broadcast of the historical drama *El monje blanco* (The White Monk) during Radio Nacional España's programme, 'Teatro breve' reveals an invested albeit ambiguous stance regarding the significance of radio in relation to cultural hierarchies:

Radio remembers; it lives off of the present and from the past. The current event is important to it, as radio is a review of happenings and goings-on. Nevertheless, it does not forget what has happened or what vibrated in the life of the nation and its history, which is, by extension the best explanation of our way of being. And thus through radio we relive events that we should not forget, as it repeats opportune expressions that those who with their ingenuity and wisdom knew how link together, thereby sowing into their writings the seed that gave universal form and meaning to Spanish literature. (Pérez Perucha 1983: 147)

Although Marquina's statements explicitly invoke nationalist sentiment, his assertion of the 'memory' of the radio and its capacity to help us relive momentous events, could have applied just as much to the history of the other side of the struggle – Republican Spain – as it did to the nationalist contingent.

The above amply suggests the ambiguous ideological subtext of *Torbellino*. It recognizes the medium's radical political capacities. (Listeners can imagine alternative realities, or recall them through songs sung during the Republic, for instance, but played again during early Francoism.) Yet radio also works in the interest of groups who seek to empower themselves through its content. Intellectuals such as Marquina or the Quintero brothers understood that radio would give their musical and artistic products an advantage over other genres, given its capacity to reach larger audiences. While the cultural purists represent a class in decline, Marquina and company form part of an emergent class in the early years of the Franco regime, similar to business leaders who made their fortune during this time. *Torbellino* plays out this emergence of a rising class of entrepreneurs, represented by the *folklórica* and the radio manager. His canny recognition of her marketability, contributing to

Torbellino's ambiguous textuality, recalls Ricardo Urgoiti's commercial strategy: to suture audience identification by positioning them as participants rather than consumers.

Consumption and Folk Relations

Music becomes commodified through the production, packaging, and distributing that disguise the behind-the-scenes labour that making music requires. Alienation is part and parcel of musical films, but Jane Feuer argues that these particular films, because they are conscious of this alienation, attempt to create 'humanistic folk relations' and the community inherent in live performance, so that the alienation of filmed performance seems cancelled out: '[t]hese folk relations ... act to cancel out the economic values and relations associated with mass-produced art. Through such a rhetorical exchange, the creation of folk relations *in* the films cancels the mass-entertainment substance *of* the films' (Feuer 1993: 3). *Torbellino*, like the Hollywood musical, becomes a mass art which aspires to be folk art, produced and consumed by the film's folk characters.

Torbellino creates 'folk relations' by representing the *folklórica* star as an ordinary girl who later becomes famous through the radio. The sequence that introduces Carmen begins as the camera pans from a makeshift microphone in Carmen's house to her face, while the spectator hears the out-of-frame voice of her aunt pretending to be a master of ceremonies. The aunt-as-MC introduces Carmen, the 'star', to a make-believe audience, which by implication is actually the extra-filmic audience. The scene is thus a reflexive commentary on the relationship that is formed when the spectator/fan places herself in the situation, identifying with the persona of the star. Scenes like this encourage audience identification by interpellating extra-cinematic audience members who have had the same fantasy of being a star, or who have 'practised' at home in front of their mirrors. In a later sequence, Carmen again imagines that she is performing before an audience. Wandering around the recording studio she sees that it is fully equipped for a performance, and as her imagination works, a pianist appears, and soon an entire orchestra. As Carmen's imagination is acted out, a conductor presents her and she transitions into performance, singing *canción andaluza* (Andalusian song). Significantly we see her watching herself from the recording booth, consuming her own star image at the same time as she projects it. The scene, then, visually portrays the idea of escaping into one's own fantasies. But the external spectator already knows that Castro has achieved success and stardom in her 'real' life, making this fantasy more than imaginary, a foreshadowing of the inevitable. The scene is understood both from the point of view of the film's character and from that of Estrellita Castro, who consumes her own fetishized image, providing a complex metaphor of star ontology. At the same time, through the visual magic of cinema, a utopian space merges with a domestic one.

The creation of a folk utopia in Castro's first song number constitutes a space in which the rhetorics of cultural hierarchy, commodification, and the role of the radio overlap with the discursive registers of gender and nation. While Carmen/Castro sings 'La Giralda es una torre con 25 campanas' (the Giralda is a tower with 25 bells) the camera follows her over to the window, then dissolves the shot of the window into a landscape view overlooking Seville. In a picturesque pan of Seville – a staple of all folkloric musical-comedy films – the camera sweeps from the Giralda to the Cathedral, performing as tourist guide and adding yet another layer of meaning to the idea of consumption. Here Marquina's efforts to index an authentic Spain give way to a series of tourist vistas that suture the imaginary tourist gaze with the subsequent commentary on consumption. The lyrics to Carmen's song, 'Sevilla es una mocita que está siempre prisionera' (Sevilla is a lass who is always imprisoned) fetishize Spain's past by referencing the medieval *romance fronterizo*, or border ballad of 'Abenámar', which chronicles the takeover of Granada by the Christians. Because we see the pan from the eyes of Carmen poised at the window, the reference to Seville as the imprisoned damsel fuses with the *folklórica*, further implicating the spatial hierarchy of North and South. The camera then cuts to two different medium-to-low-angle shots of monumental crosses, and then to a shot of people filing in and out of the cathedral, reaffirming Northern, Christian dominance over an Arab, feminized Andalusia.

But at this moment, the song expands into a portrait of folk relations as Carmen's performance merges with the songs of local street vendors, or *pregoneros*, who from the street below are advertising wares such as bottles, vases, clothing and candy. Carmen's singing becomes a romanticized song exchange with these *tíos de los pregones*, as in the tradition of oral medieval poetry. The addition of the merchants scouting out their potential customers, and their subjective presence in the scene, restate the bond between Carmen and the folk life of Andalusia, creating a kind of folk commercial: 'The SER was national coverage for the large drug, cosmetic, and liquor companies that wanted a publicity spot' (Díaz 1997: 38). In fact, radio ads of the 1940s and 1950s purposefully imitated the *pregonero* calls in an attempt to exploit the nostalgia for a pre-technological/capitalist era of advertising and marketing. The result was an ambiguous combination of clever marketing and savvy manipulation of Republican sentiment. And catchy music was ideal for remembering products:

> Soon the radio would become the executor of the pregonero's commercial jingle, just as our dear minstrels in the bygone days who twisted into meaty verses the announcement for the arrival of fresh fish or nice red, egg-laying chickens) (Díaz 1997: 211).

Radio advertisements were repeated by listeners and viewed as songs in themselves.

The multiple shots from the points of view of the anonymous vendors and the snapshots of various unnamed townspeople repeating the songs of the *pregonero* become metonyms for the 'pueblo', a term used in vanguard writing of the 1920s and 1930s, whose meanings differed according to the agenda. For intellectual elites it could mean 'a repository of things of cultural value' (Sinclair 1988: 227–8). For Lorca the *pueblo* was 'a source of immense worth: nursemaids and servants had long been carrying out the invaluable task of "taking the ballad, the song, and the story to the homes of the aristocracy"' (Ibid.). The meaning of 'pueblo' in *Torbellino* is less radical and more how Lorca envisioned it: an idealized group of working-class and peasant Spaniards who are responsible for safe-keeping and orally transmitting a corpus of songs that can later be pilfered and classified by bourgeois writers and poets. *Pueblo*, as it is used in this film, suggests a social unity. In effect, it serves the interests of the upper classes because it makes the lower classes look uniform and homogenous.

Torbellino, then, presents music as by and for the people. Carmen not only sings *cante andaluz*, but also participates with the *pueblo* as they carry out their daily activities. This carefully staged folklore sequence implies that oral tradition and folklore, although more authentic and preferable to mass culture, need the technology of modernity, such as the radio and film, to become dominant cultural discourse. Just as strongly, it implies the need for bourgeois mercantile interests to incorporate the powerful appeal of oral tradition and folklore, in order to create a dominant cultural discourse that will be used by the consumers of mass culture. The editing, shots, angles and interplay between Carmen and the 'pueblo' create the illusion that the myth of community is held together by song, even if it is performed only within the confines of the film. As

Carmen finishes her song with the street merchant, the camera transports the spectator back to the interior of her apartment where her friends clap for her, having pretended to be listeners to the make-believe radio broadcast.

Conclusion

In *Torbellino*'s discourses of individual liberalism, social mobility and the rise to stardom, audiences could imagine alternative identities and new forms of gratification. Don Segundo and Carmen were like the entrepreneurs who profited during the Republic (like Ricardo Urgoiti) or the early post-war (again, Urgoiti, or the *folklóricas* and film-makers who were able to mould their careers to the exigencies of censorship and National Catholic ideology). And clearly, the radio station and its broadcast sessions reflect the semi-autonomous status of the media under Francoism as a space where ambiguous political and cultural discourses intersected. *Torbellino* thus provides evidence that in 1940s Spain, larger and more far-reaching projects than autarchy or authoritarian sexuality were being rehearsed, namely, that of a capitalist modernity that needed its consumer-citizens to identify with the musical products marketed on radio and in films. In *Torbellino*, as in radio, mass-media products homogenize audiences and hybridize musical forms, despite efforts by the State, elites, or intellectuals such as Marquina.

Notes

1. All translations in this chapter are by the author.
2. '"Torbellino", de Luis Marquina: Una pizpireta sevillana', *Ya*. 15 June 1983.
3. This quote, in which a critic describes the right's frustration with the use of expensive film stock to represent ideologies that were anathema to Falange ideology, appeared in a Falangist journal in a 1940 article: 'Ni un metro más', *Primer Plano*, 1(7), Madrid, 1 December.
4. King Alfonso XIII, according to Balsebre, underscored radio's interclassist vocation at Unión Radio's inauguration: 'a los de más alta y elevada jerarquía social y a los más humildes' (of those of higher, loftier social standing and those of lower standing) (Balsebre 1992:

142). Through radio the king's subjects could have direct contact with heads of state, thereby foreshadowing later descriptions of radio as magical, i.e. voices being heard, telepathy (Taylor 2002: 432).

5. Similar to the debates on national cinema, the debate on the meaning of flamenco was carried out by a combination of aristocrats, social reformers, anarchists, Andalusian Nationalists, and poets (Mitchell 1994: 3).

6. Also see: *Canelita en rama* (Eduardo García Maroto, 1942) and *Serenata española* (Juan de Orduña, 1947), as Jo Labanyi points out (2002).

References

Abella, Rafael (1996), *La vida cotidiana durante el régimen de Franco*, Madrid: Ediciones Temas de Hoy.

Alvarez Caballero, Angel (1994), *El cante flamenco*, Madrid: Alianza.

Balsebre, Armand (1992), *Historia de la radio en España: Volumen I (1874–1939)*, Madrid: Cátedra.

Bermúdez, Silvia (1997), '"Music to My Ears": Cuplés, Conchita Piquer and the (Un)Making of Cultural Nationalism', *Siglo XX/20th Century*, 15(1–2): 33–54.

Besas, Peter (1985), *Behind the Spanish Lens: Spanish Cinema Under Fascism and Democracy*, Denver: Arden Press, 1985.

Boyd, Carolyn P. (1997), *Historia Patria: Politics, History, and National Identity in Spain, 1875–1975*, Princeton: Princeton University Press.

Díaz, Lorenzo (1997), *La radio en España: 1923–1997*, Madrid: Alianza.

Feuer, Jane (1993), *The Hollywood Musical*, Bloomington: Indiana University Press.

Girbal, F. Hernández (1935), 'Hay que españolizar nuestro cine', *Cinegramas*, 10(2): 3.

Graham, Helen (1995), 'Popular Culture in the Years of Hunger', in Helen Graham and Jo Labanyi (eds), *Spanish Cultural Studies: An Introduction*, New York: Oxford University Press.

Hall, Stuart and Whannel, Paddy (1965), *The Popular Arts*, New York: Pantheon.

Hopewell, John (1986), *Out of the Past: Spanish Cinema After Franco*, London: BFI.

Huyssen, Andreas (1986), *After the Great Divide: Modernism, Mass Culture, Postmodernism*, Bloomington: Indiana University Press.

Labanyi, Jo (2001): 'Música, populismo y hegemonía en el cine folklórico del primer franquismo', in Luis Fernández Colorado and Pilar Couto Cantero (eds), *La herida de las sombras: El cine español en los años 40*, Madrid: Academia de las Artes y las Ciencias Cinematográficas de España.

——(2002) 'Musical Battles: Populism and Hegemony in the Early Francoist Folkloric Film Musical', in Jo Labanyi (ed.), *Constructing Identity in Twentieth Century Spain: Theoretical Debates and Cultural Practice*, London: Oxford University Press.

Landy, Marcia (1998), *The Folklore of Consensus: Theatricality in the Italian Cinema, 1930–1943*, Albany: State University New York Press.

Lorca, Federico García (1977), 'Teoría y juego del duende', *Obras Completas, Vol. I*, Madrid: Aguilar.

Marsh, Steven (1999), 'Enemies of the *Patria*: Fools, Cranks and Tricksters in the Film Comedies of Jerónimo Mihura', *Journal of Iberian and Latin American Studies*, 5(1): 65–75.

Mitchell, Timothy (1994), *Flamenco, Deep Song*, New Haven: Yale University Press.

Ortega y Gasset, José (1983), 'Teoría de Andalucía', *Obras Completas Vol. VI*, Madrid: Alianza.

Pérez Perucha, Julio (1983), *El cinema de Luis Marquina*, Valladolid: 28 Semana Internacional de Cine de Valladolid.

Rodríguez, Juan Carlos (1994), *La Norma Literaria*, Granada: Diputación Provincial de Granada.

Romero Ferrer, Alberto (1996), *Los hermanos Machado y el teatro: (1926–1932)*, Sevilla: Diputación de Sevilla.

Salaün, Serge (1990), *El Cuplé*. Madrid: Espasa Calpe.

——(1995), 'The Cuplé: Modernity and Mass Culture', in Helen Graham and Jo Labanyi (eds), *Spanish Cultural Studies: An Introduction*, New York: Oxford University Press.

——(1996), 'La mujer en las tablas: grandeza y servidumbre de la condición feminina', in María Luz González Peña, Javier Suárez-Pajares and Julio Arce Bueno (eds), *Mujeres de la escena 1900–1940*, Madrid: Sociedad General de Autores y Editores.

Sieburth, Stephanie (1994), *Inventing High and Low: Literature, Mass Culture, and Uneven Modernity in Spain*, Durham NC and London: Duke University Press.

Sinclair, Alison (1988), 'Elitism and the Cult of the Popular in Spain', in Edward Timms and Peter Collier (eds), *Visions and Blueprints: Avante-garde Culture and Radical Politics in Early 20th Century Europe*, Manchester: Manchester University Press.

Eva Woods

Stallybrass, Richard and Allon White (1986), *The Politics and Poetics of Transgression*, Ithaca: Cornell University Press.

Taylor, Timothy (2002), 'Music and the Rise of Radio in 1920s America: Technological Imperialism, Socialization, and the Transformation of Intimacy', *Historical Journal of Film, Radio and Television*, 22(4): 425–44.

Vernon, Kathleen (1999), 'Culture and Cinema to 1975', in David T. Gies (ed.), *The Cambridge Companion to Modern Spanish Culture*, Cambridge: Cambridge University Press.

Woods, Eva María (2000), 'From Rags to Riches: Ideological Contradiction and Folklórica Stardom in Andalusian Musical Comedy Films, 1936–1949', Dissertation. DAI: Ann Arbor, Michigan.

Filmography

Albacete, A. and D. Menkes, *Más que amor, frenesí* (1996)
    Sobreviviré (1999)

Almodóvar, P., *Sexo va, sexo viene* (1977)
    Pepe, Luci, Bom y otras chicas del montón (1980)
    Qué he hecho ye para merecer esto (1984)
    Ley del deseo (1987)
    Mujeres al borde de un ataque de nervios (1988)
    Átame (1989)
    Tacones lejanos (1991)
    Kika (1993)
    Carne trémula (1998)
    Todo sobre mi madre (1999)
    Hable con ella (2002)

Amenábar, A., *Tesis* (1995)

Aranda, V., *Las crueles* (1969)
    La novia ensangrentada (1972)
    Cambio de sexo (1976)
    La muchacha de las bragas de oro (1979)
    Tiempo de silencio (1986)
    El Lute, camina o revienta (1987)
    Si te dicen que caí (1989)
    Los jinetes del alba (1990)
    Amantes (1991)
    Intruso (1993)
    Libertarias (1996)
    Juana la loca (2001)

Armendáriz, M., *Las cartas de Alou* (1990)

Bardem, J.A., *Cómicos* (1953)
    Calle Mayor (1956)

Filmography

Bardem, M., *La mujer más fea del mundo* (1999)

Bigas-Luna, *Caniche* (1979)
     Jamón jamón (1993)

Bollaín, I., *Flores de otro mundo* (1999)

Borau, J.L., *Furtivos* (1975)
     Río abajo (1984)

Buñuel, L., *Ensayo de un crimen* (1955)
     Viridiana (1961)
     Belle de Jour (1966)
     Tristana (1970)

Camus, M., *La colmena* (1982)

Colomo, F., *Tigres de papel* (1977)

De la Iglesia, E., *La semana del asesino* (1971)
     Juego de amor prohibido (1975)
     Los placeres ocultos (1975)
     El sacerdote (1977)
     La criatura (1977)
     El diputado (1978)

Delgado, J.M., *Diferente* (1962)

Diego, G., *Malena es un nombre de tango* (1996)

Díaz Yanes, A., *Baton Rouge* (1988)
     A solas contigo (1990)
     Demasiado corazón (1992)
     Nadie hablará de nosotros cuando hayamos muerto (1995)

Fenollar, A., *La tía de Carlos en minifalda* (1967)

Fernández, R., *No desearás al vecino del quinto* (1970)
     Gay Club (1980)

Filmography

Fernán-Gómez, F., *El extraño* viaje (1964)
　　　　　Crimen imperfecto (1970)

Ferreira, P., *Sé quien eres* (2000)
　　　　　El alquimista impaciente (2002)

Ferreri, M., *El cochecito* (1960)

Fons, A., *Mi hijo no es lo que parece* (1973)

Franco, J., *Tenemos 18 años* (1959)
　　　　　Awful Dr. Orlow (1961)
　　　　　Miss Muerte (1965)
　　　　　El caso de las dos bellezas (1967)
　　　　　Bésame monstruo (1967)
　　　　　El misterio del castillo rojo (1972)
　　　　　Barbed Wire Dolls (1975)
　　　　　Exorcism and Black Masses (1974)
　　　　　Cartas boca arriba (1966)
　　　　　She Killed In Ecstasy (1970)
　　　　　El muerto hace las maletas (1971)
　　　　　Vals para un asesino (1974)
　　　　　Macumba sexual (1981)
　　　　　The Vampires (1970)
　　　　　Female Vampires (1973)
　　　　　Eugénie de Sade (1970)
　　　　　El hundimiento de la casa Usher (1989)
　　　　　99 Women (1968)
　　　　　Visa Pour Mourir (1975)
　　　　　Jailhouse Wardress (1975)
　　　　　Las últimas de Filipinas (1985)

García Berlanga, L., *¡Bienvenido Mister Marshall!* (1952)

García Sánchez, J.L., *Tranvía a la Malvarrosa* (1996)

Gimenez-Rico, A. *Retrato de familia* (1976)

Grau, J., *La trastienda* (1976)
　　　　Cartas de amor a una monja (1978)

Filmography

Guerín, J.L., *En construcción* (2001)

Gutiérrez, C., *Poniente* (2002)

Iquino, I.F., *Alma de Dios* (1941)
    Aborto criminal (1973)
    Chicas de alquiler (1974)
    Fraude matrimonial (1976)

Larraz, J.R., *Vampyres* (1974)

León de Aranoa, F., *Barrio* (1998)

Lucía, L., *La princesa de los Ursinos* (1947)

Manzanos, E., *El y él* (1980)

Marquina, L., *Torbellino* (1941)
    El monje blanco (1945)

Martínez Lázaro, E., *Amo tu cama rica* (1991)

Nieves Conde, J.A., *Surcos* (1951)

Olea, P., *Un hombre llamado Flor de Otoño* (1978)

Orduña, J. de, *La Lola se va a los puerto* (1947)
    Serenata española (1947)
    Locura de amor (1948)
    Agustina de Aragón (1950)
    La Leona de Castilla (1951)
    Alba de América (1951)
    El último cuplé (1957)

Ozores, M., *Ellas los prefieren ... locas* (1976)
    Capullito de Alhelí (1983)

Perojo, B., *Goyescas* (1942)

Rey, F., *Morena Clara* (1936)
    Carmen, la de Triana (1938)

Filmography

Santillán, D., *Silvia ama a Raquel* (1979)

Saura, C., *Ana y los lobos* (1972)

Soler, L., *Saíd* (1999)

Truchado, J., *Haz la loca ... no la guerra* (1978)

Trueba, F., *Ópera prima* (1980)
Belle Epoque (1992)

Uribe, I., *Bwana* (1996)

Vadim, R. *Blood of Roses* (1960)

Vera, G., *Segunda piel* (1999)

Index

Index

Index

Index

Index

Index

Index